The City & Guilds textbook

Theatrical, Special Effects and Media Make-Up Artistry

Kelly Stokes
Tracey Gaines
Nicki Purchase

Boost

HODDER
EDUCATION
AN HACHETTE UK COMPANY

Although every effort has been made to ensure that website addresses are correct at time of going to press, Hodder Education cannot be held responsible for the content of any website mentioned in this book. It is sometimes possible to find a relocated web page by typing in the address of the home page for a website in the URL window of your browser.

Hachette UK's policy is to use papers that are natural, renewable and recyclable products and made from wood grown in well-managed forests and other controlled sources. The logging and manufacturing processes are expected to conform to the environmental regulations of the country of origin.

Orders: please contact Hachette UK Distribution, Hely Hutchinson Centre, Milton Road, Didcot, Oxfordshire, OX11 7HH. Telephone: +44 (0)1235 827827. Email education@hachette.co.uk Lines are open from 9 a.m. to 5 p.m., Monday to Friday. You can also order through our website: www.hoddereducation.co.uk

ISBN: 978 1 5104 8477 1

© Kelly Stokes, Tracey Gaines and Nicki Purchase 2021

First published in 2021 by

Hodder Education,
An Hachette UK Company
Carmelite House
50 Victoria Embankment
London EC4Y 0DZ

www.hoddereducation.co.uk

Impression number   10 9 8 7 6 5 4 3 2 1

Year   2025 2024 2023 2022 2021

City & Guilds and the City & Guilds logo are trade marks of The City and Guilds of London Institute. City & Guilds Logo © City & Guilds 2021

Cover photo © Chloe Winslade, Sean Parnell and Florence Jones

Illustrations by Integra Software Services Ltd.

Typeset in India by Integra Software Services Ltd.

Printed in Slovenia

A catalogue record for this title is available from the British Library.

Contents

Go to www.hoddereducation.co.uk/product/9781510484771 to access the following chapters.

Introduction to the qualifications

This textbook covers the following qualifications, which aim to provide a range of essential technical and practical skills and knowledge to equip you to seek employment or further training within the make-up industry.

The **Level 2 Technical Certificate in Make-Up Artistry (6010-20)** qualification studies theoretical aspects of the subject and applies them to practical tasks.

Compulsory topics include:
- working in the make-up industry
- anatomy and physiology
- research, develop and showcase designs
- the art of applying make-up
- hair artistry
- creative make-up artistry.

Examples of the areas in which this qualification could lead to a job as a make-up artist include:
- photoshoots
- magazine and publication shoots
- department stores
- make-up stores
- salons.

The following Level 3 qualifications will benefit from having an entry requirement of the Level 2 Technical Certificate in Make-Up Artistry.

The **Level 3 Advanced Technical Diploma in Media Make-Up Artistry (540) (6010-30)** qualification covers a very wide range of skills and knowledge required for working in the media make-up industry.

Compulsory areas include:
- working in the film, TV and theatre industry
- create historical hair and make-up looks
- media make-up creative hair design
- fashion and photographic make-up
- the creation and presentation of a look book and industry portfolio
- apply body art
- camouflage make-up.

Optional areas include:
- cutting and styling techniques for performers
- avant-garde hair and make-up
- the evolution of cosmetics and retail
- specialist bridal hair and make-up
- media make-up blogging.

This qualification could lead to a job working as a:
- photographic make-up artist
- editorial make-up artist
- TV make-up artist
- video make-up artist
- freelance make-up artist
- specialist bridal make-up artist.

The **Level 3 Advanced Technical Diploma in Theatrical, Special Effects and Media Make-Up Artistry (540) (6010-31)** covers a very wide range of skills and knowledge required for working in the theatrical and media make-up industry.

Compulsory areas include:
- cutting and styling techniques for performers
- avant-garde hair and make-up
- creative make-up design for productions and industry demands
- apply prosthetic pieces and bald caps
- special effects make-up
- create, dress and fit facial postiche
- body art for competition.

Optional areas include:
- camouflage make-up
- media make-up blogging
- create, cast small prosthetic pieces and bald caps
- costume design and prop making
- wig dressing, fitting and maintenance.

This qualification could lead to a job working as a:
- theatre make-up artist
- film make-up artist
- TV make-up artist
- make-up designer
- product developer
- entrepreneur.

Each of the above qualifications is divided into units, which cover different areas of your training. All units of the Level 2 qualification are mandatory which means you must complete them all. The Level 3 qualification structures are made up of mandatory and optional units. You must complete all of the mandatory units and some, but not all, of the optional units.

HOW TO ACHIEVE YOUR QUALIFICATION

To achieve your qualification, you need to successfully complete:

1 **A synoptic assignment (similar to a trade test).** This assignment is externally set, internally marked and externally moderated, and is designed to require an effective and integrated way of an appropriate selection of skills, techniques, concepts, theories and knowledge from across the whole content area.

2 **One exam, sat under examination conditions.** This is set and marked externally. The test is designed to draw out the depth and breadth of understanding across the mandatory content. This test can only be taken a maximum of two times (three for Level 3). If this is not passed, you will not achieve your qualification.

Preparing for your synoptic assignment

What is the synoptic assignment?

A typical synoptic assignment brief could be to carry out a range of services on a model in a hair and makeup artistry environment, over a period of 4–6 hours. This will require you to use your skills and knowledge of a range of treatments from across the mandatory units of the qualification, such as applying prosthetic pieces and bald caps and special effects make-up services. To achieve your Level 3 qualification you will be assessed to make sure you have the necessary breadth of skills, knowledge, values and behaviours and are ready to progress onto the next stage of your career

How is the synoptic assignment assessed?

The synoptic assignment brief is set externally. It will be internally assessed and marked by your college and externally moderated by City & Guilds to confirm the grade you have achieved. You will be marked and assessed against assessment objectives (AOs) such as your breadth and accuracy of knowledge, understanding of concepts and the quality of your technical skills, as well as your ability to use what you have learned in an integrated way to demonstrate high standards of professional practice.

What will you have to do?

You will be required to draw from your knowledge and understanding across the range of the qualification content to effectively carry out the services. To complete your synoptic assignment you will be required to bring together your knowledge and skills by applying learning from across the scope of the qualification, rather than demonstrating achievement against one specific unit.

When will you have to do this?

Before the date of your synoptic assignment, your tutor will provide you with a sample assignment to prepare you for the actual synoptic assignment. The sample assignment will be in the form of a brief that will detail exactly what you will be expected to carry out. The assignment will cover a range of services from across the units in the mandatory content of this qualification. Towards the end of your qualification, you will be prepared for the actual synoptic assignment, carrying out a variety of media hair and makeup services on a number of models within a commercially set time. This 'trade test' as part of your synoptic assessment will require you to use consultation techniques to identify client requirements and build a professional rapport. You will draw on the knowledge, understanding and practical skills you have developed during the qualification to deliver a range of personalised media hair and makeup services, adapting to any factors as required. You will be marked on the quality and accuracy of your practical performance and your ability to communicate effectively and reflect on the services carried out. It is therefore important that you carry out your work out to the highest professional standard you can. You should demonstrate how well you know and understand the subject and how you are able to use your knowledge and skills together to complete the tasks.

Preparing for your exam
What will the externally marked exam involve?

The external assessment will draw from across the key areas of the qualification, using a range of short answer questions to confirm breadth of recalled knowledge and deeper applied understanding. Extended response questions are included, giving you the opportunity to demonstrate higher-level understanding and integration through discussion, analysis and evaluation, and ensuring the assessment differentiates between 'just able' and higher achieving learners.

Understanding the exam wording or command words

In examinations, certain words, often called command words, are commonly used as prompts to give an indication of the type of response that is expected by the question. These words commonly include **describe**, **explain**, **state** and **discuss**.

- **Describe** – This command word requires you to give a representation of something in words; a 'picture in words'.
- **Explain** – This command word requires you to give reasons, or suggest causes and effects.
- **State** – This command word requires you to express or declare something in words.

- **Discuss** – A discuss or evaluate question will usually be marked and graded according to the level of response. You will be required to compose a detailed response, which considers the topic of the question. You will need to compare and contrast and consider any pros and cons; provide a discussion or argument, which is justified and supported.

While these command words give an indication of what is expected, it is important to understand that these words do not stand on their own. In preparation for your exam, you should not focus on simply learning the meanings of these words in isolation of the rest of the question, but focus on interpreting the full question or task. The command words give an indication of what is wanted and in the context of the instruction or question, the full meaning should be clear. For example, the questions below all use the word 'describe', but all require different sorts of answers.

Question	Answer required
Describe a _____.	(Describe how they look)
Describe the process for _____.	(Describe a sequence of events)
Describe the effects of _____ on _____.	(Describe the changes following some sort of impact)

Revision tips

These revision tips will help you prepare for your external exam assessment.

- Regularly check your knowledge and understanding to ensure that you still remember key content from every unit, especially content covered at the start of your qualification.
- Remember the 3 Rs – **R**ecap, **R**evise and **R**ecall. Take opportunities to recap, revise and recall, both in the classroom and using a mix of online resources and activities. Take time to find out which learning strategies work best for you - reading, practising hands on or being taught or shown.
- Use a range of different revision strategies that best meet your learning needs. For example, creating cue or flash cards can help you to remember key knowledge content. You could make use of mobile learning apps to prepare your own revision flash cards to help develop a secure understanding of key terminology, concepts and frameworks. Use a Dictaphone to record key information (most mobile phones have an app) and listen to it to reinforce your learning.
- Familiarise yourself with how to deal with different command verbs, such as the differences between responses which describe or explain.
- Always take hand written notes in class and ensure you have developed your note-taking skills. This will prepare you to capture and summarise the most important aspects of the content.

- These notes will be invaluable when you are preparing for your examination and help identify any gaps in your knowledge and understanding.
- Don't just memorise facts and figures, but try to make links and deeper connections. Visualisation and concept mapping techniques involve making links between different information and ideas – they can help you to apply your knowledge and understanding in different contexts and situations.
- You will need to manage your time effectively as independent learners. Creating a revision timetable or planners is a useful exercise to help you prioritise your learning activities, focusing on areas where there might be gaps in your understanding.
- Find a colleague to be a revision buddy with. You can ask each other questions and help each other with revision and recall.
- It's important to stay fit and healthy in order to be well-prepared physically and mentally to demonstrate your knowledge and understanding. Remember to get enough sleep, drink plenty of water, eat well and get enough downtime in the build-up to the exam. Simple relaxation techniques can help if you are feeling stressed.

How will the questions be marked?

In your exam paper it will show you the numbers of marks available per question. This will give you an indication of the depth of response expected. Half marks are never used.

- Questions requiring you to recall knowledge typically require a separate point per mark.
- Questions requiring you to demonstrate understanding may require a point or limited explanation for 1 mark, with a further mark available for more depth or explanation.
- Questions requiring you to apply knowledge, understanding and skills would expect a higher quality of response for higher marks, and these are usually marked using level of response marking.

HOW WILL THE QUALIFICATION BE GRADED?

The synoptic assignment (trade test) will be allocated marks holistically. Once all your assessments are complete, your evidence and the proposed marks from your tutor will be submitted to City & Guilds for moderation. City & Guilds will set the grade boundaries for each assessment and publish the results. Grade boundaries will be set using technical experts. Grades from your synoptic assignment and your external assessment make up your overall qualification grade. Your synoptic assignment will contribute 60 per cent to your overall qualification grade, with your external exam grade contributing 30 per cent and 10 per cent portfolio.

What about qualifications with optional units?

If optional units are required as part of the qualification, these must be completed to achieve the qualification, but the individual optional unit grades will not count towards your overall grade, although they will be displayed on your certificate.

WHERE TO GO FOR FURTHER INFORMATION

The most important sources of information you are likely to need are listed below:

- Your City & Guilds Learner Journal will provide further information about your qualification.
- Your tutor/assessor will provide you with all the important information you require about your qualification.
- You can visit the City & Guilds website for more information at www. cityandguilds.com

About the authors

KELLY STOKES

I have worked in the hair and beauty industry for 25 years. I have been qualified as a hair and make-up artist for 15 of those. In this time, I have worked for a well-known make-up and skincare brand as well as being a freelance make-up artist specialising in weddings and high fashion photoshoots. I have been the head make-up artist for several film productions alongside fashion and editorial work.

Over the past 13 years I have taught Theatrical, Media and Special Effects Make-Up at both Levels 2 and 3, teaching across a variety of awarding bodies including City & Guilds, VTCT and BTEC.

I have my own hair and beauty salon and private training academy where I have 10 members of staff working in all areas of the beauty, hair, aesthetics and make-up industry. Here I use my personal skills with my own client base as well as teaching a range of specialised private make-up courses including editorial, commercial, high fashion and specialised wedding make-up. I work for City & Guilds as a moderator for Level 3 Media Make-Up Artistry and Level 3 Theatrical, Special Effects and Media Make-Up Artistry. I was a member of the team involved in writing the technical qualifications for City & Guilds which also included creating the digital SmartScreen resources.

This is the third textbook I have written within the beauty and make-up industry. It is my passion to help others and to pass on what I have experienced and learnt over the years I have been in the industry. The media make-up industry is an amazing sector to be a part of – there are so many routes you can take which enables a hair and make-up artist to have a flourishing career which is both exhilarating and rewarding. I for one feel very blessed to be part of such an amazing industry.

TRACEY GAINES

I currently work as a full-time media make-up tutor in a college, with City & Guilds as our awarding body.

Before I diversified into teaching, I initially studied as a hairdresser then progressed to train further as a make-up artist. Utilising both skillsets, I was fortunate enough to make a career in the film, TV, theatre and fashion industries. I originally started working as a trainee on TV show *Emmerdale* which was a great experience that I learned a lot from.

I then progressed as a freelance hair and make-up artist working on many different productions for the BBC, ITV, Channel 4, Channel 5 and many more. I have had a diverse career working on daytime TV programmes, feature films, commercials, editorial shoots and theatre productions.

My wide and varied career as a make-up artist has enabled me to contribute my expertise into writing and teaching. I was involved in writing and teaching the Advanced Technical Diplomas for Level 3 Media Make-up Artistry and Level 3 Theatrical, Special Effects and Media Make-up Artistry. I have also worked as an examiner for the test papers and a moderator for City & Guilds.

NICKI PURCHASE

I have worked in the beauty and make-up industry for over 10 years. Throughout this time, I have had a passion for make-up and remain fascinated about how make-up can transform and enhance a person's appearance. Having originally started my beauty therapy training, I began working as a counter manager at a department store for Estée Lauder Companies. After I completed my training, I worked in a number of salons and spas which gave me the opportunity to work with high-end brands and to gain experience within the industry. I then went on to work at a further education college where I gained my teaching qualification which allowed me to share my industry knowledge and skills to my learners.

However, I realised that the make-up industry was where my ambitions lay so I decided to progress my make-up skills and completed various courses in London as well as the VTCT Level 3 Theatrical Media Make-Up qualification. This gave me the opportunity to take on the role as a freelance make-up artist, focusing on bridal make-up, as well as catwalk shows, TV commercials, local theatre productions and short feature films. Whilst working on these, I met and worked alongside other make-up artists who helped to enhance my skills and experience. As my knowledge and skills advanced, I then started teaching media make-up qualifications.

Currently, alongside my freelance work, I teach at a private training school, delivering their varied make-up qualifications. In addition, I have worked for City & Guilds for over five years where I had the added benefit of being part of the team developing and writing the technical qualifications for Media Make-Up at both Levels 2 and 3. I was appointed a chief examiner and principal moderator for the Technical Certificate in Level 2 Make-Up Artistry and I continue in these roles to this day.

I take every opportunity to research and update my industry skills, and I would stress the vital importance of this to all readers. I hope this book will provide you with a good introduction to the exciting world of make-up.

How to use this book

The table below shows which chapters in the book cover which units of the following qualifications:

- Level 2 Technical Certificate in Make-Up Artistry (6010-20)
- Level 3 Advanced Technical Diploma in Media Make-Up Artistry (540) (6010-30)
- Level 3 Advanced Technical Diploma in Theatrical, Special Effects and Media Make-Up Artistry (540) (6010-31).

	Level 2 Technical Certificate in Make-Up Artistry (6010-20)	Level 3 Advanced Technical Diploma in Media Make-Up Artistry (540) (6010-30)	Level 3 Advanced Technical Diploma in Theatrical, Special Effects and Media Make-Up Artistry (540) (6010-31)
Chapter 1 Working in the make-up, film, TV and theatre industries	201	301	
Chapter 2 Anatomy and physiology for make-up artists	202		
Chapter 3 Researching, planning and showcasing designs: creating a look book and industry portfolio	203	302, 320	
Chapter 4 The art of applying make-up	204		
Chapter 5 Creative hair design for media make-up	205	304	
Chapter 6 Fashion and photographic make-up		303	
Chapter 7 Historical hair and make-up looks		305	
Chapter 8 Face and body art	206	306	
Chapter 9 Camouflage make-up		307	307
Chapter 10 Cutting and styling techniques for performers		309	309
Chapter 11 Avant-garde hair and make-up		310	310
Chapter 12 Apply prosthetic pieces and bald caps			321
Chapter 13 Special effects make-up			322

At the beginning of each chapter there is an **Introduction** which provides an overview of the topics covered in the chapter and a brief summary of learning outcomes.

Throughout the book you will see the following features:

- **Handy hints** are useful tips to assist you or help you remember something important.
- **Key terms**, marked in bold purple in the text, are explained to aid your understanding. (They are also explained in the Glossary at the back of the book.)
- **Health and safety** boxes flag important points to help you follow safe working practices.
- **Activities** provide theoretical and practical tasks to support knowledge and understanding.

At the end of each chapter there are some **Test your knowledge** questions. These are designed to identify any areas where you might need further training or revision.

There are also **Practical assignments** at the end of some chapters which are short practical activities that help you prepare for the synoptic assignment.

Acknowledgements

The Publishers would like to thank the following for their invaluable contributions to the photoshoots for this book:

- Kelly Rawlings, Tracey Gaines, Nicki Purchase, Rachael Kent and Zoe Tatum-Rooney for their technical expertise.
- Models:
  - Zaria Long
  - Lauren Jones
  - Hannah Brown
  - Catherine Robinson
  - Jessica Gaines
  - Stephen Gaines
  - Lucy Jayne Blanchard
  - Claire Harrington
- Photographers:
  - Phil Jones, www.philjones-photography.co.uk
  - Mary Doggett, https://ettphotography.co.uk
  - Lucy Jayne Blanchard

Thanks also to everyone who has contributed to previous Hodder Education and City & Guilds photoshoots, on which we have drawn for this book.

Finally, thanks to Kryolan Professional Make-up (https://uk.kryolan.com) and Gorton Studio (www.gortonstudio.co.uk) for kindly supplying photos for the book.

CHAPTER 1

WORKING IN THE MAKE-UP, FILM, TV AND THEATRE INDUSTRIES

INTRODUCTION

Many exciting and varied careers are possible within the make-up industry for those with a passion for make-up, hair and fashion.

This chapter will explore the factors that contribute to a successful career within the industry, and how a professional portfolio can be used to showcase your abilities to potential employers at interviews.

You will also learn the importance of safe working practices within the make-up industry, and how to communicate effectively and build professional relationships.

This chapter is linked to all of the chapters within this textbook and covers fundamental aspects such as: health and safety; professional practice; consultation; communication; contra-indications and contra-actions; preparation of self, work area and model; recommendations and evaluation.

In this chapter, you will learn about:

1 the factors to consider when entering the make-up industry
2 how to work safely within the make-up industry
3 the expectations of working within the make-up industry
4 sales opportunities when providing make-up services
5 the factors to consider when preparing a make-up and hair application
6 how to provide recommendations and evaluate the make-up and hair application.

1 FACTORS TO CONSIDER WHEN ENTERING THE MAKE-UP INDUSTRY

The make-up industry is an amazing place to work and there are many rewarding job opportunities within it. Working for a professional brand in retail, such as MAC, Estée Lauder or Benefit, can be exciting. The hours are long but the rewards are high, and there will be opportunities to progress in your career, become a senior make-up artist and work as part of a team travelling around the country. Working in the film sector is fast-paced and varied, but the work can be very intense and working hours are also long. The theatre is also a thriving sector of the make-up industry. It too can involve long hours, with both matinee and evening performances, but there is an amazing atmosphere at every show, and the work can a take you all over the world when shows are touring.

To become a professional make-up artist, it is very important to gain the correct qualifications. The more experience you have, the better the job opportunities that will open up to you within the industry.

Progression routes

There are several progression routes open to make-up artists. Working through the different levels – Levels 2, 3 and 4, or subsidiary, diploma and extended – will give you a better depth of knowledge and experience, as well as a broad overview of the world of make-up and hairstyling.

Level 4 qualifications in theatrical and media make-up

You can take Level 4 qualifications at colleges or private training providers. Having a Level 4 qualification will make it easier to gain entry into university or an apprenticeship, for example, with the BBC or ITV. It a good qualification to obtain even if you do not want to progress to university – for example, because you want to set up your own business.

These qualifications may cover:
- techniques and materials to make TV- and theatre-grade prosthetic pieces
- life casting
- sculpting techniques
- custom bald caps and prosthetic pieces
- advanced techniques for applying, blending and colouring prosthetics and bald caps
- deconstructing scripts to see where make-up is needed
- key communication skills to convey information to a team
- presentation techniques for designs
- pitching designs to a director to fit the design brief
- research
- business management.

University degrees in related subjects

A degree course in hair and make-up prepares the make-up artist for a career as a practitioner in a variety of sectors, such as fashion, hair and make-up design, wig making, prosthetics, theatre, film and TV. These qualifications will teach you the practical skills of make-up and hair design, as well as an understanding of historical and current influences on fashion, society and the environment. Visual and academic research skills will also be covered, which will underpin your creative practice, analytical skills and critical awareness in readiness for the major assignments that you will undertake in your final year.

Increasingly, make-up artists need to be versatile and flexible to respond to the convergence of fashion with **time-based media** and new technologies and platforms. As a student, you will learn about this sector of the fashion industry and the position of the make-up artist and hair designer within it.

KEY TERM

Time-based media: the Guggenheim Museum describes this as contemporary artwork, including video, film, slides, audio or computer technologies, that have duration as a dimension and unfold to the viewer over time.

The importance of teamwork will be explored through collaborative projects that will be completed throughout the course. Students will also learn to work independently to develop skills and their own personal style in preparation for entering the industry.

ACTIVITY

Research all the universities that interest you as a make-up artist. Make a list of the qualifications they offer and the pros and cons of each.

Apprenticeships within film, TV and theatre

Apprenticeships are available in TV, film and theatre companies. They are a fantastic opportunity as they give make-up artists the chance to build up skills and experience while earning a salary. An apprentice working in the industry is expected to:

- be approachable, enthusiastic and willing to assist others in a fast-paced, exciting environment
- work long hours
- have the ability to communicate positively with the entire production team
- work closely with a team of make-up artists and supervisors
- have prior experience of working with scripts and schedules.

Gaining as much experience as possible is key to getting accepted on an apprenticeship programme. One way to do this is to join a local amateur dramatics group to learn how to read scripts and get involved with the preparation of the shows.

▲ **Figure 1.1** Working behind the scenes on a film set

ACTIVITY

Research the apprenticeships that are available to make-up artists.

Continuing professional development

Continuing professional development (CPD) is the process of tracking and documenting the skills, knowledge and experience that you have gained both formally and informally. It is a record of your experiences and learning – generally in the form of a physical folder or portfolio – that documents your development as a professional.

The make-up industry is a fast-paced, evolving industry that requires make-up artists to keep up to date. It is a freelance make-up artist's responsibility to keep informed of new innovations in products and fashions and to develop new skills. Companies will have their own CPD policies and it is their responsibility to supply CPD training on new techniques, equipment and products to the make-up artists who work for them.

The CPD process helps you to manage your development on an ongoing basis, and to record, review and reflect on your learning. There are a variety of private training providers across the UK that offer short CPD courses to continue your professional development as a make-up artist.

Private training providers

Private or independent training providers (ITPs) offer training and vocational courses to small groups or on a one-to-one basis to young people and adults. They must be fully certified to be able to give out recognisable certificates. Private training providers are not run by the council and students pay a fee to take their courses.

Types of employment, businesses and jobs

There are different types of employment within the make-up industry.

Different types of employment

Employed status

If you are employed, you have a permanent employment contract with the organisation that you work for. An employee working for a company is entitled to receive sick pay, holiday pay, a pension and possibly health care.

▼ Table 1.1 Benefits and drawbacks of being employed on a permanent contract

Benefits of being employed	Drawbacks of being employed
Regular pay Opportunities for professional development Benefits package Working alongside other professionals	May have to work regular set hours and commute daily to an office Limited number of days off Less variety so work may become boring

> **HANDY HINT**
>
> Clients expect make-up artists to be on top of fashion trends and to be in the know about the latest looks and colour palettes. The best make-up artists are those who are one step ahead of new make-up trends and who keep developing their skills. Do not hesitate to enrol on courses that will increase your skill set.

Fixed-term contract

This refers to an employment contract that starts and ends on a particular date or on completion of a specific task or project. You may be working on a fixed-term contract if you are:

- a seasonal or casual employee taken on for up to six months during a peak period
- a specialist employee needed for a specific project
- covering for maternity leave
- able to negotiate your terms and pay.

You do not count as a fixed-term employee if you:

- have a contract with an agency rather than the company you're working for
- are a student or trainee on a work experience placement
- are working under a 'contract of apprenticeship'.

Casual work contract

Casual work contracts are used when employers have varying demands for staff: for example, sometimes they will need large numbers of staff, while at other times they will not need any staff. Under a casual work contract, the employer does not have to offer work and the individual does not have to accept the work when it is offered.

Casual workers are not considered to be employees, which means that their contracts do not contain many of the standard employment contract clauses, such as those relating to pensions, collective agreements, grievances, disciplinary procedures, maternity and paternity leave, sick pay and retirement.

Self-employed status

Being self-employed as a freelance or a sole trader gives you complete flexibility over your working life, but there can be significant drawbacks. There might be times when your income is irregular, and you are not entitled to many of the benefits offered by employers, such as holiday pay, sick pay or a pension.

▼ **Table 1.2** Benefits and drawbacks of being self-employed

Benefits of being self-employed	Drawbacks of being self-employed
Tax is paid in arrears, so you pay no tax during your first year of business	Work can be irregular
	Fewer employment rights
No limit to holidays	Need to put money aside for holiday or when you want to take time off
Being your own boss	
Work when and where you choose	No sick pay
	A lot of admin, for example, invoices and self assessment tax returns

Volunteering

A volunteer is a person who freely offers to take on a task, responsibility or project, usually without being paid for the work that they provide. For example, a volunteer may work on a theatre production or as an assistant on a film set to gain experience and knowledge of the industry.

Different types of businesses

There are a variety of different types of businesses a make-up artist could venture into.

- **Sole trader (working from home or owning your own premises)** – a self-employed individual running their own business. A self-employed make-up artist may have a room at home set up as a studio where clients come prior to a make-up shoot, for a trial for wedding make-up or for special occasion make-up.
- **Renting a room** – the make-up artist pays rent each month to use a room or studio, usually within a hair or beauty salon.
- **Partnership** – when two or more people go into business together. A partnership is a legal agreement in which the partners agree to run the business as co-owners. All of the partners invest in the business, and each shares the profits and losses.
- **Limited company** – sole traders and partners can choose to set up a limited company. This business structure has a number of benefits, the main one being that it allows people to run a business without any risk to their personal finances if the company fails. This is because business debts only have to be paid by the business, not by the shareholders or owner. However, limited companies have much more complex and time-consuming accounting requirements.
- **Franchise** – a franchise is a self-employment business opportunity that allows make-up artists to start their own company trading under an established brand name and using the brand's products. For example, Body Shop is a popular franchise that allows make-up artists to work in-store and franchise from home. For small business owners, franchising can be a way to expand quickly and cost-effectively.

Different jobs available to hair and make-up artists

Make-up artistry is an extremely versatile career. The best part is that it is almost recession-proof: even when times are tough, people want to look their best. Make-up is a multi-billion-dollar industry and a make-up artist could take any number of career paths.

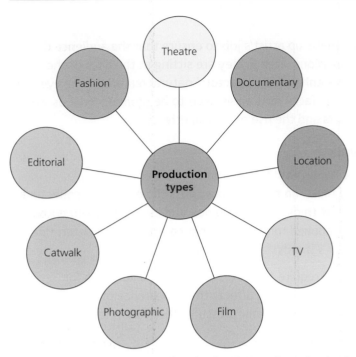

▲ **Figure 1.2** Different types of production that require professional make-up artists

TV and film

Make-up artists working on the sets of films and TV shows might be required to create all kinds of effects, from natural make-up applications that **enhance** an actor's features to special effects and prosthetics, such as in *The Lord of the Rings* or the *Harry Potter* films.

Film and TV work usually means having an irregular work schedule, working long hours for several months in a row followed by a time without work. You may have to relocate temporarily for the duration of the production.

There are four main job titles in the make-up department on a film set.

1 **Key/head make-up artist** – this person is in charge of designing each individual actor's make-up. They apply make-up to the actors and lead roles; they also delegate and oversee the whole make-up production to ensure **continuity** throughout filming.
2 **Make-up artist** – this person is responsible for applying make-up to supporting actors. The make-up artist works closely with the key make-up artist to execute their original designs.
3 **Make-up assistant** – this person organises make-up kits and assists make-up artists throughout the production/shoot. In addition to watching and learning, they may be asked take photographs of cast members to ensure continuity and consistency if a reshoot is required.
4 **Special effects (SFX) make-up artist** – this person is responsible for any special make-up effects, such as applying prosthetics, making and fitting wigs or using foam latex.

The entire make-up department will be on hand throughout filming in case touch-ups or changes are required during the shoot.

KEY TERMS

Enhance: improve or make an area stand out, for example, enhancing cheekbones using a highlighter.

Continuity: ensuring that a hair and make-up look is consistent and looks exactly the same each time the look is created. Scenes are often filmed out of sequence, so any changes to the look need to be tracked and followed in case the scene has to be reshot.

Theatre

In theatre, it is the make-up artist's job to ensure that the audience can see the actors' expressions, even if they are sitting at the back of the theatre. This involves enhancing the actors' natural features – the eyes need to be big and the facial structures need to be pronounced – as well as creating characters and the use of special effects.

Fashion/catwalk

The high fashion/catwalk world is the home of big and bold looks. As well as applying make-up that complements the designer's collection, a make-up artist must think outside the box and create wild and eccentric looks. The make-up applied to the **models** on a catwalk can determine the upcoming season's trends.

Fashion jobs generally require a high artistic ability, a keen eye for detail, knowledge of how lighting affects the appearance of make-up and an ability to work quickly under pressure. The work is fast-paced and fun.

Editorial/commercial

Editorial and commercial make-up tends to be displayed in magazines, on products, on billboards and in advertisements such as TV commercials.

In commercial advertising campaigns, the look tends to be quite simple, so as not to distract from the product itself. It may also need to 'sell' a lifestyle or particular brand image.

When shooting for magazine editorials, the make-up artist's job is to create a look that tells the editorial story. Editorial looks are likely to be more dramatic or **avant-garde** compared to commercial work.

Bridal hair and make-up

Bridal hair and make-up can be very lucrative for a professional make-up artist. A make-up artist can either specialise purely in bridal hair and make-up or carry out freelance bridal make-up work to earn additional income. A person who can combine hairdressing and make-up artistry will be in high demand for bridal packages as they can offer the whole look. Make-up artists who offer bridal make-up are normally busiest in the summer and at weekends.

Hospitals

Being a camouflage cosmetician is a very rewarding career. Camouflage cosmeticians help people with disfigurement, primarily affecting the skin and face. This specialised area entails a great deal more than just adding colour to the face or masking a minor imperfection: it can help to cover scars, burns, birthmarks and any skin disfigurement. For more on camouflage make-up, see Chapter 9.

KEY TERMS

Model: a person employed to wear clothes or make-up for fashion- and editorial-based work.

Avant-garde: out of the ordinary or experimental.

Teaching

To be a successful teacher, a make-up artist needs to understand the responsibilities of a teacher. A teaching qualification will guide you through the best assessment methods, from practical to portfolio work. Once you have a teaching qualification and understand how to assess and teach in different learning styles, the journey of teaching can begin. It is full of variety and fun, which makes it a career cherished by many make-up professionals.

Writing or publicity

If you enjoy writing, becoming an editor or writer is a very rewarding job. This varied role might involve providing content for social media channels, working with graphic design teams on layout and design, testing out new products and meeting representatives from different companies.

There are a variety of writing jobs in the make-up industry.
- **Bloggers** – these people write blogposts about techniques, experiences and products and publish these on an online platform for other people to read.
- **Make-up editors** – editors generally work for magazines, writing about the latest fashions, techniques and products.
- **Textbook writers** – these people write educational textbooks for make-up artists to refer to and to guide them through their qualifications.

Studio

A make-up artist could start up a studio and work independently, creating make-up looks for weddings, proms, photoshoots for family portraits, fashion shoots and one-to-one teaching of make-up application. They could also work in a studio alongside a photographer. This is a very diverse job that relies on word of mouth, advertising and connecting with other professionals within the industry.

Location

A make-up artist could work on location for a film, commercial, TV series or fashion shoot. The location could be an exotic beach, but could equally be a field in the middle of the night. Location work involves very long hours and the make-up artist may need to be able to jump on a plane within 48 hours and be away from home and family for considerable lengths of time.

Retail

Many make-up artists work full- or part-time in retail, selling make-up products in stores, in the cosmetics sections of department stores and at cosmetic events and shows. Retail work involves answering customers' questions, giving makeovers, demonstrating application techniques and selling the products, often on a commission basis. Other make-up artists work full- or part-time in salons and spas, building a dependable clientele list over time. Make-up looks normally range from natural to glamorous. Camouflage work may also be required in covering tattoos or skin **pigmentation** issues.

KEY TERM

Pigmentation: the natural colour of someone's skin.

Legal requirements and insurance

Make-up artists need to know about and understand the following pieces of legislation to ensure that they are working safely to protect their business and models. Note that the following information was correct at the time of publication: it is the make-up artist's responsibility to keep up to date with any changes in legislation.

Legislation

Health and Safety at Work Act 1974

This is the principal piece of legislation within the UK that covers health and safety in the workplace. The act is designed to protect workers and members of the public alike, and applies to both employers, employees and people who are self-employed.

Management of Health and Safety at Work Regulations 1999

These regulations require employers to appoint a person to be responsible for assessing the risks to the health and safety of employees, clients, visitors and anyone entering the workplace. This person is required to take the appropriate actions to eliminate or minimise any risks and they need to be trained and fully aware of all the procedures involved.

If the employer has five or more employees, the responsible person must document the findings of any risk assessment. If any risks have been identified, an action plan must be drawn up. All staff must be aware of the risks and the procedures that will be enforced to control the identified risks.

Health and safety training for all staff must be ongoing, as part of their CPD (see page 4).

Health and Safety (First Aid) Regulations 1981

These first aid regulations provide guidance for employers on how to provide first aid in the workplace. Areas that need to be considered include:
- the provision and maintenance of first aid (first aid kit, equipment, rooms, and so on)
- training for first aiders
- requirements for appointed persons
- making all employees aware of first aid arrangements
- first aid when self-employed
- cases where first aid regulations do not apply.

Personal Protective Equipment at Work Regulations 1992

These regulations state that all employers must provide suitable personal protective equipment (PPE) to all employees who may be exposed to any risk while at work. PPE could include gloves, masks, aprons, eye protection and uniforms. If the employer complies with COSHH regulations (see below), the requirements for PPE regulations will usually be covered.

Provision and Use of Work Equipment Regulations (PUWER) 1998

These regulations place responsibility for work equipment onto the company who own, operate or have control over the equipment. Work equipment is any appliance, tool or machinery that is used at work. This includes equipment that employees use at work, including anything that involves programming, stopping, repairing, transporting, modifying, maintaining, cleaning and servicing the equipment.

Control of Substances Hazardous to Health (COSHH) Regulations 2002

Many substances that are commonly thought to be harmless can be hazardous if used incorrectly or stored contrary to manufacturers' guidelines, which is why all suppliers must provide guidelines on how their materials should be stored and used. Employers are required to carry out a risk assessment to assess which substances potentially pose a risk to health from exposure and to ensure that a record of these substances is compiled. This risk assessment must be carried out regularly and should advise that:

- hazardous substances must be identified by symbols and must be handled and stored correctly
- high-risk products should be replaced by low-risk products whenever possible
- an assessment must be carried out on all members of staff who may be at risk
- PPE should be provided and staff training should be carried out if required.

A hazardous substance can enter the body through:
- contact with the eyes
- inhalation through the nose
- ingestion via the mouth
- contact and absorption through the skin
- the blood stream via injections or open wounds.

Reporting of Injuries, Diseases and Dangerous Occurrences Regulations (RIDDOR) 2013

RIDDOR requires employers and people in control of work premises to report serious workplace accidents. These include work-related deaths, major injuries and seven-day injuries (injuries that cause more than seven days' inability to carry out normal duties), diseases caused through exposure in the workplace and specified dangerous occurrences or near misses (events not causing harm, but have the potential to cause injury or ill health).

It is a legal requirement for employers to gather and record any information about incidents that have occurred in the workplace. Companies with more than ten people working on the premises must, by law, have an accident book to record these incidents.

Environmental Protection Act 1990

This act states that any person disposing of waste must do so safely and in such a way that it does not cause damage to the environment. It is important to take care when disposing of unwanted or out-of-date products: manufacturers' guidelines for disposal should always be followed. In some cases, it is possible to request that the manufacturer disposes of any waste for the business. All employees should be trained in the safe disposal of waste products.

Workplace (Health, Safety and Welfare) Regulations 1992

Employers have a general duty to ensure the health, safety and welfare of their employees at work. These regulations expand on these duties and are intended to protect the health and safety of everyone in the workplace. They ensure that adequate welfare facilities are provided for people at work, whether they are employed by a company or self-employed.

Electricity at Work Regulations 1989

These regulations ensure that precautions are taken against the risk of death or personal injury from electricity in work-based activities. The regulations require employers and self-employed people to take responsibility for the safety and maintenance of electrical systems and electrical equipment on the premises. The regulations also address responsibilities when working with or near electrical equipment. These responsibilities apply to almost all places of work and to electrical systems at all voltages.

Fire Precautions (Workplace) Regulations 1997

Employers or anyone responsible for a workplace must take reasonable steps to reduce the risk from fire and make sure people can escape safely if there is an incident. The areas that need to be addressed include:
- carrying out a fire risk assessment that identifies any possible dangers and risks
- considering who may be especially at risk
- getting rid of or reducing, the risks from fire as far as is reasonably possible and providing general fire precautions to deal with any possible risks left
- taking any other measures to make sure there is protection if flammable or explosive materials are used or stored on the premises
- creating a plan to deal with any emergency
- keeping a record of any findings and reviewing them where necessary.

Manual Handling Operations Regulations 1992

Employers must make provisions for their employees when manual handling is required, such as lifting, transporting or supporting a load. Employees should avoid manual handling if there is a possibility of injury.

If manual handling cannot be avoided, employers must reduce the risk of injury as far as reasonably possible. The regulations specify that:

- hazardous manual handling operations should be avoided so far as reasonably practicable
- any hazardous manual handling operations (including pushing and pulling) that cannot be avoided should be assessed
- the risk of injury should be reduced so far as reasonably practicable.

Employers' Liability (Compulsory Insurance) Act 1969

Employers are obliged to take out employer liability insurance against employee illness or injury. Employer liability insurance enables employers to meet the cost of compensation for injuries or illness whether they are caused on- or off-site.

Working Time Regulations 1998

The Working Time Regulations govern the number of hours most workers can work.

- They limit the average working week – in general, you cannot work more than 48 hours a week, although individuals may choose to opt out and work longer if they wish.
- They specify statutory entitlement to paid leave for most workers – in general, paid annual leave of 5.6 weeks a year.
- They limit the normal hours of night work and regular health assessments.
- They specify special regulations for young workers, who:
  - are restricted to eight hours per day and 40 hours per week, with two days off per week
  - have a 30-minute break every 4.5 hours.

General Product Safety Regulations 2005

These regulations are the main basis for ensuring the safety of consumer goods by imposing certain controls on their safety. They ensure that all products that are to be used by consumers are safe.

EU Cosmetics Directive

The EU Cosmetics Directive defines a cosmetic as 'any substance or preparation intended to be placed in contact with the various external parts of the human body ... or with the teeth and the mucous membranes of the oral cavity, with a view exclusively or mainly to cleaning them, perfuming them, changing their appearance, and/or correcting body odours, and/or protecting them or keeping them in good condition'.

Cosmetics suppliers (manufacturers, importers or exporters) who would like to sell cosmetic products in the EU must comply with the following regulations:

- EU Cosmetic Products Regulation (EC) No. 1223/2009
- REACH Regulation (EC) No. 1907/2006.

As the UK has left the EU, new UK regulations will apply. It is the responsibility of make-up artists to check whether this directive is still applicable.

Supply of Goods and Services Act 1982

This act ensures that traders provide services to an adequate standard of workmanship. However, it only applies to contracts entered into before 1 October 2015. The Consumer Rights Act applies to any contracts after that date.

Sale and Supply of Goods Act 1994

This act regulates the sale of goods in the UK. It was also superseded by the Consumer Rights Act.

Consumer Rights Act 2015

The Consumer Rights Act replaced the Supply of Goods and Services Act, the Sale and Supply of Goods Act and the Unfair Terms in Consumer Contracts Regulations.

The act makes clear that any products or services offered to consumers must be of satisfactory quality, fit for purpose and sold as described. If the service or product does not meet the standards set out under the act, the act provides clear guidelines for consumers on how to resolve the issue.

Trade Descriptions Act 1968

The Trade Descriptions Act ensures that people tell the truth about the products or services that they are selling. It is an offence for a trader to:
- make false statements about the provision of any services, accommodation or facilities
- apply a false trade description to any goods
- supply or offer to supply any goods to which a false trade description is applied.

Local Government (Miscellaneous Provisions) Act 1976

This act grants a variety of powers to local authorities in England and Wales, including the power to regulate establishments such as tattoo shops, ear piercing studios and acupuncture clinics.

Data Protection Act 2018

This act controls how the personal information of any living person is used by a business or organisation. Every staff member who has access to personal data has a responsibility to ensure that it is used legally and fairly, and cannot be accessed without permission.

The types of information covered by the act include:

- name
- address and contact information
- health and medical details
- financial information
- race and ethnic background
- religious beliefs
- criminal convictions.

The General Data Protection Regulation (GDPR) is a set of rules designed to give people more control over their personal data. The GDPR came into effect from May 2018 and was designed to modernise laws that protect the personal information of individuals.

Equality Act 2010

This act protects people from being discriminated against in the workplace. It aims to ensure that all employees are given equal opportunities and to prevent people being treated unfairly because of their:

- gender
- race
- disability
- religious beliefs
- sexual orientation
- age.

Protecting your business

In every type of business, professionals must offer high-quality services to satisfy their customers. To do so, they must have the right skills and techniques, which are usually acquired through training and experience. In addition to this, make-up artists need to understand the risks that they may encounter and the importance of protecting their business, themselves and their clients. Insurance coverage is an essential part of this.

Public liability insurance

No matter how skilled you are and how much experience you have, it only takes a split second to have a lapse in concentration, slip with the mascara wand and cause serious damage to a client's eye. This is just an example of something that could happen, but it illustrates why public liability insurance is vital for make-up artists. This is because public liability insurance protects you from serious financial and legal difficulties in the event of any accidental slips or injuries that you could be liable for. It is not compulsory for make-up artists, but it is certainly the first type of protection you should take out.

A typical make-up artist's insurance policy covers:

- public liability
- product liability
- treatment risk
- financial loss.

Employer's liability

As an employer, you are responsible for the health and safety of your employees while they are at work.

Employer's liability insurance provides cover against claims by employees who have had an injury or illness in the course of their employment, such as being injured in an accident that occurs because health and safety rules have not been implemented.

Car insurance

Car insurance is a legal requirement for any vehicle kept on the street, on a driveway or in a garage (unless you have permission to keep it off public roads). Although insurance cover is mandatory, you do have a choice in the kind of policy you buy.

Business car insurance is not the same as commercial car insurance. Business insurance covers regular driving, for example, to appointments with clients, while commercial insurance is primarily aimed at motorists who use their vehicle for commercial purposes, such as making deliveries or transporting tools and materials.

Contents insurance

Contents insurance covers the cost of replacing your possessions if they are damaged or destroyed, for example, by fire or flooding. The most important thing you need to consider when calculating how much contents insurance you need is how much the contents of your studio are actually worth.

Buildings insurance

Buildings insurance will provide money to cover the costs of repairing or rebuilding your property if it is damaged or destroyed.

Disclaimer

A disclaimer is often used when the model or customer signs to say they agree to the service and that the information they have given is true, for example, regarding contra-indications.

Working from home

If you are using your home as a base for your business – whether your business provides a service, sells or makes a product or employs six people full time – you may require specialist home business cover.

Possible insurance policies that a make-up artist working from home may need to take out include:
- professional indemnity insurance – any business providing a professional service is vulnerable to a claim of negligence if the service fails to meet the client's expectations

- employer's liability insurance – this protects a business against the cost of a compensation claim made in the event of an employee injury or work-related illness
- public liability insurance – this covers the cost of claims made by a member of the public for an incident that may have occurred at the make-up artist's premises
- cover for personal equipment, stock, goods in transit or product liability.

Requirements of becoming a freelance make-up artist

A professional freelance make-up artist can set their own hours and rate of pay, choose their clients and build a fabulous brand to be proud of. To run your own business, you must:

- register with HM Revenue and Customs (HMRC)
- register your business with Companies House if you are setting up as a limited company
- keep detailed and accurate records of your finances
- understand allowances and tax reliefs
- make tax, national insurance and pension contributions.

You may also need to:

- register a domain name for your website
- create business cards
- promote your business, such as at wedding fairs.

ACTIVITY

Research each of these requirements for becoming a successful freelance make-up artist and write a detailed description of each.

HANDY HINT

It is important for any freelance worker to have a large and well-connected network. Talking to people at events or connecting with people online will help you to build a reputable, professional business.

Communication and teamwork

Communication is how we pass on, receive and respond to information. Good communication skills are essential for make-up artists as communication can make the difference between a poor make-up application and an excellent one. Poor communication often leads to confusion, misunderstanding and mistakes.

We can communicate in a variety of ways.

- Verbal communications – spoken words and listening.
- Non-verbal communication, including:
  - body language and symbolic gestures
  - written words and images (emails, texts, letters, and promotional material such as leaflets, blogs and websites).
- Listening skills – good listening allows us to demonstrate that we are paying attention when talking with models or clients.

- Visual images – using visual aids (such as a mood board or digital images) is a great way to communicate with models or clients. This allows both parties to share their ideas.
- Multimedia – a variety of media platforms can be used when communicating with clients or models, for example, using pictures and videos found on the internet to explore different imagery.

Verbal communication

Verbal communication includes speaking and asking questions. There are different types of questioning skills. **Open questions** are used to start a conversation and include the words 'what', 'where', 'why', 'when', 'who', 'which' and 'how'. However, during consultation, you could also use the following words or phrases to draw information from your client.

- *Tell* me about your make-up requirements.
- *Explain* exactly what the theme/occasion is.
- *Describe* what you would like the end results to look like.

Closed questions are those that can be answered by either 'yes' or 'no'. They can be used to confirm information.

ACTIVITY

Sit back to back with a partner. Using verbal communication only, describe one of the following pictures by naming the shapes and explaining their position in relation to each other.

 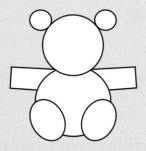 

Your partner's job is to draw the picture you are describing without looking at you or the original picture.

Non-verbal communication

This includes all movement of the body, such as:
- body language and symbolic gestures
- eye contact, eye movement and staring
- facial expressions
- signs of active listening, such as head nodding
- posture
- written words
- images.

▼ **Table 1.3** Examples of positive and negative non-verbal communication

Positive non-verbal communication	Negative non-verbal communication
Smiling	Frowning
Direct eye contact (without staring)	Staring (this kind of eye contact can be seen as aggressive)
Keeping arms and legs uncrossed	Moving away while speaking
Leaning slightly forward to show interest	Yawning
Subtle mirroring, meaning that your body language is the same as or similar to that of the person you are communicating with	Looking away
	Sneering or an expression of distaste or disgust
	Shaking head to say no
	Chewing gum

Communicating professionally

As a make-up artist it is very important to know how to communicate and behave appropriately. A make-up artist has to remain professional at all times, even after a long day on location when you may be tired and cold. Failing to behave professionally can have a detrimental effect on your career.

This means you must:
- speak clearly when talking to the model or client
- listen to models' requests
- keep your body language positive
- record details about product or make-up requirements
- follow instructions from senior make-up artists or directors
- give direction to the model/client on how to sit/stand throughout application of make-up
- use a range of professional terminology
- work as part of a team at all times.

Make-up artists also need to understand the importance of professional practice, which may include:
- checking the model's well-being throughout the service
- ensuring environmental conditions, such as temperature, are suitable for the model and the service
- using working methods that minimise the risk of **cross-contamination**
- ensuring the use of clean equipment and materials
- leaving the service area and equipment in a suitable condition
- promoting environmental and sustainable working practices
- using professional etiquette, for example, by being polite and presenting yourself in a way that makes people comfortable around you
- taking the diverse needs of models, **performers** and clients into account
- maintaining the model's modesty at all times.

> **HANDY HINT**
>
> Remember that everyone is different, so value everyone's opinion even if you do not agree with them. Treat people fairly and professionally.

KEY TERMS

Cross-contamination: when microorganisms are transferred from one place to another, through direct or indirect contact, such as through unhygienic practices.

Performer: a person employed to act in production-based work, for example, film, TV and theatre.

2 SAFE WORKING PRACTICES WITHIN THE MAKE-UP INDUSTRY

It is very important to follow safe working practices to prevent injuries, accidents and cross-infection while working as a make-up artist.

Avoiding cross-contamination

There are two ways in which cross-contamination can be avoided.

- **Decanting products where possible** – this ensures that micro-organisms are not transferred from the model's skin into the product's container. However, decanting products can be very difficult as make-up artists do not want to ruin expensive palettes and cause wastage by decanting too much product. An alternative is to spray palettes with isopropyl alcohol before and after every use, which acts as a disinfectant.
- **Using disposables** – using one-use disposables such as mascara wands can prevent the transfer of bacterial, viral or fungal infections from one person to another. There are environmental impacts of using disposables, however. See pages 32–33 for more information on environmental and sustainable working practices.

Maintaining safe working environmental conditions

Ways to keep the working environment safe include:

- using the correct lighting for the make-up application (see Chapter 6, pages 159–165, for detailed information)
- where possible, making sure the temperature is comfortable for the model or client, as this can affect the make-up application
- being aware of the model or client's personal space and, as much as possible, not being too intrusive
- ensuring there is adequate ventilation if working inside, especially if working with highly perfumed products or a spray machine.

Use and disposal of products and waste

Be sure to tidy the work area and dispose of all waste safely. Make sure that any contaminated waste is disposed of into a bin. When working with prosthetics, be aware that certain products, such as alginate and clay, cannot be disposed of down the sink.

First aid procedures

Having a first aid qualification is highly recommended. When working on premises, be sure to have a first aid box containing all of the essentials. When working on location, make sure you know who to go to in case of a first aid situation.

KEY TERM

Decant: remove a product from its original container using a spatula to avoid cross-contamination.

HEALTH AND SAFETY

Products should be decanted to avoid any cross-contamination. You can use a spatula to remove the product from its original packaging and place it on a make-up palette or the back of your hands, as long as you have washed them and they are clean.

A basic first aid kit should contain:

- plasters in a variety of different sizes and shapes
- small, medium and large sterile gauze dressings
- at least two sterile eye dressings
- triangular bandages
- rolled crêpe bandages
- safety pins
- disposable sterile gloves
- tweezers
- scissors
- alcohol-free cleansing wipes
- medical sticky tape
- thermometer (preferably digital)
- skin rash cream, such as hydrocortisone or calendula
- cream or spray to relieve insect bites and stings
- antiseptic cream
- cough medicine
- antihistamine cream or tablets
- distilled water for cleaning wounds
- eye wash and eye bath.

Fire and evacuation procedures

Employers are responsible for fire safety in the workplace including:

- carrying out fire risk assessments and reviewing them regularly – a written record must be kept if there are more than five people in the business
- putting appropriate fire safety measures in place and maintaining them – this includes a fire detection and warning system, fire extinguishers, fire exit signs and clearly marked escape routes
- planning for an emergency
- providing staff with information, fire safety instruction and training.

▲ **Figure 1.3** A fire evacuation sign

If a fire alarm goes off, all occupants must evacuate the building immediately. When a fire is detected, the following steps should be taken to keep everyone safe.

1 Call the emergency services immediately and provide all the information required.
2 Help anyone who may be injured.
3 Exit the building following the emergency evacuation procedure, ensuring that any lifts in the building are **not** used.
4 Ensure everyone is out of the building.
5 Assemble everyone at the designated location away from harm.
6 Stay away from the building until a fire marshal or firefighter tells you that it is safe to go back inside.

Firefighting equipment

There are many different types of firefighting equipment, so get the equipment that is best suited to your working environment and make sure you know how to use it.

Fire extinguishers

Most modern fire extinguishers can deal with a variety of different fire scenarios. They can be filled with powder, foam, water additive or carbon dioxide.

There are four classes of fire extinguishers. Each class puts out a different type of fire.
- Class A extinguishers put out fires in ordinary combustibles, such as wood and paper.
- Class B extinguishers are for use on flammable liquids, such as grease, gasoline and oil.
- Class C extinguishers are for fires in live electrical equipment.
- Class D extinguishers are designed for use on flammable metals.

No fire extinguisher works on all types of fire.

A fire extinguisher should never be used to prop open a door. It should be fixed to the wall, and regularly checked by a service technician.

▲ **Figure 1.4** Powder fire extinguisher

Fire blankets

Fire blankets can be used to smother small fires that start in the workplace or at home. Economy fire blankets or white kitchen blankets are a good choice for small kitchens.

Personal protective equipment for self and client

Personal protective equipment (PPE) should always be used when required for health and safety purposes, especially when using chemicals and products that can be harmful if not used correctly. PPE also protects the client and ensures that they are ready for the application.

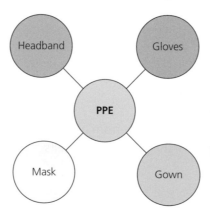

▲ **Figure 1.5** Types of personal protective equipment

▲ **Figure 1.6** A model in a gown

The importance of risk assessments and the process for carrying them out

Risk assessments are carried out to ensure the health and safety of workers and anyone else visiting the workplace. A risk assessment is a process of identifying any **hazards** in a workplace and the risks associated with them, then taking measures to remove or reduce the risk. It is a legal requirement for all employers to have a risk assessment in place.

The six steps to take when carrying out a risk assessment are:

1 identifying hazards
2 deciding who might be harmed and how
3 evaluating risks and deciding on precautions
4 recording findings
5 implementing recommendations
6 reviewing the risk assessment as required.

3 EXPECTATIONS OF WORKING WITHIN THE MAKE-UP INDUSTRY

Working with others in the make-up industry

It is very important to understand the different roles in the make-up industry and the importance of working effectively with others as part of a team. Depending on the job and location, there can be a vast number of people working together, whether it is for TV, film, theatre or music videos. As a make-up artist, it is important to work closely with all the other teams involved. Some of the professionals that a make-up artist may work with include:

- stylists
- hairdressers
- nail technicians
- photographers
- runners
- editors
- models
- producers
- directors
- light technicians
- sound engineers
- floor managers
- choreographers
- set designers
- performers or actors
- costume designers
- agents.

Skills and attributes of a make-up artist

A make-up artist needs to have certain skills and **attributes** to work professionally and to gain recommendations and a good reputation. Skills are the things that you have learnt through work, training or education and general life experience. They are tangible and can be backed up by qualifications and real-life examples. Attributes are the characteristics or qualities that you might naturally have – perhaps you're a naturally chatty person or you might be very resilient – that benefit you in life and work.

The following skills and attributes are essential for a make-up artist.

- **Time management** – it is important to work to a schedule.
- **Punctuality** – arrive at work early enough to set up and be ready for the day. Never rush in exactly on time or late.
- **Efficient work practices** – be professional at all times and adhere to all specific working practices.
- **Reliability** – the job of a make-up artist is very specialised and the reputation of the client is at stake, so you must avoid letting them down. No one will employ a make-up artist who is unreliable.
- **Attendance** – attendance is key as a make-up artist; only take time off when completely necessary to prevent any disruption to the job, whether it is on location, at a theatre or on a film set.
- **Organisation** – make sure all make-up is organised prior to turning up to a job, and that your kit is appropriate to the job you are carrying out.
- **Forward planning** – make sure your journey to the job is pre-planned; know exactly where to go and what parking is available, and whether food and refreshments will be available if working on location or somewhere secluded. Make sure everything is planned before the job starts.
- **Flexibility** – you need to be flexible as a make-up artist. The location, the model, the make-up application or all three may change at the last minute, so aim to be versatile and adaptable.
- **Troubleshooting** – be aware that looks may change and that the make-up look will be discussed as a team and worked out together. Make sure that you contribute to these discussions.
- **Professionalism** – be professional at all times, even when you are feeling tired and stressed. Professionalism is key to progress in the make-up industry. You should:
  - work as a team
  - show respect
  - be reliable
  - be honest
  - be ethical
  - be attentive
  - be polite.
- **Creativity and imagination** – your make-up ideas need to be imaginative and creative and should showcase your skills.
- **Research skills and up-to-date knowledge** – the industry changes very quickly, so it is important to keep up to date with current techniques and to research new looks.
- **Personal presentation** – although there is no set uniform for a make-up artist, and many artists have their own individual style, it is important to look professional at all times. This includes having:
  - good personal hygiene
  - neat hair and nails
  - appropriate clothing
  - positive body language.
- **Etiquette** – be polite and professional at all times.
- **Confidentiality** – make-up artists work closely with a lot of people, including very famous people, so be sure to keep everything that you discuss with your model or client confidential.

Effective interview techniques

Being interviewed for a job can be nerve-racking. You may feel uncomfortable 'selling' yourself and the prospect of having to meet and impress new people may make you anxious. However, being interviewed is a skill you can learn. With the right techniques, you can become a master at sharing your value with potential employers, presenting yourself effectively and getting the jobs you want.

▼ **Table 1.4** Dos and don'ts for interviews

Do	Don't
Listen to the questions that you are being asked	Don't be late
Make sure you understand the question and take time to answer	Avoid being arrogant or coming across as overconfident
Answer questions clearly and concisely	Don't discuss controversial topics such as religion, politics or gender relations
Be enthusiastic	Don't criticise former employers
Use positive body language	Try not to appear too nervous
Prepare answers for questions you may be asked	Don't slouch or look uninterested
Be positive and confident about yourself and your experiences	Don't swear or use slang words
Prepare some questions to ask the interviewer	Don't lie
Dress smartly	Don't read from notes
Make sure you have read up about the company and understand the role	Don't argue with the interviewer
Try to always make eye contact and not look away	
Make sure you arrive in plenty of time	

Production demands

A lot of planning is required in order to develop the design ideas for the make-up in a production. This could include:

- attending scheduled meetings and rehearsals
- working to timescales
- understanding the roles and responsibilities of others
- taking instruction
- taking meetings minutes
- working as part of a team.

Table 1.5 outlines the production demands that need to be considered when working as a make-up artist. When working as part of a production team, the make-up artist needs to be aware of many different elements in the production process.

▼ **Table 1.5** Parts of the production process for a make-up artist

Discussion with design team	This involves meeting with the teams that designed the set, backdrops, stage, management, make-up and hair.
Text analysis	This allows the make-up artist to interpret the words the writer has given them and transform them into live action.
Design analysis	This involves analysing the space, costumes and props that you see when you watch a performance.
Script breakdown	Breaking down the script into bite-size pieces and discussing the characters in detail allows the make-up artist to get the full picture of the characters' looks and the theme.
Continuity	For make-up artists, this means ensuring that the look of the actors in the same scene is consistent when it is shot over several days or out of sequence.
Interpretation of character role	Make-up artists need to design the make-up to suit the character, so their own interpretation of the character look is key.
Budget	It is important to work to a budget (an amount of money or expenditure allowed to complete the job). You may need to adapt the look accordingly in certain situations, such as for a low-budget production.
Costings	The make-up artist lists the products to be used and creates a costings sheet.
Equipment	This is the equipment available or needed for the production, for example, airbrush machines, hairdryers and tongs.
Lighting	What lighting will the make-up be applied under? What lighting will be used when it is filmed or shot? Will it be inside or outside? Is it daytime or nighttime?
Costume designs	Will the models or performers be in costume before or after the make-up is applied? Is the costume restrictive?
Call sheets	A call sheet is the daily schedule in film-making. It details the shooting schedule and shot list associated with each scene that will be filmed that day.
Safety issues	Are there any health and safety elements that need to be adhered to, for example, will any additional PPE be required?
Suitability of the design	Does the planned make-up look suit the model or performer's features and skin type? It is a good idea to meet or see pictures of the models or performers before creating a suitable make-up look for them, so that you can take into account their face shape and characteristics, their skin tone and type their eye shape, their gender and age and any allergies they may have. Products will be chosen to suit the skin type/tone of the performer.
Cast and crew list	How many cast members are there to design looks for? How many make-up artists will be required for the application?
Shooting schedule	A shooting schedule allows make-up artists to know who to get ready and in what order.
Confidentiality	A make-up artist has to be aware of client confidentiality, particularly when working with famous clients. Also, a make-up artist may get a script before the film has been advertised, so the storyline has to be kept confidential.
On-set etiquette	Always be well presented and behave in a professional manner while on set. Come with the correct kit and be familiar with the shooting schedule.

Benefits of social media

Social media is a fantastic tool for businesses, allowing them to send messages about their brand to the right people at the right time. For make-up artists, it offers the opportunity to showcase their work to a lot of people. This attracts professional and personal connections, as well as potential clients all over the world.

▲ **Figure 1.7** Benefits of using social media

For more information on different social media platforms, see Chapter 15, pages 336–338. Of course, there are many more conventional methods of promoting yourself as an established make-up artist as well.

Facebook

Facebook is a social networking site that allows users to create personal or business profiles, upload photos and videos and send messages. The advantages for a make-up artist of using Facebook include being:

- discoverable – when people search for you on the internet, they'll be able to find you on Facebook
- connected – you can have one-to-one conversations with your customers, who can 'like' your page, read your posts and share them with friends and check in when they visit your premises
- timely – your page can help you to reach large groups of people frequently, with messages tailored to their needs and interests
- insightful – analytics on your page will give you a deeper understanding of your customers and your marketing activities.

Twitter

People use Twitter to talk about what's happening around them right there and then, as well as to share photos and videos. It allows make-up artists to connect with others and can be a powerful way to engage with the public. It can influence conversations and help to build a very successful business.

Instagram

Instagram allows make-up artists to share pictures and videos of their work instantly from their mobile devices. Instagram can be used to promote a business by:
- inviting users to view all make-up looks
- taking users behind the scenes of the make-up artist's work
- offering exclusive benefits to followers.

LinkedIn

LinkedIn is a network of about 45 million professionals. It can be used to:
- build an online business reputation
- meet key contacts in your industry
- get business and sell products
- find quality candidates for jobs
- promote professional identity
- find relevant online communities of others in your profession.

KEY TERMS

Blog: a regularly updated website or online journal where a writer shares information on a specific subject area.

Vlog: a video blog shared on a platform such as YouTube®.

Blogging and vlogging

Many businesses use **blogs** – a regularly updated website or online journal – to communicate with their customers and the general public. **Vlogs** (video blogs) are recorded as videos, rather than written, and shared on platforms such as YouTube.

Blogging on a frequent basis is a relatively easy, inexpensive way to enhance your business and attract prospective customers. You can use it to:
- develop relationships with potential and existing customers
- establish your business as an industry leader
- connect people to your brand
- create opportunities for sharing your work.

For more on blogging and vlogging see Chapter 15.

Z-CARD

A Z-CARD® is a type of business card. Just like a portfolio, they showcase the make-up artist's versatility.

YouTube

YouTube is a website designed for sharing video material. It is a fantastic tool for make-up artists and many use it to showcase their work.

Dropbox

Dropbox is a cloud-storage service that allows you store and share files – whatever they are – and access them at any time from different devices via the Dropbox app and website. You could upload pictures, your CV or testimonials from your clients, and be able to share them with prospective employers straight away.

Pinterest

Pinterest is a website that allows you to 'pin' things online, just as you might pin pictures to a real-life bulletin board. Pinterest saves your pins on your account so that you can access them easily. You can also follow friends on Pinterest and 're-pin' things that they have already pinned on their Pinterest boards or browse a live feed of items that are being pinned by others when you're searching for inspiration.

Model Mayhem

Model Mayhem is a subscription-based social network for models, make-up artists, stylists, photographers and other creative professionals. It can be used showcase your work or portfolio online and to advertise when a job is coming up.

HANDY HINT

Before posting photos on social media, you may need to edit them to show your work at its best.

Advantages of photo editing:

- It can be useful for minor editing effects such as reducing red eye, whitening teeth or eyes and enhancing colour.
- You can change a colour photo to a black and white photo.
- Photos can be cropped to remove backgrounds or other items not required in the picture.
- Backgrounds and effects can be added to enhance the overall look.

Disadvantages of photo editing:

- Editing programs can be expensive to purchase.
- Photo editing requires a good skill level.
- Those not trained in the use of editing software will not be able to use all the available tools effectively.
- An edited photo does not provide a true representation of a make-up artist's skill level.
- A professional-looking image can be very time consuming to achieve.

---

4 SALES OPPORTUNITIES WHEN PROVIDING MAKE-UP SERVICES

A make-up artist working on a counter in a shop or a department store should be able to advise on the best products to suit a customer's skin type or skin tone. They need to be able to demonstrate techniques and to sell products.

The key to creating sales opportunities is knowing the products and services that are on offer and asking the customer questions to make it easier to assess which products they will benefit from the most. This avoids the need for awkward hard-sell tactics. Often, the customer will not even realise that they have had products promoted to them.

Principles of sales

Every sale follows the same pattern. The seven steps outlined in Table 1.6 will enable you to build a relationship with the customer and complete the sale.

▼ **Table 1.6** The seven Ps of selling

Probe	Interview the customer: ask questions and listen to the answers carefully to find out everything you can. These questions should be asked as a part of the consultation with the customer when finding out about their make-up routines at home.
Prescribe	Use the information gained to recommend products or services that you feel will benefit the customer.
Present	Demonstrate the product to the customer so that they have instant, first-hand experience of the products you are offering them.
Participate	Keep the customer involved in the selling process by giving them the products to hold.
Problem solve	A customer is unlikely to hand over cash for a product you have just introduced to them immediately; they are probably going to put obstacles in the way. The key is to anticipate these obstacles and be prepared to offer a solution to their problem.
Purchase	The customer will purchase the recommended product or products.
Promote	Record the purchases and recommend other products or services. This provides repeat business.

Creating a rapport with clients

It is very important to create a rapport with clients as soon as they walk into the room. This is done by:
- meeting and greeting the client with confidence and professionalism
- using positive body language, such as smiling, standing straight and looking happy.

HANDY HINT

Reading people's eyes is important. If there is eye contact in a retail situation, the client is being open and attentive and may be interested in making a purchase.

Consulting with clients to investigate wants and needs

Talk to clients to find out what they want from the make-up service. Why have they come in for a makeover or to purchase make-up products? Is it a special occasion? You should:

- find out what make-up range the client is using currently
- use both open and closed questions
- actively listen to the client's responses
- summarise the client's requirements for them.

Matching and presenting products to clients

This might involve:

- colour matching the product against the client's skin tone
- demonstrating product application
- describing features and benefits
- link selling, for example, selling a foundation with the matching powder.

Closing sales

To complete the sale, the make-up artist must be able to:

- identify buying signals – what does the client want?
- identify any objections
- ask for the sale
- identify repeat business opportunities.

5 FACTORS TO CONSIDER WHEN PREPARING A MAKE-UP AND HAIR APPLICATION

See the section on preparing make-up services in Chapter 4, pages 103–108.

Briefing techniques

The client's requirements are known as a brief. You will need to know the following to successfully conduct a briefing session.

- **Understand the importance of communicating with models in a professional manner** – for more on communicating with your model, see the section on communication and teamwork, pages 17–19.
- **Know how to conduct a briefing session, taking into account the model's diverse needs** – make-up artists need to understand how to deal with a range of diverse needs, understanding why models should not be discriminated against because of their culture, religion, age, disability or gender.
- **Know the legal requirements for providing services to minors under 16 years of age** – models under 16 years of age must be accompanied by a parent/guardian at all times.

- **Understand the importance of agreeing the service and outcomes to meet the model's needs** – it is very important that the model is aware of the service being carried out, so they know what to expect. The make-up look may have been chosen by the client rather than the model, but you should always talk to the model about it and agree on the application.
- **Know the legal requirements for storing and protecting personal data if needed** – it is a legal requirement to keep all models' or clients' personal data private. It should be stored on a computer that has a password to keep it secure or kept in a lockable cabinet. The introduction of the GDPR in 2018 changed the way that businesses handle the information of their customers – for more information see the section on the Data Protection Act, pages 14–15.
- **Know how to complete record cards** – it is important to fill out a record card. This should include all of the information regarding the service, for example, whether it is a camouflage treatment or make-up for a special occasion. This information is used to agree the service and write down any special requests. The artist and the model/client will both sign the record card after the discussion to agree the service. It is also a good place to write down the products used for further reference. This information is then kept in a lockable cabinet for data protection reasons, as it will have the models'/clients' names on.
- **Know how to complete a consultation form** – this will include all medical information regarding the client, for example, what medication they are taking, any previous operations that may affect the service, their general health, any contra-indications that may prevent or restrict the service from going ahead, the name and address of their doctor and any information about skin sensitivity testing. This document must be signed and dated by the model or client and the make-up artist. As this has confidential information on it, it must be kept in a lockable cabinet.

Environmental and sustainable working practices

Sustainability refers to our ability to meet our current needs without reducing the ability of future generations to meet their needs. Sustainable working practices that make-up artists should consider include minimising pollution, reducing and managing waste in compliance with the Environmental Protection Act (see page 12), and reducing energy usage.

Temperature

Depending on what job the make-up artist is on, it is important to think about the temperature of the area being worked in. This is because the temperature can affect the application and sustainability of the make-up.

- If the location is cold and prosthetic pieces are being applied, the product may need to be warmed up first.

- If the location is very hot and it is a fashion shoot, the make-up artist will need to be on hand to blot powder on any shiny areas of the model's skin.

Ventilation

If the make-up artist is using highly flammable products, ventilation is very important to remove the fumes from the area. If airbrush make-up is being used, open a window to remove any particles from the air. On location it can sometimes be difficult to do this, but it is important to work as safely as possible.

Minimising pollution

- Choose to drive efficient, low-polluting vehicles.
- Use reusable canvas bags instead of paper or plastic bags.
- Buy rechargeable batteries for frequently used devices.
- Buy green electricity produced by low-pollution facilities.
- Use public transport, walk or cycle when possible.

Reducing and managing waste

- Choose products that have less packaging or products with packaging that can be refilled and reused.
- Recycling conserves energy and reduces production emissions. Choose to use materials that can be recycled, such as paper, plastic, glass bottles, cardboard and aluminium cans.

Reducing energy use

- Use energy-efficient equipment and low-energy lighting.
- Turn off appliances and lights when you leave the room.

Contra-indications

A **contra-indication** is something that can **prevent** the make-up from being applied or **restrict** the service that can be provided.

It is important to establish any contra-indications prior to carrying out a make-up service, as they may prevent the treatment from being carried out and may require medical attention.

An infectious **disease** can be passed on from one person to another by droplets in the air, for example, via coughing or sneezing. Contagious diseases are passed on through direct or indirect contact, for example, by touching the infected area or by sharing materials such as make-up brushes.

A **disorder** is usually not infectious, but may still mean that the service can't be carried out. Not all disorders are contra-indicated however, so it is vital that you are familiar with the diseases and disorders that you may come into contact with while working so you can take appropriate action.

> **HANDY HINT**
>
> Recycling can reduce the amount of waste going to landfill. Having separate bins in your working area for recycling, clinical, domestic and perishable waste is essential.

KEY TERMS

Contra-indication: something that can prevent or restrict the service from being carried out, for example, an infectious disease.

Prevented contra-indication: a contra-indication that means you cannot carry out the make-up service.

Restricted contra-indication: a contra-indication that means you can carry out the make-up service, but you may have to limit it or work around the area.

Disease: a condition that produces specific signs or symptoms.

Disorder: a non-infectious condition of the skin, hair or scalp, such as skin tags, colouration and strawberry marks, as well as conditions such as psoriasis.

Disorder	Description
Eczema (atopic dermatitis) 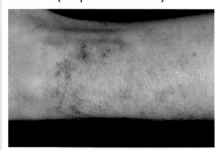	A red, swollen area of skin, which may be cracked. In some instances, weeping may occur from the blisters that can be present, which later form hardened scabs. Eczema can be inherited, or outbreaks can be related to stress or allergens. Once the source of irritation is identified and removed, it may disappear. Medical referral is needed if the condition is severe or there are open sores, and the service must be contra-indicated. If the condition is mild, the service can go ahead but must avoid the affected areas.
Erythema 	An area of the skin in which the blood vessels have dilated due to either injury or inflammation. The area appears red and it may affect one area locally or appear generally all over the skin. The cause of the condition needs to be identified as it may be an allergic reaction. If the cause is unknown, the client should be referred to their doctor.
Contact dermatitis 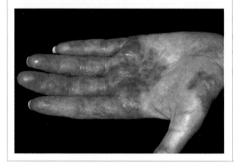	An inflammatory skin disorder in which the skin becomes itchy, swollen and red. It is caused when the skin comes into contact with a certain substance – either an irritant or an allergen. Irritants directly damage the skin's outer layer. Common irritants include soaps and detergents. Allergens trigger a response from the immune system, which causes an allergic reaction that appears as a rash.

Discussing contra-indications with clients

When talking about contra-indications, it is very important to understand that a make-up artist is not a doctor or a nurse and therefore cannot diagnose a condition. You can only advise the model or client to seek a medical diagnosis.

It is very important to communicate with tact and diplomacy when discussing contra-indications with the model or client. The contra-indication could be a sensitive topic for them to talk about or they may not realise that they have a contagious condition or need to seek medical attention. The model or client should feel comfortable throughout the consultation.

If the model or client is unaware of a prevented contra-indication, the make-up artist needs to explain that the service cannot be carried out until the condition has been treated or has cleared up.

If it is a condition that would restrict the service, explain any modification or adaptation to the service that you will be making to the model or client. Be tactful as it could be a sensitive topic for the model or client.

▼ **Table 1.8** Actions to take in response to specific contra-indications

Encourage the model or client to seek medical advice	As a make-up artist, you are not allowed to diagnose a contra-indication, so it is very important to encourage the model or client to seek medical advice.
Explain why the service cannot be carried out	Once the consultation has been completed and you have realised that the service cannot be carried out, it is important to explain why the service cannot be continued at this time.
Modify or adapt the service	If modifications are required, make sure the model or client is aware at the start of the service, as this may affect the final make-up look.

Skin sensitivity testing

It is very important to carry out skin sensitivity testing prior to the application of products, as a negative reaction may prevent a performer from playing their role or a model from modelling the make-up. Always follow manufacturers' instructions for product use and application. Even if they produce the same look or effect as another product, they may have very different ingredients.

Tests must be carried out 24–48 hours before to the application and must be done again if the actor/model changes medication, becomes pregnant or becomes sensitised, as this can have an effect on the skin, or if there has been a period of time when the product has not been used.

▲ **Figure 1.15** Skin sensitivity testing

Products that require a skin sensitivity test include adhesives, adhesive removers and latex.

This is the procedure for carrying out a skin sensitivity test.
1 Apply a small amount of product to the inner crease of the elbow or behind the ear, 24–48 hours before the product is to be applied, and allow it to dry.
2 Ask the model to keep the product on the test area for the next 12 hours.
3 Inform the model of possible **contra-actions** that could occur.
4 Record the test on the model's information card, including the time, date and any reaction that may occur.
5 If a reaction occurs, try an alternative product.

Negative reactions to a product include swelling, redness, heat or a rash. If any of these develop during a service, stop using the product immediately. Clean the area, removing the product from the skin.

KEY TERM

Contra-action: a reaction to a product that occurs either during the service or immediately afterwards.

6 PROVIDE RECOMMENDATIONS AND EVALUATE THE MAKE-UP AND HAIR APPLICATION

Make-up artists need to be able to make appropriate recommendations following a make-up and/or hair service, as outlined in Figure 1.16.

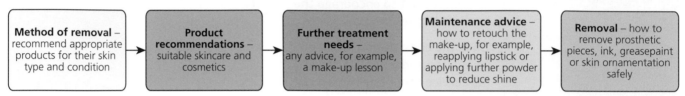

Method of removal – recommend appropriate products for their skin type and condition → **Product recommendations** – suitable skincare and cosmetics → **Further treatment needs** – any advice, for example, a make-up lesson → **Maintenance advice** – how to retouch the make-up, for example, reapplying lipstick or applying further powder to reduce shine → **Removal** – how to remove prosthetic pieces, ink, greasepaint or skin ornamentation safely

▲ **Figure 1.16** Providing recommendations

HEALTH AND SAFETY

Do not allow models or clients to pull off prosthetic pieces, as this can damage the skin.

HANDY HINT

Make sure all prosthetic pieces and ornamentations are removed with the appropriate remover. For example, if it was applied with spirit gum, remove it with spirit gum remover.

Contra-actions

Models or clients should also be given advice regarding contra-actions should one occur, for example, watery eyes. You need to be able to recognise the difference between **normal contra-actions** and **adverse contra-actions**, including those that are a result of poor practice.

A normal contra-action can be touch sensitive, therefore techniques and product selections need to be adapted accordingly throughout the service.

You also need to understand appropriate actions that should be taken in response to any contra-actions that occur either during or after the service.

▼ **Table 1.9** Contra-actions and appropriate responses

Contra-action	Response
Stinging	Remove product and apply a **cold compress**. Wait for the stinging to subside, then reapply using different products. If the contra-action persists, seek medical advice.
Watery eyes	Adapt product and application techniques.
Stinging eyes	Remove product around the area. Apply an eye bath if required.
Erythema	Remove product and apply a cold compress. If appropriate, cover erythema with camouflage make-up and continue the service.
Allergic reactions	Remove product and apply a cold compress. If the contra-action persists, seek medical advice.

KEY TERMS

Normal contra-action: a reaction to a product that creates sensitivity, such as a reddening of the skin or watery eyes. These can be dealt with by the make-up artist, but if the contra-action worsens, the model or client should seek medical advice.

Adverse contra-action: a severe reaction to a product. If this occurs, remove the product immediately, apply a cold compress and advise the model or client to seek medical attention.

Cold compress: a cotton pad or cloth dampened in cold water, used to cool an area affected by a contra-action.

Evaluate effectiveness of make-up and hair application

Self-evaluation requires you to critique your own make-up and hair application. You may find it useful to look back at photos of your work to see if and where you could have done better. This will help you to grow and continuously improve your performance.

In order to evaluate yourself effectively, you must understand the criteria used to gauge your performance and different methods used for self-evaluation.

- **Visual evaluation** – examine the finished make-up look in detail, looking at each area and each technique.
- **Verbal evaluation** – ask for feedback from the model or client or from the director to assess whether what has been created matches the design brief.
- **Written feedback** – ask the model for written feedback. This is frequently done through social media reviews. They are usually very helpful and give other prospective clients a good overview of the kind of work and professionalism of the make-up artist. Professional make-up artists use feedback to improve their skill level and ensure they are delivering the expected or desired looks.
- **Repeat business** – being booked again by the same designer, photographer, stylist, director or model is a good indication of how successful the previous work was.

HANDY HINT

Self-evaluation also applies to your studies. Reflect on your work and judge how well you have performed in relation to the assessment criteria. Try to identify what constitutes a good (or poor) piece of work.

ACTIVITY

Create an evaluation form that can be given to your models or clients to help you collect feedback and improve your skills. Make sure you allow for self-evaluation too.

Test your knowledge

1 List three progression routes for a make-up artist.

2 Explain three differences between being employed and being self-employed.

3 Describe three different career paths that a make-up artist could take.

4 List four different types of production that require professional make-up artists.

5 Describe three different bacterial contra-indications.

6 Describe how to perform a skin sensitivity test.

7 Explain four pieces of health and safety legislation that affect make-up artists.

8 Describe three requirements of becoming a freelance make-up artist.

9 Explain the difference between verbal and non-verbal communication.

10 List the possible contra-actions that may occur either during or after a make-up service.

CHAPTER 2

ANATOMY AND PHYSIOLOGY FOR MAKE-UP ARTISTS

INTRODUCTION

The skin is a canvas for make-up artists, so it is important to have an understanding of the functions of the skin and its underlying structures. The appearance and condition of the skin will have an impact on the choice of products and application techniques used. This section also covers different hair types and how the hair growth cycle works, enabling you to create the best hairstyles for clients.

It is also important to understand facial anatomy and proportions. The shape of a person's face is created by their underlying bone and muscle structure. When styling hair, knowing the bones of the skull, as well as the proportions of the face and head, will ensure that you achieve a balanced look.

In this chapter, you will learn about:

1   the structure and functions of skin and hair
2   the skeletal system
3   the muscles of the face and upper body.

1 THE STRUCTURE AND FUNCTIONS OF SKIN AND HAIR

Skin

The skin is the largest organ in the body and is the outer protective wrapping for the body's internal organs. It consists of three layers: the epidermis, the dermis and the subcutaneous layer. The skin contains a huge network of nerve cells that detect changes in the environment. It has the ability to self-repair, and is constantly being shed and replaced. The appearance of our skin alters with our general health, as well as with our emotional state, and poor skin condition can be a sign that something is wrong.

▲ **Figure 2.1** Healthy skin

KEY TERMS

Collagen: protein responsible for giving skin resilience and elasticity, which accounts for about 75 per cent of the weight of the dermis.

Elastin: protein that holds bundles of collagen fibres together and makes up less than five per cent of the weight of the skin.

Elasticity: the ability of skin or hair to spring back to its original state straight away once it has been stretched.

Sweat glands: simple coiled tubular glands that open directly onto the surface of the skin. They regulate body temperature and help eliminate waste products.

Sebaceous glands: small sac-like pouches found all over the body, except on the soles of the feet and the palms of the hands, that produce an oily substance called sebum.

HANDY HINT

Dermal papillae give the papillary layer its name. These uneven projections are responsible for our fingerprints.

Dermis

Often referred to as the true skin, the dermis lies directly beneath the epidermis and is the thickest layer of the skin. The dermis is 20–30 times thicker than the epidermis. It is composed of a dense network of specialised proteins – mainly **collagen** and **elastin** – organised into in bundles that run horizontally throughout the dermis. These are important for giving the skin its strength and **elasticity**. Damage to collagen and elastin fibres is the primary cause of skin ageing and the appearance of wrinkles.

The dermis is made up of two layers: the papillary layer and the reticular layer.

The key function of the **papillary layer** is to provide vital nourishment to the living layers of the epidermis above. It is a highly active and important area of the skin.

The papillary layer:
- is located directly below the epidermis and is made up of loose connective tissue
- supplies nutrients to the epidermis and has a specialised vascular system that assists in the control of body temperature by increasing or decreasing the blood flow in the layer
- contains mast cells, which are responsible for releasing histamine (associated with allergies) in response to tissue damage.

The deeper **reticular layer** is formed of tough, fibrous connective tissue, which gives the skin strength and elasticity, and helps to hold all structures in place. It:
- is located below the papillary layer and above the hypodermis
- contains sensory receptors for deep pressure
- contains blood vessels and lymph vessels, which form a network through the reticular layer to facilitate the removal of waste from the skin
- contains fibroblast cells, which produce collagen and elastin.

Skin appendages found in the dermis include:
- hair follicles, which are tube-like structures from which a hair grows
- hair shaft, which is the part of the hair that can be seen at the skin's surface
- **sweat glands**, which secrete sweat
- **sebaceous glands**, which are attached to hair follicles and produce sebum
- nerve endings that send messages to the brain in response to sensations such as pain, touch and heat
- dermal papillae, which are cone-shaped projections that contain a network of blood vessels that nourish hair follicles in the skin and bring nutrients and oxygen to the lower layers of epidermal cells
- arrector pili muscles, which connect hair follicles to the dermis. When the muscles contract, which happens when the body is cold, for example, this causes the hairs to stand on end.

Subcutaneous layer (adipose tissue)

This specialised layer under the dermis contains a network of collagen fibres and fat cells (**adipocytes**). It protects the body from external trauma and insulates it from the cold. It is the main storage site for fat and, therefore, energy. Many blood and lymphatic vessels, and nerves, pass through the subcutaneous layer.

- It divides the dermis from the muscular fascia beneath.
- The main cells in this layer are adipose cells, which protect against damage to underlying body structures and provide insulation, which is why it may also be referred to as the adipose layer.
- It is thicker in women than in men.
- It has a rich blood supply and contains some sensory nerve endings.

The number of fat cells contained in the subcutaneous layer differs in different parts of the body. The **distribution** of fat cells also differs between men and women.

Function of skin

The skin is the first line of defence against toxins, radiation and harmful pollutants. Each layer of the skin performs an important role in keeping our body healthy.

The skin performs seven primary functions.

- **Sensation** – the skin contains lots of nerve endings, which allow the body to detect sensations such as cold, heat, pressure and pain.
- **Heat regulation** – the skin regulates the body's temperature by sweating. When sweat on the skin evaporates, it cools the body down.
- **Absorption** – thousands of pores on the surface of the skin can absorb acids, vitamins, water and oxygen to protect and nourish the skin.
- **Protection** – the skin protects all of the body's internal organs.
- **Excretion** – the skin is the body's largest waste removal system. Toxins are excreted through the skin's sweat glands and pores.
- **Secretion** – the skin secretes sebum, keeping it soft and supple. The layer of sebum on the outermost layer of the skin is known as the acid mantle.
- **Production of vitamin D** – the body produces vitamin D when the skin is exposed to sunlight. Vitamin D helps the body to absorb calcium from our diet, which is important for healthy muscles, bones and teeth. A lack of vitamin D can cause bones to become soft and weak.

KEY TERMS

Adipocytes: fat cells.

Distribution: the way in which something is shared out.

Excretion: expelling waste from the body.

Secretion: the production of substances that the body uses, for example, sebum.

KEY TERM

Keratin: a protein that makes up the hair, skin and nails.

HANDY HINT

Hair is 95 per cent keratin.

Hair

The human body is covered in hair, which is made mostly of the protein **keratin**. Longitudinally, the hair is divided into three parts.

- **Hair bulb** – the enlarged part at the base of the hair root. Living cells divide within the bulb and grow to form the hair shaft. The hair bulb forms the base of the hair follicle.
- **Hair root** – the part found below the surface of the skin.
- **Hair shaft** – the part of the hair lying above the surface of the skin.

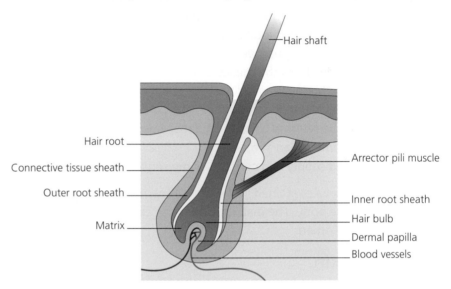

Hair shaft

Hair root

Connective tissue sheath

Outer root sheath

Matrix

Arrector pili muscle

Inner root sheath

Hair bulb

Dermal papilla

Blood vessels

▲ **Figure 2.4** Hair anatomy

Types of hair

- **Lanugo** – the hair that develops on a foetus while it is still in the womb. It protects the skin from amniotic fluids and is usually shed before or shortly after birth.
- **Vellus** – the fine, fluffy hair that covers most of the body. It develops in childhood and remains on much of the body throughout adulthood. Vellus hair differs in length and thickness from person to person. The main role of vellus hair is to keep the body warm and to protect the skin.
- **Terminal** – the longer, thicker, pigmented hair found on the head, under the arms, eyebrows, pubic regions, arms and legs. The growth of terminal hair is influenced by hormones.

Structure of hair

Internally, the hair has three layers: the cuticle, cortex and medulla.

- **Cuticle** – the hair's protective layer, composed of overlapping cells. A healthy cuticle is smooth and flat. It gives the hair shine and also minimises the movement of moisture in and out of the cortex, maintaining the hair's hydration, balance and flexibility.
- **Cortex** – consists of long keratin filaments containing the pigment melanin, which gives the hair its colour.

Medulla

Cortex

Cuticle

▲ **Figure 2.5** Structure of hair

The filaments are held together by **disulphide and hydrogen bonds**. The cortex forms the main bulk of the hair and gives it strength.

- **Medulla** – the innermost layer of the hair. It is only present in thicker hair types.

Hair growth cycle

The hair on our body grows at different rates. Each hair on the human body is at its own stage of development. Once the cycle is complete, it restarts and a new strand of hair begins to form. There are three different stages of hair growth.

- **Anagen (active)** – the anagen phase is the active stage of hair growth. The cells in the hair bulb divide rapidly, making new hair. Hair grows actively for an average of two to seven years before the hair follicles become dormant. The length of this phase differs from person to person, depending on the person's maximum hair length.
- **Catagen (changing)** – the second phase of the hair growth cycle is short, lasting only two to three weeks on average. In this phase the hair stops growing and removes itself from the blood supply, leaving a club hair.
- **Telogen (resting)** – the hair enters its third and final stage. In the resting period, the club hair rests in the follicle while new hair begins to grow beneath it. It can last anything up to 100 days.

Each hair follicle is independent, so they all go through the growth cycle at different times. This means that you do not lose patches of hair all at once. We shed approximately 50–100 hairs in every day.

KEY TERM

Disulphide and hydrogen bonds: protein bonds, which are the strongest structures of the hair shaft.

HANDY HINT

On average, 88 per cent of scalp hair is in anagen phase.

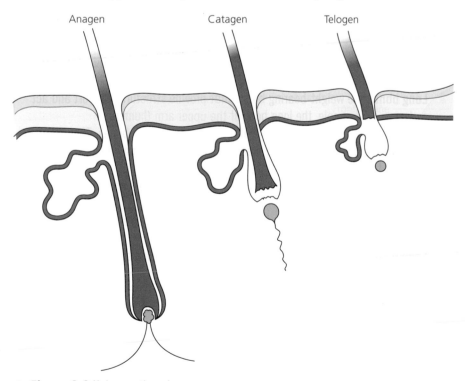

▲ **Figure 2.6** Hair growth cycle

Examples of primary research include:
- personal experiences, such as:
  - childhood memories
  - films watched and books read
  - your understanding of stereotypical interpretations of particular characters, for example, a pantomime dame or a princess
- talking to other creatives in the industry, such as:
  - photographers
  - hairstylists
  - fashion designers
  - make-up artists
  - artists
- talking to family and friends who have experienced different fashion eras or different cultures and traditions, for example, by creating a questionnaire for them to complete or looking through photo albums to see the hair, make-up and fashion trends that they have known.

Secondary research

Secondary research involves collecting and using information that already exists. Make-up artists use these sources to generate ideas for their designs.

Examples of secondary research include:
- books/libraries
- magazines and comics
- the internet
- social media
- film and TV
- theatre
- musicals
- fashion shows
- hair and make-up shows and seminars
- bridal shows
- museums
- make-up competitions
- music videos
- art galleries
- exhibitions.

ACTIVITY

Think back to your favourite childhood film. Using various research sources, create a new character for that film, focusing on their hair and make-up look.

Different research sources will be used depending on the make-up design that is required. It is important to understand the type of production and the make-up requirements when creating authentic characters for a given design brief. For example, you would choose different make-up products and techniques when creating a character for a stage performance or for a film. Make-up artists must learn how to combine their research with their own ideas and inspiration to create something totally original. Research should include both historical and present-day looks.

Types of characters that could be created for different productions include:
- pantomime characters, such as a pantomime dame, a fairy godmother or a pantomime villain
- gender reversal (female to male or male to female)

- a very elderly character
- an animal
- a drag queen
- conventional make-up for a performer
- Halloween characters, such as a witch, a monster, a vampire, a werewolf, a zombie or an emaciated (starved) character
- a mythical creature, for example, a unicorn or a dragon
- a supernatural character, for example, an angel or a goblin
- a clown
- a bald person
- a casualty victim.

▲ **Figure 3.1** Pantomime dame

Types and examples of productions include:
- ballet, for example, The Royal Ballet and Matthew Bourne
- opera, for example, English National Opera
- musicals, for example, the work of Cameron Mackintosh and Andrew Lloyd Webber
- pantomime, for example, local theatre productions
- dance, for example, Michael Flatley and Diversity
- historical, for example, Shakespeare and Charles Dickens
- film and TV, for example, Warner Brothers and Steven Spielberg.

Influences on current make-up trends

Some research sources can have a huge impact on influencing current trends.
- Social media is one of the most common sources used by make-up artists when researching design ideas. As well as providing inspiration, it helps you to keep up to date with current trends and to expand your own individual style by learning new skills.

HANDY HINT

Chapter 15 has further information about blogging.

- Blogging and vlogging are popular ways for make-up artists to promote themselves and their products, and to network with other professionals in the industry. This form of media is a reliable way to get an honest opinion on current trends from like-minded people.
- Magazines are another way for make-up artists to keep up to date with trends in beauty, hair, make-up and fashion, as well as gain knowledge of new products and brands, which is important if you want to work in the fashion or editorial fields. Magazines are also a source of inspiration and ideas for your own designs.

Historical looks can also influence current trends. For more on this see Chapter 7.

2 PLANNING MAKE-UP DESIGNS
Planning for make-up and hair design

The initial part of the planning process is for you to interpret the brief you have been given. The brief could be anything, from a bride's ideas for their wedding day to creating an accurate representation of a complex character for film or TV.

Models can often change on the day, so you will need to be prepared to adapt your products and techniques because the look you had planned may not work on another model. Some make-up artists prefer to complete more than one design in case this happens.

There are several factors that could affect the make-up artist's original design ideas.

- **Skin and hair type** – if an original hair design was to create a hair-up look on a model with long hair and the model's hair on the day is short, techniques and products would need to be adapted, for example, using a texturising product to add grip when putting the hair up and to hold the hair in place. Similarly, if the model's skin type is different to what was originally expected, for example, if they have sensitive skin or an allergy, it may be necessary to use a different product suitable for their skin type to achieve the look agreed.
- **Skin tone and hair colour** – make-up artists should always be ready to work on models with different skin tones and have a range of products in their kit to suit everyone. Hair colour could affect the colours that are chosen, as well as the overall look of the hair and make-up.
- **Face and eye shape** – corrective techniques may need to be carried out when working on different face shapes. Eye shape is very important to consider as certain techniques may not be as effective. For example, if someone has hooded eyelids a cut crease eyeshadow technique would not be the best one to use and other techniques may be better suited to enhance the eye.

HEALTH AND SAFETY

You always need to check whether your model has any allergies to any products. If they have, you will need to find alternatives and make adjustments.

HANDY HINT

Return to Chapter 1 for more detailed explanations on production demands that affect creating design ideas (pages 25–26) and factors to consider when preparing for hair and make-up application (pages 31–39).

- **Age** – depending on the job and the look that is being created, the model or performer's age may need to be considered. Certain products are best avoided on mature skin, such as too much face powder or illuminating products, as these can enhance areas that the model may prefer to hide.
- **Gender** – it is important for make-up artists to have experience of working on both men and women as there are differences in bone structure, skin type and skin characteristics. For example, when working on a male model, make-up artists may be required to camouflage stubble or a beard shadow, so understanding how this can be done is important.
- **Environmental conditions** – weather, temperature, lighting and ventilation can all affect the application and use of products, so it is important for make-up artists to be prepared to adapt to any of these situations. More details can be found in Chapter 4, pages 106–107 and Chapter 6, page 160.

HANDY HINT

You can create templates that you can transfer your designs onto. You should have at least three or four templates that include both men and women and different head positions. This can be achieved by finding a head shot from a magazine and tracing round the outline of the face and features. You can use this as a template and start creating your design, letting your own individual style come through.

Mood boards

After interpreting the brief, you can start researching design ideas. You could start by creating a mind map in order to generate ideas and concepts. Then you can create a visual representation of images, using a range of sources, in the form of either a **mood board** or a look book. Face, body and hair charts can then be completed to start putting ideas together on how the final look will be achieved. These help you to communicate your ideas to an audience. They can also be shared with the model or production team, who will provide you with feedback that you can use to adjust and finalise the design.

Mood boards are a great way to express ideas visually, and they can show your creative side. For any make-up look, you will need to discuss your ideas, whether this is with the model or client or with a producer. Mood boards should be eye-catching and tell the creative story of where ideas originated and how they have led you to come to your final design.

KEY TERM

Mood board: a collage of images, text, sketches and material that communicates your ideas for a given theme.

HANDY HINT

Use A1-size card to produce your mood boards, so you have plenty of space to showcase your ideas.

Mood boards should include the following elements.

- **A title or theme** – the theme should be obvious and needs to be relevant to the brief that has been provided.
- **Visual images** – this does not just mean pictures found on the internet. Magazine cut-outs or photographs could also be included. Photographs help to capture thoughts about or impressions of the theme. Pictures of test shots can also be used to show ideas and techniques that may be used.
- **Text and annotations** – the use of key words can capture the meaning of a given theme. Annotations can help to explain where inspiration came from and clarify what it represents.
- **Textures, accessories and materials** – including different textures and materials can show off your creative flair. It is eye-catching for the audience and makes the designs noticeable. Accessories that will be used for the make-up look could also be included.
- **Sketches** – sketches of designs and inspirations could be included to show off your artistic flair. For example, you could sketch the costume design if you do not have a visual picture of it.
- **Face, body and hair charts** – these show your ideas for the look you wish to create based on your research.
- **Techniques and products** – these provide an insight into how you will complete the look created on the face, body and hair charts.
- **Budget and costings** – this will allow you to work out costs and create a suitable budget to fit your design ideas.

▲ **Figure 3.2** Examples of face charts

HANDY HINT

Be careful not to breach copyright restrictions when using other people's photos and images. You should not copy or publish the work without the permission of the copyright holder or under the terms of their license agreement. You can create your own images based on an original image, but they should not be identical.

Face, body and hair charts

Face, body and hair charts help make-up artists to plan the make-up and hair look. Details of products, colours and techniques are added, which provide you with a point of reference to use when creating the look.

These charts also help with continuity – ensuring that the hair and make-up is applied consistently – particularly if you are required to complete the same look more than once. They also ensure that another make-up artist could recreate the same look by following the details provided.

When working in film, TV or fashion shows, face and hair charts and photographic images will often be created by the head make-up artist, who designs the look. The charts are then given to a team of make-up artists to recreate the look.

To complete a face chart, you will need:
- translucent powder
- eyeshadows and pigmented powders
- brushes
- lipgloss applicators or flocked doe foot applicators
- calligraphy pen or black liquid liner
- watercolour painting or fine grain drawing paper
- correction fluid.

However, make-up artists can be as creative as they like and use a range of different products and techniques.

Here are some tips on creating a face chart.
- You can download a template of a face chart and print it on textured paper or create your own face chart. Textured paper is better than regular paper as powdered make-up products will hold to it.
- Use liquid liner or fine artist pens when creating lashes.
- Firmer brushes are good for applying the products as they help to push the colour into the paper.
- Gradually build the colour and blend.
- Use cotton buds to blend.
- Colour in the eye using coloured pencil to make the face chart look more alive.
- Draw eyebrows faintly with a pencil to get the ideal shape, then fill in with an angled brush and eyeshadow to create realistic hair strokes.
- An eraser will come in handy if any mistakes are made.
- The face chart can be set by using hairspray for powdered products and clear nail varnish for lip products to stop them from smudging.

> ### HANDY HINT
>
> Watercolour painting paper is good to use when creating face charts.

ACTIVITY

Create your own face chart template and complete a make-up design based on the theme of 'pride'.

When creating a hair chart, you will need to use a head template that shows different angles of the head in order to sketch your design. Using art pencils is the best way to create a realistic representation of the hair design.

When creating a body chart, you will need to use a body template that shows the front and back of the body. You can then use pencils and pens to sketch your design. Accessories and textures can be added if these are being used for the look.

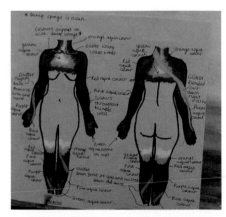

▲ **Figure 3.3** Example of a body chart

Look book: a collection of visual resources that communicates and demonstrates a make-up artist's progression from the initial design stage through to the finished look.

▲ **Figure 3.4** Look books

Look books

A **look book** presented in the form of a sketch book is another way to showcase your design ideas. It is similar to a mood board, but includes more detail and is presented slightly differently. Look books enable make-up artists to communicate and demonstrate their progression from the initial design stage through to the finished look. Look books should be eye-catching and creative, enhancing the appearance of the designs.

Information that can be included in a look book includes:
- collages of research ideas and pictures (mood board)
- samples of materials and textures
- face, body and hair charts
- sketches
- budget and costings
- a list of hair and make-up products, as well as equipment and tools, that will be used to create the look
- justification of choices of specific products and equipment
- test shots taken while the look is being created and of the finished look
- pictures of the design ideas that can be used as a reference for recreating the look.

Budgeting for make-up artistry services

As a freelance make-up artist, you must create a budget. A budget is a plan for estimating the costs and income for a particular job. It will be necessary to consider a wide range of factors in order to work out income as well as costs. These factors will depend on the job being undertaken.

When carrying out bridal make-up, for example, you will have to create your own budget and consider all factors, such as travel costs, kit costs, time needed and the number of models. However, when working for a production company for TV, you will often already have a budget for make-up and hair, as well as the overall costs for crew, equipment and location. Some companies may pay for things such as food and drink while the make-up artist is on set and others may not. However, to ensure that you make a profit, consider the factors in Figure 3.5.

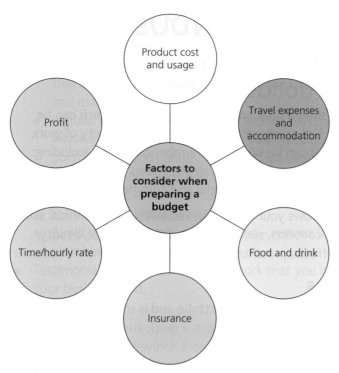

▲ **Figure 3.5** Factors to consider when preparing a budget

- **Product costs and usage** – the best way to work out product costs is to choose the main products that will be used and calculate ten per cent of the total cost. For example, if a foundation costs £28, the cost per usage would be £2.80. You should also allow for the costs of other products such as consumables (cotton wool, cotton buds, gown, disposable applicators, tissues, spatulas) and specialist products (special effects make-up, accessories).
- **Travel expenses and accommodation** – travelling long distances may require an overnight stay, so hotel costs need to be considered in addition to the cost of travelling to the location.
- **Food and drink** – this may be supplied, depending on the job. However, this aspect should still be considered, particularly if the job involves working long hours.
- **Insurance** – all make-up artists are required to have insurance. This covers any claims made against them for causing injury or damage, as well as product loss or damage to any kit. This can cost £100–200 a year, depending on what the policy includes. The cost of insurance should be averaged out across the year and apportioned to each individual job.
- **Time/hourly rate** – this will vary from job to job, and depends on how experienced you are. Travelling time to the location, especially if it is long distance, should be included in this. Once an hourly rate is decided, then the other factors in Figure 3.5 should be considered to provide the total cost.
- **Profit** – when all the factors above have been considered, the make-up artist can calculate the profit they will make from the job.

HANDY HINT

When starting out, make-up artists often work for minimal pay or for free to build up experience and to get recognised within the industry.

- **Oily skin** is caused by the overproduction of sebum. This can be due to hormonal changes, for example, during puberty.
- **Combination skin** is the most common skin type. It is the combination of two or more skin types and has a mixture of the different characteristics of each skin type.

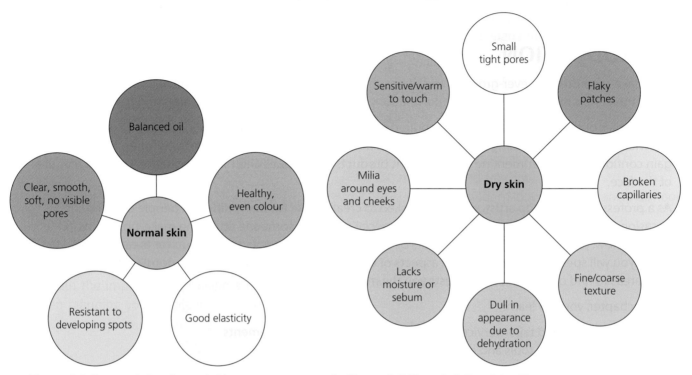

▲ **Figure 4.1** Characteristics of normal skin

▲ **Figure 4.2** Characteristics of dry skin

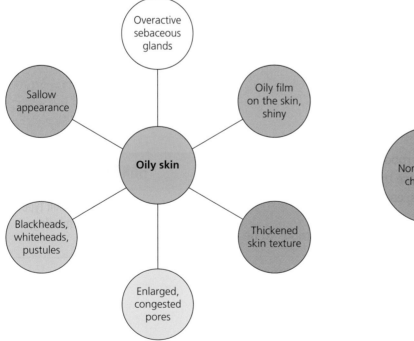

▲ **Figure 4.3** Characteristics of oily skin

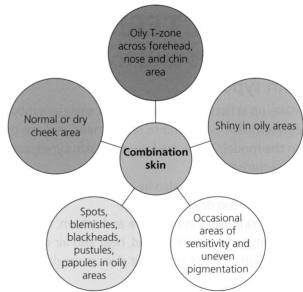

▲ **Figure 4.4** Characteristics of combination skin

▲ **Figure 4.5** Dry skin

▲ **Figure 4.6** Oily skin

▲ **Figure 4.7** Combination skin

The condition of the skin

In addition to skin type, the condition of the skin tends to be affected by internal and external factors.

Sensitive skin

We all need a certain amount of sensitivity in our skin for it to function correctly, and many models may say that their skin is sensitive. A truly sensitive skin will react to even the mildest stimulus. It is often associated with pale or dry skins that lack enough protective sebum, although it can still be oily. It can have a high flushed look, with a tendency to colour easily. Extra care will need to be taken when treating.

Dehydrated skin

Dehydration describes a lack of moisture or fluid. Many factors can cause this, for example, insufficient water intake, air conditioning, weather changes, excess alcohol intake, smoking, illness, medication, using incorrect products, exposure to sunshine or dieting. The skin may still have the correct amount of sebaceous secretions but suffer from flaking and tightness due to lack of surface moisture. This may be a temporary or a long-term problem.

Mature skin

Sebaceous secretions slow down as we age and this is coupled with a loss of skin elasticity. The skin becomes finer in texture and wrinkles form. The epidermis becomes thinner, with a lack of springiness and support from underlying muscles, which causes the skin to be looser. Areas of **hyperpigmentation** and broken capillaries are often present.

> **HANDY HINT**
>
> Remember to test for allergies or sensitivity to make-up products 24–48 hours before treatment. See page 39 for details on carrying out a skin sensitivity test.

KEY TERM

Hyperpigmentation: patches of skin that are darker than the overall skin tone.

Face shape	Characteristics	Corrective techniques
Square	• Jawline is square and angular. • Width of cheekbones and forehead are similar. • Width of cheekbones and jawline are similar.	Techniques to help soften the angles of the face include: • applying shader to the angles of the jawbone • applying highlighter to the centre of the forehead and chin • applying blusher to the cheekbones in a circular pattern, taking it up towards the temple.
Oblong	• Face is noticeably longer than it is wide. • Width of cheekbones and forehead are similar. • Width of cheekbones and jawline are similar. • Can have either angular or rounder features.	Techniques to create the impression of width and shorten the face length include: • applying shader to the point of the chin and top of the hairline to reduce the length of the face • highlighting the temple and lower jaw to create width • adding blush to the apples of the cheeks to create the appearance of fullness.
Triangle	• Forehead is wide and tapers to a narrow chin. • Also referred to as a heart face shape. • Pointed chin.	• Shade under the cheekbones and the angles of the face, tip of the chin and corners of the forehead. • Highlight cheekbones. • Apply blusher in a circular pattern to the inner cheekbone.

Techniques for different eye shapes

▼ **Table 4.3** Techniques for different eye shapes

Eye shape	Techniques
Wide-set	A light- to medium-colour shadow should be applied to the outer corners of the eyes and blended upwards, slightly beyond the socket line, but not outwards. Medium- to dark-toned colours should be applied to the inner eye and blended softly towards the centre of the eyelid to give the illusion of bringing the eyes together. Dark liner can be applied to the inner section of the eyes and mascara added.
Close-set	A light-colour shadow should be applied to the inner corners of the eye. Medium and dark tones should be applied to the outer part of the eye and swept outwards to 'pull' the eyes apart and give a lengthening effect to the eye. Eyeliner can be applied to the outer corners of the eye and mascara added.
Deep-set	Apply a light-colour shadow over the entire eyelid. Apply a medium tone slightly above the socket line and blend. Apply a darker shade along the outer part of the eyelid on the top and bottom lashes and add mascara.
Prominent	A matte shadow should be applied over the entire eyelid. A medium tone should then be applied to the outer corners of the eye and blended across the eyelid, covering about half the original colour. A darker colour should be applied along the top of the lashes. Highlight the brow bone to draw attention to the area and add mascara.
Hooded	Apply a light-colour shadow over the entire eyelid. Apply a medium colour slightly above the socket line and blend upwards, creating a higher crease. Apply a darker tone along the outer part of the eyelid on the top and bottom lashes and add mascara.
Small	Apply a light-coloured shadow all over the eyelid. Dark colours should be avoided as this will make the eyes appear smaller. A medium-colour eyeshadow can be applied to the outer corner of the eye and blended upwards and outwards just above the socket line. This will help make the eyes appear more open and wider. Eyeliner can be applied just to the outer corners of the eyes. Highlight can be applied to the brow bone and finish with a mascara.

Techniques for different lip shapes

▼ **Table 4.4** Techniques for lip shapes

Lip shape	Techniques
Uneven	Using a lipliner, even out the lips to make them symmetrical on both sides. Finish by applying lip colour.
Small	Using a lipliner, outline both the upper and lower lips and extend the lips at the corner of the mouth. Finish by applying lip colour.

→

Lip shape	Techniques
Thin	Using a lipliner, outline the upper and lower lips very slightly. Use a lighter lip colour to help make the lips appear larger.
Thin upper lip	Using a lipliner, outline the upper lip to balance with the lower lip. Finish by applying lip colour.
Thin lower lip	Using a lipliner, outline just outside the lower lip line to make it appear fuller. Fill in with a lip colour to create balance between the top and lower lips.
Fine lines around the lip	Using a long wearing lipliner, outline the lips to help prevent the lipstick from bleeding into the fine lines. Lighter lip colours will work better and will not show the lines as much.

Techniques for nose shapes

▼ **Table 4.5** Techniques for nose shapes

Nose shape	Techniques
Broad	Shade down either side of the nose.
Crooked	Apply a shader to the crooked part of the nose to help mask the appearance.
Short	Apply highlighter to the bridge of the nose down to the tip of the nose.
Long	Apply shader to the tip of the nose.

Techniques for mature models

You need to have a good understanding of corrective techniques when working on mature models. The eyelids are sometimes hooded – when the crease of the eyelid is hidden by skin folding down from the brow bone to the lash line – so eyeshadow should be applied carefully to enhance the eye area. Lines and wrinkles are often a concern too, so make-up artists need to avoid using products that emphasise this, as well as avoiding the use of too much product in these areas.

Here are some tips and techniques when working on mature models.
- Use a primer to help the foundation last longer and create a smoother finish. This helps to smooth out fine lines and wrinkles.
- Less is always more when using foundation on mature skin. Avoid heavy coverage foundations and applying too thickly. Instead, use a lightweight foundation to avoid emphasising lines and wrinkles.
- Use a colour corrector to cover any age spots, redness or blemishes.
- Use a yellow colour corrector under the eyes to neutralise bluish–purple tones, then add a regular concealer in a colour similar to the foundation. Avoid using a concealer lighter than the model's **complexion** as this will accentuate lines.
- Avoid using too much powder as it can sit in lines and wrinkles, drawing attention to those areas and making lines more obvious. A fine, translucent powder can be applied sparingly only to areas where there is noticeable shine.
- Avoid using products with too much shimmer or glitter as this emphasises lines, wrinkles and drooping contours. Some highlighter can be added to the bony areas of the face as they do not move. Highlighter can be matte, which works well on mature skins.
- Use a lipliner to prevent lipstick 'bleeding' into the lines around the mouth.
- Colour can be lost on lips, so add colour.
- Use softer colours for eyeliner and mascara to create a more flattering look, such as brown or dark grey in place of black.
- A pencil or kohl will give you a softer eye line look as opposed to using a liquid or gel liner that gives a more defined dramatic look.

KEY TERM

Complexion: the natural colour, texture and appearance of a person's skin.

ACTIVITY

Find pictures of different celebrities, or even your family and friends, and create a treatment plan for them, stating what products and techniques you would use to create a basic make-up look. Things to consider include face shape, eye shape and colour, skin tone and colour, and any other facial features or factors that may need to be enhanced or corrected.

KEY TERM

Spoolie brush: similar to a mascara wand with a tapered head and soft bristles.

The choice of brushes is important. A make-up artist can never have enough blending brushes, but you can start off with three different-sized brushes – a large soft fluffy brush, a medium fluffy brush; and a small, dense brush.

Standard day eye make-up commonly uses three colours: a pale shade as a base colour, a mid-tone often applied to the eyelid, and a darker shade to add depth to the contour/socket of the eye. Always start at the outer corner of the eye because the area where the brush is first placed will be more concentrated. Then lightly blend the product inwards towards the inner part of the eye.

Applying eyeshadow to the lower eyelid as well creates a soft focus and frame to the eyes. A darker colour can be applied first, close to the lash line, followed by a lighter colour to soften and blend the line.

When applying loose pigment:
- use a flatter brush and press firmly into the pigment to get enough product on the brush
- gently dab and press the pigment onto the eyelid
- blend the edges with a blending brush.

When applying cream eyeshadow:
- apply with a brush or your fingertips
- use a clean blending brush to buff the shadow and soften any harsh lines and edges.

When applying crayon:
- apply directly to the eye area using a technique called sketching then blend out with a brush
- powder eyeshadow can be added on top for a more intense colour.

When applying glitter:
- mix the glitter with a mixing gel or apply a glitter gel to the eyelid first
- use a synthetic brush to apply glitter, dabbing it onto the eyelid
- do the eyes before the base to avoid glitter fallout. If there is still glitter on the skin, press masking tape or roll a **spoolie brush** onto the skin, to pick up any excess.

Eyeliners

Eyeliners help to define and emphasise the eye area and come in various colours.

Types
- Eye pencils – made of wax. They are the most common type of eyeliner.
- Liquid – long-lasting and waterproof. It comes with a small applicator brush for creating precision lines.

- Kohl pencils – a soft, creamy pencil liner that provides an intense colour and can be easily smudged to give a soft smoky effect. They come as a pencil to be sharpened or as a retractable pencil that does not require sharpening.
- Gel/cream liner – a waterproof liner that gives the look of a liquid liner but is easier to apply using an angled brush.
- Cake – comes dry and is mixed with water to apply. It dries quickly and cannot be smudged.
- Sealers – can be mixed with eyeshadow to protect from smudging or lifting.

▲ **Figure 4.19** Pencil eyeliner

Application

Depending on the model's eye shape, the positioning and application of eyeliner can be used to enhance the eye area. If a model has particularly small eyes, applying eyeliner across the whole of the eyelid can actually make the eyes look smaller. In this case, applying eyeliner to the corners of the eye will create the illusion of wider and more open eyes. The thickness of the eyeliner can also be adjusted to correct the eye shape.

The general rule when applying eyeliner is to start in the middle of the eyes, over the upper eye area, and stroke outwards, then from the inner part of the eye to the middle. The skin needs to be taut and supported when applying eyeliner to ensure that a smooth, even line is created.

Eyeliner needs to be applied close to the lash line to create a tight line effect. To achieve this, rest your thumb carefully on the closed eyelid, lifting slightly. The brush or pencil can then be pressed and applied tightly into the lash line.

Creating a winged liner will help to widen the eye. This can be a hard skill to master as it takes time and patience to ensure that the wings are symmetrical. Mark out the positioning of the wing on both eyes to check that they are even before you draw the wings.

Liquid eyeliner often has its own applicator brush, but you should wipe this over with a cleaning product before use to avoid cross-contamination. Alternatively, decant the product onto a palette and apply with an angled or precise eyeliner brush. Gel/cream liner can also be applied by decanting the product onto a palette first and then applying with a brush.

An eyeshadow can be used to create a softer eyeliner effect around the eyes. Dampen an angled brush, then pick up the eyeshadow product and apply to the eyelids.

Mascaras

Mascaras are used to lengthen and volumise the natural lashes. Mascara brushes come in different shapes to create different effects. As a professional make-up artist, you should use disposable wands.

HANDY HINTS

- Pencil eyeliner needs to be sharpened as it becomes blunt with use. This also helps to avoid cross-contamination between models.
- Use a cotton bud or a flat angled brush with a non-oily eye make-up remover to correct and create a defined wing.
- Surgical tape can be used as a guide for creating a winged eyeliner.

HEALTH AND SAFETY

- Decant lip products onto a spatula and apply with a lip brush to avoid cross-contamination.
- Sharpen lip pencils before and after each use to prevent cross-contamination.

Application

Lip colour needs to last. The following application method will help you achieve a long-lasting finish.

1 Apply a lip primer using a lip brush. A lip scrub could also be used if the lips are dry or chapped.
2 Line the upper lip with a soft pencil. Use light feathery strokes, working from the corners of the lips towards the centre.
3 Accentuate the curve of the lower lip and work from the outer corners to the centre.
4 If the lip pencil is a good match to the lipstick, turn the pencil sideways and apply a light coat to the entire lip area.
5 Shape and correct the lip shape if necessary.
6 Apply a coat of lipstick using a lip brush and blot.
7 Using a tissue, dab some translucent powder over the lips as this will help the lipstick last longer.
8 Apply a second coat without blotting.
9 Finish with a coat of gloss if required.

HANDY HINT

Highlighting just above the upper lip line will enhance shape and draw attention to the lips.

Body products

You may also need to consider products that may help to enhance the skin on the body. These are some products that can be used.

- Bronzer – gives the body a healthy glow and can be used to shade the contours of the body.
- Shimmer – helps to add definition and accentuate bone structure.
- Tanning products – provide colour and give the skin a healthy glow. Tanning products help models to avoid looking 'washed out' under harsh studio lighting.

ACTIVITY

Research a range of make-up brands, both high street and professional, to start getting an idea of products you will need to build up your kit.

Step by step: day/special occasion make-up

Day make-up should be kept subtle to highlight the model's natural features and conceal flaws and blemishes on the skin. Make-up should be kept to a minimum, using natural colours that complement the model's skin tone, hair and eye colour.

The following step by step shows techniques that can be used to create a day make-up look. This look can also be used for a special occasion, such as a bridal look.

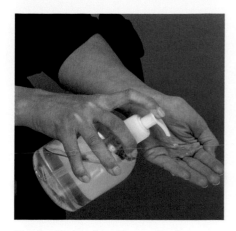

Step 1 – Wash and sanitise your hands.

Step 2 – Clip the model's hair back away from their face.

Step 3 – Remove any eye and lip make-up using make-up remover. Warm a small amount of cleanser in your hands and apply to the model's face using slow sweeping and circular movements to cleanse the skin and remove excess make-up and dirt. Remove the cleanser with damp cotton pads or sponges. Then apply moisturiser and finish by applying a primer to suit the model's skin type and condition.

Step 4 – If required, apply colour-correcting concealers to neutralise unwanted colour tones.

Step 5 – Find a foundation with the same tone and shade as the model's skin. Apply a small amount of foundation to the jawline to match with the model's skin tone. You may need to mix foundation colours to get the perfect match.

Step 6 – Using a foundation brush, apply foundation to the face starting from the nose, sweeping onto the cheeks, forehead and chin. Either blend with a sponge or a stipple brush to ensure an even, flawless finish.

Step 7 – Apply your preferred brow product to the brows using an angled brow brush, filling in any gaps and shaping the brows to the desired shape.

Step 8 – Using a concealer or an eye base, carve around the brows with a small, flat brush and blend the excess onto the eyelid.

Step 9 – Apply an eye primer to the lid using your fingertips.

Step 10 – Using a small eyeshadow brush, apply a light colour over the whole eyelid.

Step 11 – Using a small, tapered blending brush, apply a darker colour to the socket line starting on the outer edge of the eye and sweeping the brush across. Create a 'V' shape onto the lid, bringing the colour towards the middle of the lid and blending just above the socket line. Apply the eyelid colour and ensure there is an even colour transition between the lid and socket line colour by blending together.

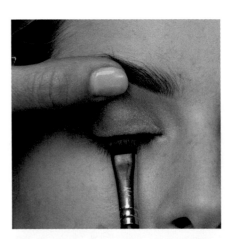

Step 12 – To create an eyeliner effect for a day make-up look, you could use an eyeshadow to create a softer, natural-looking effect. Lift the lid slightly with your thumb then apply a dark brown or black eyeshadow into the tight line (close to the lash line) of the eye using a flat definer brush.

→

Step 13 – Apply mascara to the lashes with a disposable mascara wand. Coat the top lashes first then, once they have dried, coat the lower lashes.

Step 14 – Apply a concealer under the eye, and elsewhere if necessary, to correct any imperfections.

Step 15 – Use a contour brush to apply a powder-based shader. Shade under the cheekbones, starting from just above the ear, sweeping down under the cheekbones and circling just under the cheek. Also apply to the corners of the forehead, under the jawline and down either side of the nose if required. Apply highlighter to the cheekbones, Cupid's bow and down the nose again if required.

Step 16 – Apply blusher to the apples of the cheeks using a fan brush and blend upwards slightly towards the temple.

Step 17 – Use a lip liner to define and shape the lips. Then apply lip colour using a lip brush.

Step 18 – Apply a translucent or setting powder to areas where there is shine. You could also use a setting spray.

Step 19 – The final look.

Step by step: evening make-up

Evening make-up can be bold and dramatic and applied heavier than a day make-up. There is a range of techniques that can be used to create the desired look. This step by step shows one way to create an evening smoky eye 'spotlight' look.

Techniques that were used for the day/special occasion make-up look can also be applied here, but using darker eyeshadow colours. There are lots of other techniques that can also be used to create an evening make-up look.

First, complete steps 1–9 from the day/special occasion make-up look above.

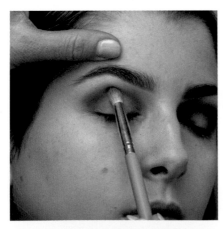

Step 1 – To create a spotlight eyeshadow look, first apply a light-colour eyeshadow across the whole lid just above the socket line using a large blending brush. Then, using a medium blending brush, apply a medium-colour eyeshadow just under the lighter colour but still above the socket line. Next, apply a darker eyeshadow colour to the socket line with a smaller blending brush. Lightly feather the darker colour into the medium colour just above the socket line to create an even colour transition.

Step 2 – Apply a concealer or eye base to the centre of the lid which will help make the eyeshadow 'pop' when applied on top. Then apply the chosen lid colour using a flat brush, pressing the eyeshadow onto the lid.

Step 3 – Using an angled or flat defined brush, apply a cream eyeliner to the top and bottom lash lines, including the water line, to create a more dramatic effect to the eyes. A liquid liner could also be used.

Step 4 – Apply strip lashes and add mascara to the bottom lashes.

Step 5 – Starting from just above the ear and using a linear brush stroke movement, apply cream-based shader under the cheekbones and circling just under the cheek. Apply to either side of the forehead close to the hairline and on the jawline if required. Blend the edges using either a sponge or clean brush, ensuring not to over blend so the placement of shader can still be seen and colour is not mixed with the foundation.

Step 6 – Apply a highlighter to the cheekbones, down the centre of the nose and the top of the Cupid's bow using a small cheek brush. Alternatively, if using a liquid highlighter, apply by dabbing the product onto the skin with your fingertips.

Step 7 – Apply blusher to the apple of the cheeks using a fan brush or blusher brush and blend up towards the temple.

Step 8 – Outline the lips with a lip liner, starting from the outer corners of the mouth up towards the Cupid's bow using light feathering movements and corrective techniques if required. Apply lip colour or gloss to the lips with a lip brush.

Step 9 – Apply powder with a powder brush using a downward movement and focusing on areas where there is shine, such as the forehead and nose.

Step 10 – The final look.

Tools and equipment for make-up artistry

Make-up artists often have their own preferences for the types of brushes and make-up brands to use. As there are so many different types of product on the market, it is worth taking time to research what products to use.

The items you will need to have on hand may include:

- small hand towel for own use
- make-up gown, couch roll or small towel to protect model's clothing
- hair clip to keep hair away from the face (although if you work with a hairstylist you must learn to work around the finished hair look and not pin the hair back)
- cotton wool pads for cleansing the skin
- cotton buds
- bowls for water to dampen sponges and for use in case a reaction occurs
- tissues for blotting the skin and lipstick
- palette for mixing colours
- brush stand or belt
- spatulas for dispensing products
- orange sticks
- disposable applicators and mascara wands
- brushes
- eyebrow tweezers (**sterilised**)
- scissors
- eyelash curlers
- sharpener for pencils
- cleanser
- toner
- moisturiser
- foundations
- blushers
- eyeshadows
- highlighters and shaders
- concealers
- mascaras
- lip pencils
- eye pencils
- lipsticks
- lipglosses
- powders
- hand mirror
- foundation sponges
- facial spray
- face chart/treatment plan and pen
- make-up chair
- mirror
- trolley
- airbrush and airbrush make-up.

Brushes

There are many make-up brushes available on the market. The type of hair used in the brush will determine its price.

- **Synthetic hair brushes** – man-made from synthetic bristles made from materials such as polyester and nylon. The bristles can be soft or stiff depending on the type of brush. They tend to work best for applying liquid or cream-based products. They are easy to clean and the bristles tend not to fall out.
- **Natural hair brushes** – made from animal hair. They are soft to the touch and are best used for powder-based products. They are good for blending and creating softer effects. However, they can sometimes shed bristles and are not as easy to clean as they hold pigments more.

KEY TERM

Sterilise: to kill all micro-organisms.

It is worth investing in a decent set of professional brushes as these will make a difference to the end result. Make-up artists often have a preference for which type of brush to use to create different effects. Table 4.6 lists the main types of brushes needed in a make-up kit and their uses.

▼ **Table 4.6** Brushes needed in a make-up kit

Brush	Uses
Foundation brush	Used to apply foundation to create a heavier coverage.
Kabuki brush	Has a round head. Used to apply loose powdered products to the face. Helps to blend the product evenly on the skin to create a natural coverage.
Large stipple brush	Can be used to apply foundation for a lighter application or buffing the skin after applying foundation. Good for blending powders and pigments.
Small stipple brush	Can be used to work on smaller areas of the face. Good for blending any formula.
Concealer brush	Can be used to apply concealer as well as to define and correct areas of the face.
Precise eyeliner brush	Used to apply liquid, gel or cream eyeliner. Allows precision when drawing fine lines around the eye area.
Fan brush	Can be used for a light application of blusher or highlighter, as well as removing excess product.
Blusher brush	Can be round or angled. Can be used to apply blusher to the cheeks.

→

Brush	Uses
Contour brush	Used to apply powder products to the face and blend them once on the face.
Angled brush	Used to line or shape the eye and eyebrows.
Tapered eyeshadow blending brush	Can be large, medium or small. Used to blend powders or cream-based products.
Flat definer brush	Can be used to apply colour or as a defining tool.
Powder brush	Used to apply and remove loose and pressed powder.
Lip brush	Used to apply colour for a lasting effect.
Lash brush	Defines and brushes lashes and brows into shape.
Beauty sponge	Used to provide a flawless application of foundation or to blend cream contour products.

HANDY HINT

Baby shampoo is good for cleaning brushes as it is gentle on the brush fibres.

KEY TERM

Sanitise: to kill some, but not all, micro-organisms.

Care of products, tools and equipment

Tools, products and equipment must be looked after to ensure health and safety standards are maintained and to prolong their use.

- **Brush cleaners** – used to clean and condition brush fibres. Brush cleaners are often used during a make-up service so that brushes can be reused without having to wait for them to dry. This **sanitises** brushes only, so cleaning them properly after each use should be carried out to ensure they are sterilised and ready for their next use.

- **Warm water and gentle soap** – used to wash make-up brushes after every use. Ensure that make-up brushes are reshaped after use and laid either flat or bristles facing down. If brushes are placed upright, the water can dissolve the glue holding the brush fibres in place, which will cause the brush fibres to fall out.

- **Sterilisation sprays** – specific brush cleaners or products such as surgical spirit or isopropyl alcohol can be used either during or after make-up application.

▲ **Figure 4.23** Brush cleaner   ▲ **Figure 4.24** Isopropyl alcohol

> **HEALTH AND SAFETY**
> Flammable products should be stored in a cool, dry place and away from direct sunlight. Always check the manufacturer's instructions and the expiry date. If the packaging is damaged or broken, throw the product away.

3 CREATE LOOKS USING MAKE-UP TECHNIQUES
Prepare for make-up services

When working as a professional make-up artist, you must be well-prepared. This shows professionalism and will help you to gain a good reputation and future work.

Design brief and research

When a make-up artist is booked for a job, they will be given a brief to work from so they know the occasion and the type of make-up required. The make-up artist should then carry out research to gather ideas and inspiration for the look they are required to create.

A mood board helps to pull all their ideas together and to communicate their thoughts to the model or client. Face charts also need to be completed to show how the final make-up will look and the products and techniques that will be used.

Identifying client characteristics

You need to consider the model's characteristics and any other factors that may influence the final design. Be prepared to adapt your product choices and techniques accordingly.

These are some of the influencing factors that a make-up artist would need to consider.

- **Model preferences** – depending on the type of job, you may need to check the model's likes and dislikes so that you are aware of colours or products to avoid. This is more relevant for bridal or special occasion make-up. For fashion and photographic make-up, the model does not really get a say in the look that is being created.

- **Illness** – illnesses can affect the condition and look of the skin. Certain products may need to be avoided or used to help the overall appearance of the skin.
- **Skin condition** – sensitive, dehydrated, congested and mature skin may require you to adapt your products and techniques to achieve the best finish.
- **Skin type** – again, adaptations to products will need to be considered to achieve the best make-up finish.
- **Skin tone** – ensure that you use the correct colour of products to complement the model's skin tone.
- **Lighting** – this can affect the way the make-up is seen, so you may need to adapt your product choice and application techniques, depending on the light the make-up is intended to be seen under.
- **Personality** – a model's personality can affect your product and application choice. Someone who is more extroverted may prefer a bolder and brighter make-up application.
- **Occasion** – the application of make-up will vary according to the occasion. You will be given a brief so that you can create a suitable look. The model's clothing also needs to be considered so the make-up can complement this.
- **Weather** – can affect product choices. For example, if it is a hot day, you should consider using products that will help to mattify the skin to avoid excess shine and oil.
- **Age** – the model's age will influence the techniques and products used. Some products will be best avoided as they could look unflattering.
- **Allergies** – if a model is allergic to a certain product, an alternative must be used instead.
- **Face shape** – the model's face shape will determine which corrective techniques to use to enhance their facial features.
- **Eye shape** –the model's eye shape will influence which eyeshadow and eyeliner techniques are used to enhance the eye area.
- **Hair and eye colour** – the model's hair and eye colour will help you to decide which colours to use to complement the model's colourings.

Safe working practices

You must follow safe working practices at all times.

- Sterilise tools and equipment to avoid cross-contamination.
- Clean brushes after every use with a sterilisation spray, then wash them in warm, soapy water at the end of the job.
- Keep metal tools in disinfectant solutions.
- The work area should be wiped down and kept tidy.
- Wash your hands prior to starting the service.
- PPE needs to be worn by you and the model.

Preparing yourself and the model

Position yourself and your model correctly to ensure the correct application of make-up and to avoid any discomfort. A chair should be used to position the model. Ideally, it should be high enough for the model to be at eye level with you.

Preparing the work area

Lay out your make-up to ensure easy access and that the correct tools and equipment are in place and ready to use. However, when working on set or on location shoots space constraints may mean that this is not possible. A brush belt is useful for easy access to brushes, and make-up should be stored in clear make-up bags so that products can be seen easily and any make-up spillages will be contained.

▲ **Figure 4.25** Make-up chair

▲ **Figure 4.26** Make-up area set-up

Prepare the model by checking for any contra-indications, as well as analysing the skin for any characteristics that could mean having to adapt their product choice and techniques.

You also need to prepare your own personal protective equipment (PPE), such as clean clothing, an apron and gloves (if necessary), while the model should have a gown to protect their clothes as well as a headband or clip to keep their hair away from their face.

The final design can then be discussed with the model and agreed.

▲ **Figure 4.27** Make-up artist discussing the treatment plan with the model

Environmental conditions

Environmental conditions need to be considered when providing a make-up service as these can affect the choice of products and techniques used.

Lighting

This is the most important factor to consider as different lighting can have a huge impact on the way the make-up looks. See Chapter 6, pages 159–165, for detailed information about this.

Temperature

Make-up artists need to be prepared to adapt their choice of products and techniques depending on the temperature of the environment.

▲ **Figure 4.28** A model being photographed under studio lighting

If the make-up will be worn in hot temperatures, such as on an outside location shoot in the summer or under studio lighting, the make-up artist should consider the following points.

- More powder needs to be applied to help take away excess shine and set the foundation.
- A matte primer should be used to prevent the face looking too shiny.
- Use a setting spray to help absorb oil and help longevity of the make-up.
- Oil-free and waterproof products are best to use to help prevent smudging and to make the make-up last longer.
- Bright light from above will cast shadows on the face, which means over-contouring should be avoided. In some cases, light-reflecting products should be used to help prevent shadowing.
- Avoid too much shimmer as this will highlight areas, causing too much shine. Titanium dioxide should be avoided to prevent flash back on camera images.

- Make-up may need to be applied more heavily as it will not look as bold under bright sunlight.
- Using preparation products with an SPF will protect the model's skin from overexposure to the sun and harmful UV rays. However, an SPF over 20 should be avoided when using flash photography as it will create flashback on the model's face.

During the winter months, when it is cold and lighting is dull, a make-up artist should consider the following points.

- The model's skin may be dehydrated and dull-looking due to central heating and exposure to the elements outside. Consider using a primer with hydrating and brightening properties to give a more radiant effect.
- Colour-correcting primers and concealers can be used to help correct skin imperfections.
- Use cream or liquid foundations to give skin a nice dewy hydrated-looking finish.
- Avoid powder-based foundations as the powder will cling to areas of dry skin.
- Use a lip balm to help with chapped lips before adding lip colour.
- Use a liquid highlighter to create a healthy glow and a dewy look.
- As the light tends to be duller in the winter months, darker colours will look more intense. Use soft, warm colours instead.

Ventilation

Ventilation is particularly important when using products that contain strong fumes and when using airbrush make-up. Ensure that windows are open or that there is a constant airflow in the room being used.

Skin preparation

The make-up artist needs to prepare the model's skin so that it is ready for make-up application. The process should not be as in-depth as a facial but it does need to clean excess make-up and dirt from the surface of the skin. Ideally the model will have no, or minimal, make-up on already, which will allow more time for the application of make-up.

Eye make-up remover

This product is specifically designed to remove make-up from the delicate eye area. It can also be used to remove lip products. It is gentler than a cleanser, to avoid any sensitivity in the skin around eyes, and can remove stubborn mascara and eye make-up. Non-oily eye make-up remover is best to use as oil can affect the application of some eye products.

Cleansers

Cleansers are used to remove dirt and excess make-up from the skin. There are many types of cleanser, but a cleansing lotion or cleansing water are best due to their light texture and because they are quick and easy to use. Cleanser can be applied using fingers and massaged into the skin, then removed with either damp cotton wool or sponges.

▲ **Figure 4.29** Preparing a model's skin for make-up application

HANDY HINT

It is useful to have cleansing wipes in your kit. They are an effective way to remove dirt and make-up quickly if you do not have much time to prepare the skin.

Test your knowledge

1 List three characteristics of an oily skin type.
2 State three different skin conditions.
3 State five different face shapes.
4 Explain the effects that the following types of lighting have on make-up application:

   a Natural

   b Fluorescent

   c Incandescent.

5 Explain three techniques that a make-up artist would use when working on a mature skin.
6 Discuss four benefits of using a foundation.
7 Explain three uses of different lip products.
8 Describe the difference between natural hair and synthetic hair brushes.
9 List six influencing factors a make-up artist needs to consider when providing a make-up service.
10 Explain the aftercare advice a make-up artist needs to provide after completing a make-up service.

Practical assignment

Scenario

You have been contacted by a client who is attending their daughter's wedding in July. They would like their make-up done for the occasion.

Task

Discuss the factors you should consider when planning for the make-up application.

CHAPTER 5

CREATIVE HAIR DESIGN FOR MEDIA MAKE-UP

INTRODUCTION

This chapter will introduce you to the wide variety of fundamental hairdressing skills that a make-up artist needs to style hair. These fundamental skills will enable you to create your total looks. It covers the basic hairstyling skills that are essential for a make-up artist as well as the products, tools and equipment needed to achieve these looks.

In this chapter, you will learn about:

1 the use of products, tools and equipment
2 how to style hair to complement make-up
3 how to achieve creative hair design.

1 THE USE OF PRODUCTS, TOOLS AND EQUIPMENT

Products for creative hairstyling

Table 5.1 details the products you can use styling the hair and the effects that they have on the hair.

KEY TERMS

Humid: having a lot of moisture in the air.

Volume: body and lift in the hair.

▼ **Table 5.1** Hairstyling products and how to use them

Product	How to use	Effect achieved
Setting lotion	This is a liquid that is usually poured and rubbed into wet hair. It can come in a spray. Run your fingers through the hair and apply the setting lotion to the full head of hair, working it into the roots and through to the ends of the hair. Comb through the hair afterwards with a large all-purpose comb to ensure that the setting lotion has been distributed through the hair evenly.	This enables the hair to take on a new form, for example, with a wet set using rollers. It can give a firm hold with root lift and add body to freshly shampooed hair. A shampoo and set will achieve a stronger hair set, which is good for longevity and helps to keep the shape. It can also help to hold styles in damp and **humid** weather.

Having the correct products, tools and equipment with you demonstrates that you are organised and that you have everything to hand for your client's hair. This also demonstrates professionalism and gives your client confidence in you.

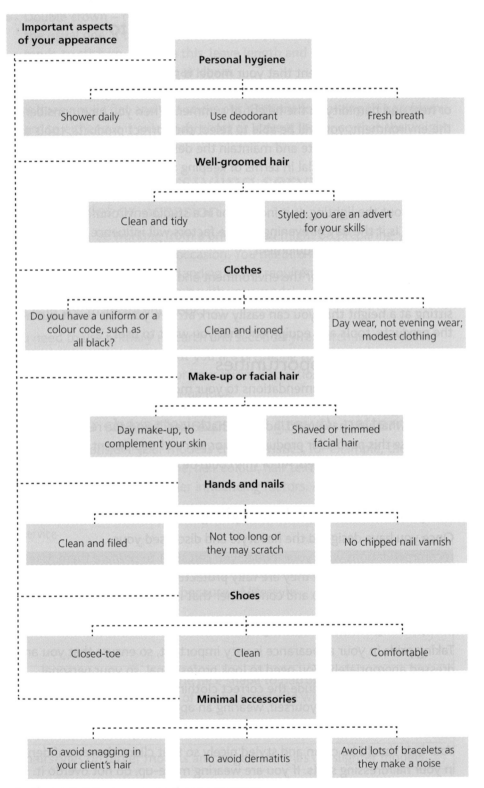

Important aspects of your appearance

Personal hygiene
- Shower daily
- Use deodorant
- Fresh breath

Well-groomed hair
- Clean and tidy
- Styled: you are an advert for your skills

Clothes
- Do you have a uniform or a colour code, such as all black?
- Clean and ironed
- Day wear, not evening wear; modest clothing

Make-up or facial hair
- Day make-up, to complement your skin
- Shaved or trimmed facial hair

Hands and nails
- Clean and filed
- Not too long or they may scratch
- No chipped nail varnish

Shoes
- Closed-toe
- Clean
- Comfortable

Minimal accessories
- To avoid snagging in your client's hair
- To avoid dermatitis
- Avoid lots of bracelets as they make a noise

▲ **Figure 5.2** The importance of your appearance

HEALTH AND SAFETY

Always use your PPE when working.

Provide hairstyling services

Setting

This is usually done when the hair has been shampooed, depending on the length of the hair and the results you want to achieve. You need to choose the correct size of rollers to create anything from large waves to tight curls.

▲ **Figure 5.3** Setting long hair using rollers

▲ **Figure 5.4** Setting using spray

In a conventional set, the rollers are put in from the very front of the hair in the middle of the forehead, working back down the head on top and also down the sides to the nape of the neck.

Setting can vary depending on the chosen technique. Brick setting is where the rollers are positioned alternately like house bricks in a wall.

> **HANDY HINT**
>
> Brush dry hair before shampooing to detangle it and use a wide-toothed comb when the hair is wet.
>
> If you notice there is still conditioner in the hair, rinse it again, otherwise it may make the hair lank and limp.

Directional setting is set in the direction of partings, set straight down the head or directed away from the face.

The rollers need to be secured in place with plastic pins and a hairnet. The model will then sit under a hood dryer to fully dry the set. This can take anything between 20 minutes and one hour, depending on the thickness, length and condition of the hair, and how hot the model likes the dryer to be.

Step by step: wet brick setting technique

Step 1 – Take a small section of wet hair using a tail comb. Place the roller mid-length, take to the end then wind to the root and secure with plastic pins.

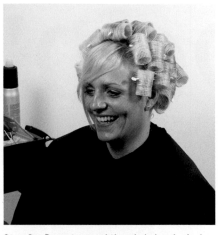

Step 2 – Repeat around the whole head, placing the rollers alternately in a brick pattern. Place a hairnet on top then position the model under a hood dryer until the hair is dry.

Step 3 – Once the hair is dry, take the rollers out and let the curls cool.

Step 4 – Brush through the set firmly with a paddle brush to remove the roller marks. Finish off the set with a comb and spray.

ACTIVITY

Create a shampoo and set using a conventional setting technique. Include a combination of plastic rollers and Velcro rollers, and apply a setting lotion.

Fully dry the hair and brush out, leaving no roller marks. Use the correct finishing products to hold the set firmly in place, making the hair look healthy and shiny.

Step by step: dry conventional setting wind technique using heated rollers

Step 1 – Ensure the hair is dry. Take a small section and place the roller mid-length. Take to the end then wind to the root and secure with a clip.

Step 2 – Continue placing the rollers, pulling upwards for root lift and ensuring that all the ends are completely around the roller before securing.

Step 3 – Allow the rollers to cool completely, then gently remove them. Brush out thoroughly to remove any roller marks then finish with a comb and spray to hold in place.

Step by step: dry conventional setting wind technique using Velcro rollers

Step 1 – Starting at the top front of the head, wind sections of hair around the roller and secure at the root. Pins are not needed. Continue down the centre of the head.

Step 2 – Continue down the sides in a directional manner. Apply heat to fix the set further.

Step 3 – Allow the rollers and hair to cool completely, then slowly remove the rollers, taking care not to catch the Velcro on the hair. Brush through to remove any roller marks then apply finishing products.

Plaiting and twisting

Plaiting and twisting are very fashionable styles for special occasions and, once they are done, they can last for a couple of days or more. Scalp plaits are generally done using three sections of hair starting at the top front and working down the head to the nape. They are secured with a band at the end.

▲ **Figure 5.6** Plaiting

▲ **Figure 5.7** Final plait in place

> **HANDY HINT**
>
> If dressing hair into a hair-up style, recommend that your model or client washes their hair the day before to avoid it being very soft and flyaway.

Step by step: plaits, knots and curls

Step 1 – Use tongs to create loose curls in the hair.

Step 2 – Section the hair at the top to create height.

Step 3 – Backcomb the hair to create height on top and to the front of the hairstyle.

→

Step 4 – Smooth hair over the backcombed section.

Step 5 – Secure the hair in place at the back with kirby grips.

Step 6 – Create a plait from one side of the head and secure in place at the back.

Step 7 – Create a plait from the other side of the head and secure at the back. Tie a small section of hair underneath into a ponytail.

Step 8 – Gather small sections of the loose hair then twist and roll into curls at the back of the head.

Step 9 – Continue twisting and curling small sections of the remaining hair and secure in place.

Step 10 – Ensure the hair up is secure but no grips should be visible. Leave some hair loose at the back.

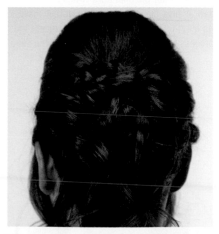

Step 11 – Ensure the hair up section is balanced and blends nicely into the loose section below.

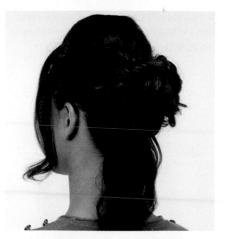

Step 12 – Apply finishing spray to the completed look.

Step by step: plait and twist

Step 1 – Brush through the hair to ensure it is knot-free.

Step 2 – Place the hair in three equal sections at the back of the head and secure with clips.

Step 3 – Plait one-third of the right section of hair against the scalp to the crown then down its length. Secure with a band.

Step 4 – Take the next third of the right section of hair, above the first plait, and create a twist from the front of the head to the crown using two strands. Secure with a band.

Step 5 – Plait the final third of this section of hair against the scalp to the crown then down its length. Secure with a band, then repeat the process from step 3 on the left side of the head.

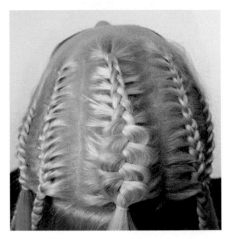

Step 6 – Plait the middle section of hair from the front of the head to the crown and secure with a band.

Step 7 – Tease the middle plait to loosen it.

Step 8 – Use tongs to curl the loose hair underneath.

Step 9 – Apply finishing products to hold the style in place.

Backcombing

Backcombing is used to create volume and body to the roots only. It can also be used for securing padding in place when you are creating hair-up styles. If done correctly it will brush out easily and not damage the hair.

Pin curling

Pin curling is used to create waves. The hair is shampooed, then split into small, circular sections using a tail comb. It is then coiled in a clockwise direction close to the scalp and secured with a pin curl clip. You can do a full head of pin curls, or a combination of half pin curls and half setting rollers. Pin curling creates waves that do not have a lot of root lift, unlike a blow-dry.

Pin curls were used in the basis of many different classic styles, from the eighteenth century all the way up to the 1960s. For more details, see Chapter 7.

▲ **Figure 5.8** Backcombing hair

Step by step: pin curls to create flat movement

Step 1 – Take small sections of hair at the nape of the neck and roll clockwise into a circle.

Step 2 – Work upwards, keeping the hair flat to the head, and secure the hair flat at the roots with a pin curl clip.

Step 3 – Continue until the full head is completely wound in pin curl clips.

Step 4 – Remove the clips then brush through the hair to create waves.

Step by step: stand up pin curls (barrel curls) to create volume

Step 1 – Take a small section of hair from the crown and roll it around the fingers from end to root into a barrel curl.

Step 2 – Secure with a pin curl clip to hold in place. Repeat the process down the head as required.

Step 3 – Remove the clips, tease the hair then apply finishing spray.

Using temporary hair additions

Temporary hair additions, such as hair extensions, can be used to add volume, length or colour to the model's own hair.

▲ **Figure 5.9** Hair extensions

Using heated styling equipment

A range of heated styling tools are available to produce a variety of looks.

- **Heated rollers** add root lift, body and volume to a hairstyle. The size of the rollers and length of hair will determine whether waves or curls are created.
- **Straighteners** are used to create smooth straight hair.
- **Tongs and conical wands** create waves and curls in dry hair. They create different-sized curls depending on the size of the barrel of the tong and the model's hair length.

The use of heated styling equipment is described further in Tables 5.2 and 5.3 on pages 115–119, as well as in the following step by step guides.

Step by step: using straighteners

Step 1 – Use clips to section the hair then spray with heat protector.

Step 2 – Using a comb followed by the straighteners, slowly work straight down the hair from the roots to the ends.

Step 3 – Continue working around the head, section by section.

Step 4 – When all the hair has been straightened, apply a finishing product for hold.

Step by step: using a curling wand or tong

Step 1 – Ensure that the hair is completely dry and brushed through and apply heat protector.

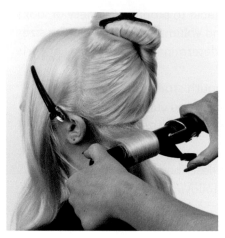

Step 2 – Use clips to section the hair then, starting at the nape of the neck, place the tong midway down the length, slide to the ends then slowly wind the hair around the tong up to the roots.

Step 3 – Continue in small sections around the back of the head.

Step 4 – Continue around the sides of the head.

Step 5 – Make sure all sides of the head are balanced with curls of equal size.

Step 6 – When all the hair has been curled, allow to cool then use your fingers or a brush to gently loosen the tong marks to create waves.

Providing hairstyling to complement make-up for different occasions

A range of hairstyles could be used for special occasions. The choice depends on the model, the time of year and the type of event. Here are some suggestions for particular events.

- **Natural** – to achieve an informal natural look, the hair is generally left down, if it is long. A shampoo and soft blow-dry or finger dry would be appropriate. The make-up should be a light daytime look that enhances the model's natural features. Clothing may be less formal and more casual, although the model may want a formal look.
- **Bridal/wedding** – this could be for the bride, bridesmaids or wedding guests. Preferred hairstyles are usually more formal hair-up styles, for example, a vertical roll secured with grips and pins. Hair ornamentation can be included to make it more of a special occasion hairstyle. The make-up might resemble a photographic look, with prominent shading and highlighting on the eyes. The colours used should complement the clothing and flowers.
- **Day at the races** – a mix of hairstyles are worn at the races. Hair can be left down, tonged into tousled curls or set in heated rollers to create large, bouncy waves. Hair-up styles such as vertical rolls, pleats, twists and plaits are also worn. Make-up should complement the colour of the outfit as well as the model's hair, skin and eye colour.
- **Prom** – the more formal looks outlined for a day at the races are also suitable for special occasions such as a prom.

Provide aftercare advice and recommendations

Further product and service recommendations

Describe the products, tools and equipment that you plan to use during your initial consultation with the model. You can discuss your recommendations openly with them; generally speaking, they will be eager to hear your advice on looking after their hair. Recommend the correct shampoos and conditioner for their hair type, as well as styling and finishing products.

Possible reactions

Although reactions to hair products are very rare, you should provide advice on possible contra-actions and what to do if they occur. The first signs of a reaction are warmth or itching in the affected area, with these symptoms becoming worse and more discomforting. If this occurs, they should rinse out the products immediately, inform you and possibly see their GP regarding the adverse reaction or if a reaction persists.

HANDY HINT

When providing aftercare advice, be sure to:
- provide clear and accurate information
- give feedback that is open and constructive
- use positive body language
- use open and closed questions.

HEALTH AND SAFETY

Advise your model on what to do if a contra-action occurs.

Test your knowledge

1 Describe a brick set.

2 How can colour in the hair affect styling techniques?

3 What is a cowlick?

4 What health and safety guidelines should be followed when using electrical equipment?

5 Why would you use hair wax as a finishing product?

6 Give three examples of hair ornamentation.

7 What are temporary hair additions?

8 What effects does backcombing have on the hair?

9 What are the benefits of using hairspray?

10 What product could you use if the hair is too soft and flyaway to style and dress?

Practical assignment

Scenario

You have been asked to create a 1920s hair and make-up look.

Task

- Produce a mood board for your inspiration, including primary and secondary research on the 1920s.
- Design the hair and make-up for a 1920s look.
- Create your 1920s look.

CHAPTER 6

FASHION AND PHOTOGRAPHIC MAKE-UP

INTRODUCTION

Fashion and photographic make-up is an exciting and creative way to showcase your skills. The fashion industry is ever-changing, so make-up artists must keep up to date with current trends. What may be fashionable one season may look outdated the next.

It is imperative to have a good understanding of lighting and the effect that it has on the way the final make-up looks. You need to know how to adapt products and techniques to suit each type of lighting, to understand the different requirements of colour and black and white photography and to understand the effects of different backgrounds when working in photographic studios.

In this chapter you will learn techniques that can be used to create your own unique looks for a range of styles, such as photographic shoots, fashion shows, commercials, music videos, TV and film, and bridal or special occasion looks.

In this chapter, you will learn about:

1   the factors affecting the application of facial contouring
2   how to apply fashion and photographic make-up
3   how to capture a photographic image.

1 FACTORS AFFECTING THE APPLICATION OF FACIAL CONTOURING

Factors that affect the application of facial contouring include:

- face shape
- eye, nose and lip shapes
- skin types and conditions
- colour theory and correction.

Face and feature shapes, skin types and conditions and colour correction are covered in Chapter 4, pages 71–81, while colour theory is covered in Chapter 9, pages 223–227.

2 APPLYING FASHION AND PHOTOGRAPHIC MAKE-UP

Preparing to apply fashion and photographic make-up

When working on set for TV or film or for a photographic shoot, it is important to arrive on time and be well-prepared. If the location is somewhere unfamiliar, it is a good idea to check the route out beforehand and allow plenty of time to get to the destination. It is unprofessional for a make-up artist to arrive late and it can also have an impact on timings for other members of the team.

It is also useful to do some research about the venue beforehand, checking things such as:

- the parking that is available on site
- the type of lighting that is available
- whether there will be electricity
- whether there will be hot and cold water
- whether there will be a designated space to lay out make-up products
- whether there will be mirrors
- whether there will be chairs for the model to sit on.

A brief will have been provided and finalised before the day of the shoot, so you should know what look is required. Mood boards, face charts and any reference material should be bought along for reference.

It is important to prepare your kit beforehand, ensuring that it is organised and clean and that it contains all products and items that may be required. If particular hair and make-up items or props are needed, you may need to source these beforehand and allow enough time for them to arrive. Make-up artists must also be prepared for the brief to change, so they should be ready for every eventuality.

There is not always a designated space to lay out make-up products, so you may need to make do with the space that is available. Use brush belts and keep make-up in clear plastic bags so that it can be seen easily. Once the make-up has been completed, have a set bag ready to do touch-ups to maintain the look on the shoot or set.

▲ **Figure 6.1** An on-set make-up bag

You also need to ensure that you prepare yourself by wearing appropriate clothing. Hair should be tied back and jewellery kept to a minimum to avoid catching in the model's hair and costume. If working on an outside location, the weather should be considered, as warm coats or waterproofs may be needed.

The length of time the make-up artist has to complete each look will vary depending on what make-up is required and may not be very long, so it is important to be prepared and ready to start. When working on a fashion show, a running order will be provided, containing details of start and on stage times, as well as the models' names and whether they have any costume changes. You need to keep on top of this to ensure everything runs smoothly. When working on commercials, TV or film, a call sheet will be provided for you to follow.

Types of fashion and photographic make-up looks

Fashion and photographic make-up has a number of specialised areas that a make-up artist could consider working in. It is important to understand the different demands of each.

High fashion

High fashion make-up is the application of on-trend make-up looks. Make-up artists may work with fashion designers to create different **runway** looks for models or for glossy magazines. Clothing collections are usually launched twice a year – spring/summer and autumn/winter – with the designs being worked on a season in advance. Fashion is also about hair and accessories, so make-up artists work as part of a team with fashion designers to create make-up looks for models that will co-ordinate with the designs in a unique way. Designers can be quite demanding about the way they want the make-up to look and will require specific creative or artistic looks.

Strong artificial lighting is used on the runway stage. This can cause the make-up to look less vibrant, so a stronger or exaggerated application is required. This can be created with bolder colours so that the make-up stands out. The make-up seen by people sat further away from the stage will be less apparent, so accentuating the make-up for eyes, brows and lips are important.

▲ **Figure 6.2** High fashion make-up

KEY TERM

Runway: a narrow platform between seating areas that is used by models to demonstrate clothing during a fashion show.

ACTIVITY

Research different fashion designers and write down a list of current fashion trends.

▲ **Figure 6.3** Commercial make-up

▲ **Figure 6.4** Beauty editorial make-up

KEY TERM

Adornments: items used as decoration to enhance a look.

Commercial

Commercial jobs might include providing make-up artistry for music videos, magazine covers, advertising products (either make-up or other products), book covers, TV commercials and catalogue work. Make-up application for advertising is often more natural and is toned-down to avoid overpowering and distracting from the product itself.

Make-up artists need to learn how to create a perfect 'no make-up look'. Although this sounds easy, it is not a look that make-up artists create frequently and they have to restrain themselves from applying too much make-up. For example, if you are designing make-up for an advertisement selling foundation, the focus should be on the skin and not draw too much attention to the model's eyes or lips.

Editorial

Editorial make-up is make-up that is not typically worn every day. It can be used for magazine spreads and runway looks. The look focuses on a theme that a client, brand or photographer requires. The purpose of editorial is to tell a story, so the make-up is designed to capture the feeling and interpret the story. The make-up can be natural or creative.

- When the story focuses on clothes, it is known as **fashion editorial**.
- When the story focuses on make-up, it is known as **beauty editorial**.
- When the focus is on hair, it is known as **hair editorial**.

Fashion editorial

The main focus of fashion editorial is clothing and fashion. The make-up should emphasise the clothing being worn, not take attention away it. The make-up style tends to be more natural, creating a pretty and flawless finish.

Beauty editorial

The main focus is the make-up, so the emphasis is on facial beauty and perfection, keeping the skin as true to reality as possible. Head and shoulder shots and close-up images are taken, so it is important for the make-up to look perfect as any flaws will be noticed. The make-up can be colourful and creative and may sometimes focus on a specific area, for example, the brows or lips.

Avant-garde

Avant-garde describes make-up that is out of the ordinary. It can be extreme and dramatic, and can express an individual's creativity. Make-up artists can be experimental with ideas and methods, and 'think out of the box' when creating designs. Avant-garde make-up may be used for runway looks, magazines, advertisements and other performance events. The make-up artist will often use **adornments** such as gems, glitters, feathers and other types of accessories to make more of an impact. You can read more about avant-garde make-up in Chapter 11.

Bridal make-up

Bridal make-up is carried out for a bride on their wedding day. The make-up artist will discuss the look the bride wishes to have and brides will often show the make-up artist pictures of their inspiration. The make-up artist will then create a design that suits their client's individual requirements. A trial run is usually carried out so that any amendments can be made.

▲ **Figure 6.5** Bridal make-up

The make-up artist needs to consider the best products and techniques to use for when the bride is being seen in person under various lighting conditions (indoors and outdoors) as well as when they are being photographed. The longevity of the make-up is very important – it has to last the full wedding day and on into the evening.

For more information on bridal make-up, see Chapter 16, which is available online at www.hoddereducation.co.uk/product/9781510484771.

Period make-up

Period make-up is designed to resemble a specific historical make-up look. The make-up artist needs to research the trends that influenced that era, focusing not just on make-up but also on hair and fashion, to gain a good understanding of the requirements needed to complete the look. Elements of period make-up influence fashion, editorial and even bridal looks. More information about period make-up can be found in Chapter 7.

Fantasy make-up

Fantasy make-up focuses on creating make-up looks for characters such as fairies, witches, aliens and clowns. Fantasy make-up may be required on TV and film sets, stage performances or for photographic looks. Make-up artists often use products such as latex, prosthetics, airbrushing and body paint to transform their model into a character.

TV and film make-up

High-definition technology in TV and film will pick up any make-up imperfections, so specialised high-definition make-up using micro-pigment particles should be used to provide a flawless finish. However, be careful not to use high-definition make-up products when using flash photography, as this will cause flashback on the face. Airbrush make-up is often used for TV as the products have good longevity under strong studio lighting.

▲ **Figure 6.6** Fantasy make-up

Application techniques

Many different application techniques can be used to create the look that is desired. Make-up artists often pick up tricks of the trade from others and may use slightly different techniques. There is no right or wrong way – the main thing is the quality of the final make-up look.

Contouring

Highlighters and shaders can be used to enhance or diminish facial features.

Products required:
- liquid highlighter
- cream-based shader and highlighter
- contour stick
- powder-based shader and highlighter.

Tools required:
- sponge
- flat brush
- fan brush
- stipple or rounded brush.

Application

- Highlighter and contouring should be applied on top of the foundation.
- Shader and highlighter can be applied either by a brush or sponge, depending on which type is being used and personal preference.
- Highlighter can be applied in a 'C' shape from the temples to the cheekbones, down the nose and on top of the Cupid's bow.
- Shader can be applied under the cheekbones, sides of forehead and jawline.
- When using a cream-based highlighter and shader, use a small rounded brush or sponge to blend them into each other. Take care not to change the base colour of the foundation.

Blending

This is an essential technique for any make-up artist and applies to all parts of the make-up, for example, the foundation, contouring, eyeshadow and blusher. Blending helps to provide a smooth transition of colour and to soften harsh edges.

Products required:
- make-up products.

Tools required:
- stipple brush
- sponge
- tapered blending brush (large, medium or small).

Application

- Apply the make-up and build product as required.
- Use soft, sweeping movements with a brush to distribute the colour evenly and create a seamless colour transition.
- Remember to use a clean brush when blending to avoid mixing colours together.
- A sponge can be used in a dabbing movement to blend foundation, concealer and cream-based shader and highlighter products.

▲ **Figure 6.7** Blending eyeshadow

Step by step: rainbow eye look

This look is a great way to practise blending techniques using a variety of bright colours to create a rainbow effect to the eyes. First, complete steps 1–8 from the day/special occasion make-up look on pages 95–96.

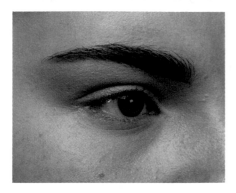

Step 1 – Prime the eye using a concealer or eye base.

Step 2 – Apply a pink eyeshadow to the inner corner of the eye. Then apply a light purple, then a dark blue to create depth into the socket line. Follow with a green colour and finish with a yellow to the outer corner, making sure you blend to create a smooth transition between each colour.

Step 3 – Using an eye base or concealer, carve around the inner part of the eyelid towards the centre to clean and create a base in order to apply a lighter eyeshadow.

Step 4 – Apply the dark blue eyeshadow to the outer corner of the lid, along with the green to create a winged effect.

Step 5 – Apply a white or pink coloured pigment or eyeshadow on top of the base to the inner corner of the eye. Then apply a light purple shimmer to the centre of the lid and blend into the dark blue.

Step 6 – Apply eyeshadow using the same colours and technique to the lower lash line to create balance to the eyes.

Step 7 – Apply a black eyeshadow to the top and bottom lash line using a flat or angled definer brush, and apply strip lashes.

Step 8 – Complete the look by following steps 5–9 of the evening make-up look on pages 95–96.

KEY TERM

Cutting in: when creating a cut crease eyeshadow look, you define the crease line by 'cutting' across it with a concealer or foundation using a flat definer brush and then apply a contrasting eyeshadow colour to the lid.

HANDY HINT

Mix a powder eyeshadow with a liquid eye primer or a mixing medium to create a cream-based eyeshadow. Remember to then set the cream with a powdered product for a long-lasting effect.

Cut crease eyeshadow techniques

The cut crease eyeshadow technique is used to define the eye socket in a dramatic way by **cutting in** the crease of the eyelid with contrasting colours. It can be used to create a more traditional evening make-up look or, if using brighter colours, more of a fashion look.

Cut creasing is an eyeshadow technique that has been around since the days of silent films. It was used to draw attention to female actors' eyes in black and white films. The style was softer than the modern version but had the same premise.

Products required:
- lid primer (eye base or concealer)
- eyeshadows – powder (compact or loose), pigment, glitter, cream
- petroleum jelly
- gel liner
- highlighter.

Tools required:
- a selection of different size brushes.

Step by step: cut crease eyeshadow

Various techniques can be used to create a cut crease look. The following step by step shows one example. First, complete steps 1–8 from the day/special occasion make-up look on pages 95–96.

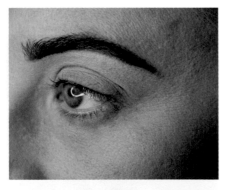

Step 1 – Prime the eye with a concealer or eye base. If using powder-based eyeshadows, apply a translucent powder over the base to set it. This will also help with blending the eyeshadows.

Step 2 – Apply a dark blue eyeshadow into the socket line with a small blending brush. Stretch the brow slightly with your thumb to help place the product. Pick up the product little and often, working in sections across the eye to build it up. Use a rounded blend movement across the socket, and a flicking movement at the outer corner to create a blown out edge.

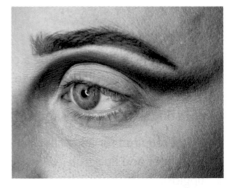

Step 3 – Apply a pink eyeshadow for the second blend, layering it halfway over the dark blue. Use a back and forth motion, following the shape of the first blend. Extend the tail slightly further out towards the temple, ensuring the edge is soft.

Step 4 – Apply an orange eyeshadow for the third blend, repeating the technique in Step 3. Layer it halfway over the pink in back and forth motions following the existing shape. Touch up each colour for brightness and ensure the blend is flawless.

Step 5 – To carve away the cut crease, apply petroleum jelly to a flat brush and glide around the shape of the cut crease from the inner to the outer corner, flicking outwards. Carefully remove all of the petroleum jelly from the eyelid with a make-up remover wipe before applying any other products.

Step 6 – With a flat brush, apply a pigmented eye base (a lighter base is best) or concealer to cut the crease. For a neat line, use only the tip of the brush. Use a stamping motion across each section of the lid to blend the base across and buff any excess product to remove harsh edges.

Step 7 – Pat a light purple eyeshadow over the lid to set the base and achieve even coverage. Apply a loose pink pigment to the centre to highlight and make the lid 'pop'. To balance the eye, apply the dark blue eyeshadow to the lower lash line with a back and forth motion. Then apply the pink, overlapping the blue, and finally the orange, creating a soft, seamless blend. Apply black liner to the lower lash line into the water line. Apply a black eyeshadow to the top lash line, blending out for a soft, smoky finish.

Step 8 – Correct any imperfections then apply lashes to finish the look.

HANDY HINT

When creating a sharper cut crease look, apply a concealer and ask the model to look up. This will help to provide a guide as to where to cut the crease.

Wet-look technique

This technique is good for an editorial make-up look. As well as the eye make-up, the face and hair should also be considered to complement the overall wet look.

Products required:
- face primer (illuminating)
- facial mist
- foundation
- glycerine
- eyeshadow product of choice
- aqua or greasepaint
- lipgloss
- petroleum jelly.

▲ **Figure 6.12** Wet-look make-up

153

Tools required:
- a selection of brushes.

Application

1 Apply an illuminating primer to give the skin a dewy effect.
2 Apply a foundation that also gives the skin a dewy effect rather than a matte effect.
3 Apply highlight and contour techniques to the face.
4 Apply an eye primer to the entire eyelid.
5 Apply the desired eyeshadow colour (a block colour is usually effective).
6 Apply either a lipgloss or a specific wet-look product on the lips.
7 Use a face mist or add glycerine before the look is to be seen to add a further effect to the wet-look make-up.

Faux freckles

This technique is used to create fake freckles on the skin.

Products required:
- foundation and base make-up products
- brown eyeliner
- freckle pen
- eyeshadow.

Tools required:
- spoolie brush
- foundation brush.

▲ **Figure 6.13** Faux freckles

Application

Freckles should be placed where the sun naturally tans the skin and intensifies natural freckles, which often appear towards the centre of the face, around and on the nose and close to the mouth. The fake freckles should be different sizes in order to resemble real freckles.

You can create faux freckles by using:
- either a brown eye pencil to make small marks across the area that you want to cover
- or a brown eyeshadow and dampened spoolie brush or a brown aqua colour paint using a flicking movement with the brush to flick the product randomly onto the skin.

If the freckles look too dark, apply foundation lightly over the top, tapping it onto the skin until the right colour is achieved.

Stencilling

Stencils can be used to create unique shapes and effects on the face or body. Different materials can also be used as a stencil to make patterns, for example, lace and fishnet stockings.

Products required:

- aqua or greasepaint
- eyeshadow
- glitter.

Tools required:

- stencil
- sponge
- brushes
- cotton buds.

Application

Hold the stencil securely on the area and use either a powder-based or cream-based product with a sponge or brush to place product onto the area exposed by the stencil.

Ornamentation

A range of adornments can be added to complete the total look, for example, glitter, gems, jewels, feathers, flowers, gold leaf and face lace.

Products required:

- adhesive
- petroleum jelly
- cotton buds
- ornamentation.

Tools required:

- orange stick
- bowl of water
- tweezers.

Application

- To use ornamentation such as gems, feathers and face lace, an adhesive needs to be applied to the skin or accessory first. Allow this to go slightly tacky before applying the ornamentation to the area.
- A dampened orange stick can be used to apply small gems.
- When using gold leaf, apply petroleum jelly to the area of the skin first. Break the gold leaf into pieces then use a cotton bud, orange stick, fingers or the end of a hair pin to pick up the gold leaf and place it onto the desired area.
- To cover an area using larger pieces of gold leaf, cut out the shape while the gold leaf is still in the protector, then place the gold leaf side down onto the area and press using the fingertips. A brush can then be used to buff away the edges.

▲ **Figure 6.14** Stencil effect

▲ **Figure 6.15** Gems used as ornamentation to finish a look

HEALTH AND SAFETY

Always ensure the model has been patch tested before using an adhesive and explain the correct removal of any accessory added to the body.

Products, tools and equipment

As well as the products, tools and equipment required to create basic make-up looks (see Chapter 4 for a list of products and brushes, pages 82–103), the make-up artist will also need some specialist products in their kit to complete fashion and photographic looks.

▼ **Table 6.1** Additional products required for a make-up kit for fashion and photographic make-up

Product	Use
Latex	Used to create special effects and 3D effects on the skin.
Glycerine	Used to create special effects such as sweat or wet-look effects.
Adhesive	Spirit gum or Pros-Aide are used to stick adornments and ornamentation to the skin. Specific eyelash adhesive is used to apply strip or individual lashes.

Product	Use
Mixing medium	Used to transform the texture, finish and application of pigments and glitters.
Barrier cream	Applied to the skin to protect it from sensitivity and staining when using face and body paints.
Aqua colour paint	A water-based product rich with colour pigments that can be used on the face and body to create different looks. It is long-lasting and smudge-proof.
Greasepaint	An oil-based product with colour pigments that can be applied to the face and body using a brush or sponge.

Product	Use
Coloured inks	Long-lasting colours that can be used on the face and body.
Modelling wax	Used to create 3D effects and for blocking out eyebrows.
Clay	Used to create 3D effects and different textures on the skin or in the hair.
Stencils	Used as a guide to transfer patterns onto the skin.

Product	Use
Strip lashes	A range of strip lashes can be used to complement make-up looks.
Adornments	Used to create more of an impact as part of the overall look. Examples include gems, glitter and feathers.
Hair accessories	Used to create different effects on the hair to complement the make-up. Examples include ornamentation, coloured hair chalks and coloured hair sprays.

3 CAPTURING A PHOTOGRAPHIC IMAGE

Effects of different lighting

The main requirement for photographic make-up is lighting because it is essential that the make-up and lighting work together. You must understand how lighting will affect the overall look and how to adapt the products and techniques used to create the perfect make-up application.

Avoid reflective products containing titanium dioxide, zinc oxide or any type of light-reflecting particles, especially for black and white photography. These products cause a glare when used with flash photography so should be kept to a minimum and contrasted with matte products.

Natural light

Natural light enables all colours to be seen in their true form. It intensifies every colour used as this type of lighting contains all the colours of the rainbow. Outdoor light varies according to the time of day, and this will change the colour of the make-up when it is photographed.

Morning light

Soft tones should be applied to enhance and complement the surroundings. At this time of day, make-up will photograph darker than it appears to the natural eye because the light is soft. A liquid foundation can be used to create a dewy look. Soft, warm tones can be used for the eyes, remembering not to apply them too strongly as the lighting will accentuate the colours. Lips should be kept light, soft and natural looking.

Midday light

Midday light is the strongest natural lighting as the sun is at its highest point during this time. If the sun is directly above the model's head, it can cast shadows onto the face. Make-up needs to be perfectly blended and have no harsh lines as these will show up in photos. A lightweight foundation with powder and a matte finish is best. Blush should also be matte: a cream blusher is ideal as it will blend into the skin well and look natural. However, if the skin is oily, use a powder blusher. Avoid too much shimmer as it can look shiny on the skin.

Afternoon light

This is the best light; because it is at its most golden as the sun starts to set. The light is at its kindest so make-up can be more dramatic. This time of day is ideal for models with skin problems and flaws as more concealer and foundation can be applied while still achieving a natural look. More colour is required: darker shades of eyeshadows and blushers, including bronzers with a slight shimmer, will photograph nicely. Lip colours can be stronger as the light is very forgiving so they will not look too harsh.

Fluorescent light

This lighting gives a cooler effect to the skin or make-up as it contains the colours blue and green. It can take away the depth of colour of the make-up and make the complexion look dull as it intensifies the tones.

Incandescent light

This lighting provides a warm look to the skin or make-up as it contains the colours red, yellow and orange. It helps to soften colours and hide flaws, which makes this light more forgiving.

Studio lighting

Studio lighting is used in photographic studios as well as in TV and film studios. This type of lighting can be harsh. It is usually fixed on set and consists of overhead, side and floor lights.

▲ **Figure 6.16** Studio lighting

Studio lighting can also produce a lot of heat, so make-up artists need to consider products that help to mattify and reduce shine. Powder should be applied regularly to absorb oil and oil-based products are best avoided.

High-definition technology in TV and film means that more details can be seen on the screen and the camera will pick up any make-up imperfections. The use of heavyweight foundations and powders should be avoided because the make-up will create a 'mask' effect and can look unnatural. Specialised high-definition make-up, which uses micro-pigment particles, is available. The reflecting characteristics of this make-up give the effect of a smooth surface on the skin and help to cover lines, hide minor imperfections and revive colour, creating a flawless finish to the skin. High-definition products are more durable and do not wear off as quickly.

Airbrush make-up is a popular choice when applying make-up for TV and film as it has many benefits. It is less visible to the naked eye because it is made from tiny particles that are sprayed on the skin, but it still provides good coverage without clogging the pores and allows the skin to breathe. This method allows for a smoother application without any brush or sponge marks. It also has hygienic benefits, as conventional application techniques using brushes, sponges or fingers risk spreading bacteria across the face. Another benefit is its formulation – it lasts a long time and is heat and water resistant, which is perfect when under the intense heat of studio lighting. See Chapter 8, pages 203–205, for more on using an airbrush.

Corrective make-up techniques such as highlighting and contouring need to be used to define bone structure and facial features. Natural shadows created by skin folds can be seen on camera, so a highlighter will help to **detract** from this and soften those areas. Colour correction can also be used to correct imperfections such as dark circles, blemishes and redness.

It is important to ensure that the make-up application is seamless, as the camera will pick up on any flaws. Photographers do not want to spend time editing make-up corrections, so it is expected that the make-up will be applied perfectly. This is also important when creating photographic pictures for your portfolio that show your true make-up skills, as no filters or edits can be used.

Black and white photography

Make-up artists must consider a number of factors when designing make-up for black and white photography. To ensure that it stands out in the photographs, they must look beyond the colours and concentrate on the tones, shades and **contrasts**. Light colours will not show, so it is important to use dark shades and tones, and to highlight areas to reflect the light. The colour applied will become irrelevant, but the shade is very apparent.

HANDY HINT

Be careful not to use high-definition make-up products when using flash photography as it will cause flashback on the face.

KEY TERM

Detract: take away.

HANDY HINT

Minor tweaks are part of the job. Test shots allow you to see what needs to be adjusted but are not always possible, so the more understanding and experience of colour and lighting you have, the better.

KEY TERM

Contrast: the difference between colours.

▲ **Figure 6.17** Make-up shot in black and white

▲ **Figure 6.18** Back light

▲ **Figure 6.19** Front light

Even when creating make-up looks for colour photography, make-up artists should ask to see the photos as black and white images to see the different tones that their choice of colours achieves.

- It is advisable to use neutral colours on the eyes, such as browns, blacks, creams and greys, as it is a lot easier to judge their tone level.
- Reds and browns on the lips are the best colours to use as they are high in richness and show up in black and white.
- Contouring the face is important: it is usually advisable to go four shades darker than the model's skin tone so it will show up in the photos. Four shades lighter can be used when highlighting as well.
- Use matte colours when creating a look for black and white photography as shimmery colours can look dull and lifeless.

ACTIVITY

Take pictures of your eyeshadow palette in both colour and black and white. See which colours stand out and which don't when looking at them in black and white. Write down the best colours in your make-up palette to use for black and white photography.

Lighting effects

When working in studios, film, TV, stage and with photographers, it is important to understand the effects of lighting on the make-up. A number of lights are used in the studio or on stage to create a variety of effects. Most lighting set-ups will consist of the following components.

- **Key light** – the main light source provided. This light is used to highlight the dimensions and form of the subject.
- **Fill light** – a secondary light, usually less powerful than the key light, that defines features and creates contrast between the image subject and the background.
- **Back light** – this lights the background, separating it from the person being photographed. The source of light comes from behind and creates a silhouette of the person. This type of lighting is often used when trying to set the mood or to add a creative touch to the photograph. The model's face will often be shadowed, so the make-up cannot be seen as well as it might otherwise be.
- **Front lighting** – this type of light does not cast any shadows on the face as the light projects evenly all over the face. For photographic work, make-up needs to be applied more heavily as the boldness of the colours may not be seen as well as the light is bright. However, when working with TV and high-definition cameras, the make-up should not be as heavily applied and needs to be precise, as the camera will pick up on the detail of the make-up.

- **Side light** – the brightness comes from the side of the person, which can have a dramatic effect on photos. This is good for showing texture and adding depth. One side tends to be cast into darkness and shadow, while the other side is in the spotlight. If complete darkness is not wanted on one side, use something to reflect light onto the darkened side: a white post or other light-reflecting surface can bounce light back to the model to soften the effect of side lighting.
- **Diffused lighting** – sometimes light can be too harsh for the effect that you want to create. Diffused lighting can be used to soften the incoming light to create a more pleasing photo. Bright sunlight is the worst kind of light for a photographer as it makes colours appear washed out and casts shadows onto the face. It is better to take photos in the shade or when the sun is behind clouds. If there is no shade, an umbrella or a similar object can be used.
- **Camera flashes** – flashes can cause 'red eye'. The further away the flash is from the lens, the less likely this is to happen. Flash photography can also wash colour from the face. It is important not to use light-reflecting make-up products, for example, SPF products over 25, translucent powder or products containing titanium dioxide or zinc oxide or any illuminating products that contain light-reflecting particles. Using these products will give the model's face a 'ghostly' appearance.

Colour temperature

Colour temperature can affect how make-up looks. Different light sources produce 'white' light made up of different colours and this can make the make-up appear different. These different colours can be expressed using a number known as the colour temperature.

Colour temperature is measured on the Kelvin scale, symbolised by the letter 'K'. The higher the Kelvin value, the whiter the light source is. For make-up application, a colour temperature of 4800–5000 K is recommended as it is not too warm or too cool.

▲ **Figure 6.20** Side light

▲ **Figure 6.21** Make-up with a 'ghostly' appearance caused by flash photography

KEY TERM

Colour temperature: a term used to indicate the type of white light that a light source emits.

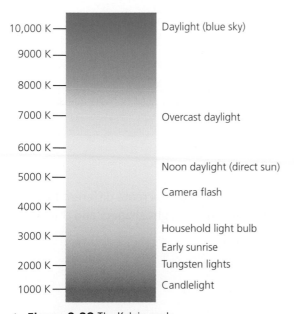

10,000 K	Daylight (blue sky)
9000 K	
8000 K	
7000 K	Overcast daylight
6000 K	
5000 K	Noon daylight (direct sun)
4000 K	Camera flash
3000 K	Household light bulb
	Early sunrise
2000 K	Tungsten lights
1000 K	Candlelight

▲ **Figure 6.22** The Kelvin scale

▲ **Figure 6.23** A ring light

▲ **Figure 6.24** Make-up with a coloured light background

The human eye is good at adjusting colour, so most objects look similar under different lightings when we look at them. However, cameras see objects as being different colours depending on the lighting. This can lead to photos having a colour cast, that is, an overall blue or orange tint, which makes the shot appear unnatural and unpleasing to the eye. Using a **white balance** setting on a camera will tell it what type of lighting the scene has and allow it to use an appropriate colour temperature when taking the shot.

Some artificial lighting, such as a ring light, has an adjustable colour temperature from 3000–5500 K, so the make-up artist or photographer can choose whether to have a warmer light or to mimic daylight.

Use of gels and filters

Gels and colour filters may be used on camera lenses and lights to create different effects and backgrounds to complement the make-up and set a scene. They are often used in editorial shoots. Using a gel or filter can totally change how the colour of the make-up appears. For example, if you are using black and white film, the colour of the gel used will darken the same colour on the subject. So, if the model is wearing red lipstick and the lens is covered with a red filter or red gel, the red lipstick will appear darker when the film is processed.

Here are some other colours and their effects.
- Blue – using blue filters makes the colours blue and green appear lighter and cools down the skin tone. It can change red tones, making them appear darker.
- Green – using green filters makes colours appear darker, particularly blue, red and purple. However, green can appear lighter.
- Red – using red filters makes blue and green tones appear darker and the face look lighter.
- Peach or orange – peach filters help to warm the skin and tend not to alter the colours of the make-up.

The make-up artist and photographer need to discuss this to ensure the correct colours and application of make-up is used.

HANDY HINT

It is important to look at make-up through the lens of the camera or in the environment it will actually be seen in because you may need to make adjustments to account for this.

KEY TERM

Light shaper: a piece of equipment used in photography to create different lighting effects.

Light shapers

Light shapers are used in photographic studios to create different light sources. Table 6.1 lists some different types of light shapers and their uses.

▼ **Table 6.2** Different light shapers and their uses

Light shaper	Use
Barn door	Barn doors are light modifiers that create focused light and help to shape and direct light. They are fixed to the front of studio or theatre lights and can make a variety of shapes.
Soft box	Soft boxes provide a nice soft, even light that, when moved close to the model, helps to reduce contrast and shadows and to conceal skin blemishes. They come in various sizes to give different results. Small closed soft boxes can be used when photographing products.
Umbrella	These are similar to soft boxes and are used to create a softer light by spreading the light out over a larger area. They are easy to set up and are portable. The light created can be more flattering to most skin types when taking portraits.
Snoot	This attachment is used to create a beam of light to highlight an object or person. It is often used in fashion and portrait photography to create a 'hair light', meaning that the light is directed onto the back of the head, helping to illuminate the hair and make it stand out from a dark background instead of blending into it.
Beauty dish	A beauty dish gives off a harsher and more contrasted light than a soft box, which can be more flattering on the subject as it gives them better-defined features. It can also create a circular catchlight in the eye.

CHAPTER 7

HISTORICAL HAIR AND MAKE-UP LOOKS

INTRODUCTION

Creating historical looks is an essential skill for a make-up artist. As well as being required for theatre, TV or film, aspects of historical looks are also used in fashion magazines and on the catwalk, influencing modern-day trends.

It is important to research historical hair and make-up to have a basic knowledge and understanding of how to create these looks. Make-up artists work behind the scenes for historical TV series such as *The Crown* and *Downton Abbey* to make the make-up and hairstyles as authentic as possible.

In this chapter, you will learn:

1 how make-up, hairstyles and fashion trends have changed through the eras
2 the range of products used to create historical hair and make-up looks
3 how to apply techniques and skills to create historical hair and make-up looks.

1 HOW MAKE-UP, HAIRSTYLES AND FASHION TRENDS HAVE CHANGED THROUGH THE ERAS

For a make-up artist to understand current trends, they must know and appreciate the history of make-up, hair and fashion. Styles have changed dramatically over time, of course, but fashion always recycles – whether we like it or not – and trends from the past are very much alive in the styles we see today.

People in ancient civilisations painted their faces with powders made from ground-up minerals, while the products that we recognise today, such as lipsticks, mascaras and nail polishes, began to emerge in the twentieth century.

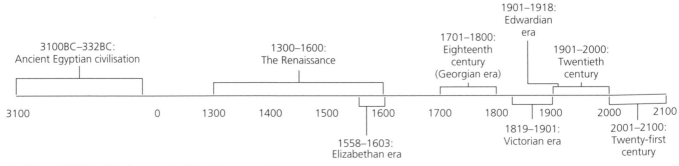

▲ **Figure 7.1** Timeline from ancient Egypt to present day

Looking through the eras

Ancient Egyptians

The ancient Egyptian civilisation lasted almost 3000 years, from around 3100BC until its conquest by Alexander the Great in 332BC. Queens Cleopatra and Nefertiti were notable ancient Egyptian leaders. It is known that Cleopatra wore lipstick coloured by ground-up carmine beetles.

Make-up

- Eye paint is the most **iconic** feature of Egyptian-era make-up. Tutankhamun's death mask and Elizabeth Taylor as Cleopatra in the 1963 film both show the same extended eyeliner techniques.
  - Green eye paint was made from the green mineral malachite, a carbonate of copper.
  - Kohl, a material used to create eyeliner, was made from a soot and the ore galena, which is the source of the metal lead.
  - These mineral powders could be added to water or animal fat to make a creamy paste that was applied to the eye area with special wood or bone tools.
- Red ochre from natural clay earth pigment was used to stain cheeks and lips. Ochre comes in many shades of yellow, orange to brown.
- **Henna**, a naturally occurring plant dye, was used to paint nails and dye hair.

Hairstyles

- Wigs were sometimes worn. These were made from human hair, vegetable fibres or wool. They could be curled, dyed, braided or beaded. Hair colour was usually black, but wigs were sometimes dyed shades of green, blue and red, and eyeshadow was often matched to this.
- A common look for both men and women was to thread beads into hair that had been separated into tiny braids. Wealthy people had wigs made of real human hair adorned with gold gems. Poorer people also decorated their hair and would thread clay beads and dried berries into their braids.
- Henna was used to colour and condition the hair. Oil was used to prevent hot winds from drying out hair.

▲ **Figure 7.2** Elizabeth Taylor in the 1963 film *Cleopatra*

HANDY HINT

Jewellery was very popular across all social classes. It was very heavy and bold, and both men and women wore bracelets, earrings, rings and necklaces. People who could not afford gold and precious stones would make their own jewellery from coloured pottery beads.

Influence of art and cultural movements on fashion

Fashion – including hairstyles, make-up, clothing and accessories – changes constantly. Designers are influenced by the major cultural and artistic movements of their times, current celebrities and past fashions and reflect these influences through the styles they design.

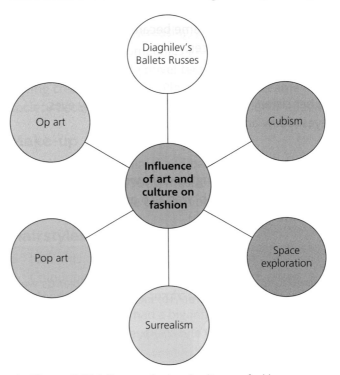

▲ **Figure 7.16** Influence of art and culture on fashion

Visual arts

Music and art can inspire the clothes and make-up that we wear.

- **Pop art** emerged in the 1950s and has been very popular within the fashion industry. Pop art introduced aspects of mass culture and advertising into art and brought art closer to a new generation.
- **Op art**, short for optical art, was popular in the 1960s. Victor Vasarely, Bridget Riley and Jesús Rafael Soto were three of the most important op artists. It uses optical illusions and is abstract, with many pieces created in black and white. Op art gives the impression of hidden images, movement and vibrating patterns.

▲ **Figure 7.17** Pop art make-up

- **Diaghilev's Ballets Russes** was a ballet troupe that influenced twentieth-century art, theatre, fashion and interior design.
- **Cubism** has influenced the world of fashion since it appeared over 100 years ago. Cubist artists such as Pablo Picasso took an avant-garde approach to everyday subject matter.
- **Surrealism** is characterised by perplexing semi-realistic images, inspired by dreams or the unconscious mind, to deliberately play with set ideas about the world that the viewer might have. Salvador Dalí is probably the most famous surrealist artist.

Cultural developments

Space exploration in the 1960s and 1970s, especially the Apollo 11 mission to land on the Moon in 1969, inspired many fashion designers. Pierre Cardin, Paco Rabanne and André Courrèges all created looks inspired by the space race and science fiction.

▲ **Figure 7.18** The influence of space exploration on fashion

Social and cultural influences

There are many ways in which make-up, hair and fashion styles can be influenced by person's social and cultural background and context.

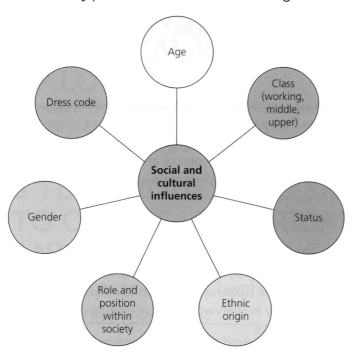

▲ **Figure 7.19** Social and cultural influences on make-up and hair

Status

From the earliest era of the Egyptian empire onwards, men and women from all classes have applied make-up in ways that displayed their social status. In the Elizabethan era, wealthy women would be distinguished by their white faces, as the lower classes would have a more sun-kissed look from working outside. The body art of Indigenous Australian people indicates social status as well as their ancestors and spiritual symbols.

Eye techniques

- Eyeliner flicks.
- Cut crease eyeshadow technique – a step by step guide is given in Chapter 6, pages 152–153.
- Smoky eyeshadow technique.
- False lashes – a step by step guide for applying strip lashes given in Chapter 4, pages 92–93.
- Drawn-on lashes.
- Coloured mascara.
- Kohl-rimmed eyeliner.
- Heavy make-up on top and bottom eyelids.

▲ **Figure 7.26** Eyeliner flicks

▲ **Figure 7.27** Cut crease eyeshadow

▲ **Figure 7.28** Smoky eyeshadow

▲ **Figure 7.29** False lashes

▲ **Figure 7.30** Drawn-on lashes

▲ **Figure 7.31** Coloured mascara

▲ **Figure 7.32** Kohl eyeliner

▲ **Figure 7.33** Heavy make-up on top and bottom eyelids

Step by step: how to draw on lashes

1 Using a fine brush with a black gel or sharpened eyeliner, carefully draw line by line along the lower lash.
2 Make the hair strokes slightly diagonally so that they flare outwards instead of straight down.
3 Be mindful to make the lines a little longer towards the outer corners of the eyes.
4 Space the lashes evenly to make room for a second colour if required.

Highlighting and contouring

Photos from the 1980s are very easy to spot. Bright make-up was a key look of this era, especially bright blusher, which was used to contour the cheekbones and temples. Bright cheeks were a way of making the bone structure pop as well as complementing the extreme eyeshadow and lip colours.

Contouring has been reinvented with a more natural look. Modern contouring now includes a darker shade under the cheekbones and a highlighter along the top of the cheekbone. Bronzer is also used where the sun would normally hit the face to give a sun-kissed glow.

Tattoos

- **Stencil** – a design that has already been created, which the make-up artist either sprays or sponges colour over to create the design on the skin exposed by the stencil.
- **Transfer** – pre-made designs that can be transferred onto the skin. They are usually water-activated.
- **Freehand** – you can also draw the design freehand onto the skin.

▲ **Figure 7.34** Shading in the 1980s

Step by step: how to apply a transfer tattoo

1 Dry the area of skin to which the transfer will be applied. Any oils or creams on the skin will affect its adhesion.
2 Transfer tattoos are activated by water.
3 Cut around the tattoo as close as possible to the design.
4 Place the tattoo face down on the area of skin where it is to be applied.
5 Apply medium pressure to the backing of the tattoo using a wet cloth or sponge for approximately 60 seconds. (Note that some products require either isopropyl alcohol or surgical spirit to activate the tattoo – follow the manufacturer's instructions.)
6 Gently peel the paper away to leave the design on the skin.
7 Allow the tattoo to dry naturally.

Transfer tattoos can be removed using baby oil.

HANDY HINT

Manual transfer paper, known as hectograph or freehand transfer paper, works in the same way as a carbon copy sheet by transferring information that is written or drawn on the top sheet onto the sheets below.

▲ **Figure 7.35** Pin curls

▲ **Figure 7.36** Vertical roll

▲ **Figure 7.37** 1960s beehive

ACTIVITY

Make your own transfer tattoo using carbon paper.

1 Remove the inner section of paper from the carbon paper. Place the drawing of your design between the tracing paper and the carbon paper. It can be secured in place with clips.

2 Use a ballpoint pen to trace over the drawing. Press firmly and fill in any thick lines.

3 Remove the design and cut out the traced drawing with a pair of scissors.

4 Apply a small amount of isopropyl alcohol on a piece of cotton wool and apply over the area of skin you wish to transfer the design to.

5 Lay the design on the skin and apply pressure to the drawing. Continue pressing the drawing onto the skin for up to 30 seconds or until you can see the drawing transferring onto the skin through the paper.

6 Peel away the transfer paper and let the stencil dry. Once fully dry, the design can be coloured in or adapted as required.

Hair techniques

- Finger waves.
- Pin curls – step by step guides to creating pin curls for volume and flat movement are given in Chapter 5, pages 135–136.
- Horizontal rolls – for example, chignon.
- Vertical rolls – a step by step guide to creating a vertical roll is given in Chapter 5, page 129.
- 1960s beehive.
- Men's quiff – there are four different styles:
  - classic quiff – short on the back and sides and high at the front, and made famous by Elvis Presley
  - short quiff – short on the sides and top with only 2.5–5 cm of coiffed hair
  - pompadour – a big wavy quiff, worn by the likes of James Dean and Johnny Cash
  - undercut – most of the hair on the sides of the head is close shaved, fading into short hair on top with a small, short quiff.
- Backcombing.
- Ornamentation.
- Crimping.
- Colouring.
- Mohican.
- Braids.
- Hair extensions.
- Flick.
- Mullet.

▲ **Figure 7.38** Backcombing

▲ **Figure 7.39** Ornamentation

▲ **Figure 7.40** Crimping

▲ **Figure 7.41** Colouring

▲ **Figure 7.42** Mohican

▲ **Figure 7.43** Braids

▲ **Figure 7.44** Hair extensions

▲ **Figure 7.45** Flick

▲ **Figure 7.46** Mullet

Step by step: finger waves

The finger-waved hairstyle was popular in the 1920s. In that era, women worked with wet hair, a lot of hair gel and their own fingers. Finger waves can still be created with this method but the stylist must have a reasonable amount of skill. Finger waves can be created more easily using a curling iron instead of fingers.

1. Comb a moderate amount of thick gel through damp hair. The hair should be damp but not sopping wet.
2. Create a deep side parting in hair. The parting can be to either side of the head.
3. Start to create waves on the side with more hair. Lay the middle finger flat (horizontally) across the hair, then take a comb and press it against the side of the finger. Drag the comb (with the teeth straight down) sideways (horizontally) along your finger until you create a ridge or C-shaped curve.
4. Place the middle finger back (horizontally) to continue building a ridge towards the back of the head. This will create one horizontal ridge that moves in one direction and a C-shaped wave in the opposite direction.
5. Move the finger along the hair about an inch down and create another ridge in the same direction as the curve above it. This will now create an S-pattern wave.
6. Repeat the previous step right up to the ends of the hair, as well as on the other side.
7. Allow the hair to dry thoroughly, then spray with hairspray for extra hold.

▲ **Figure 7.47** Finger waves

Step by step: chignon

A chignon is a hair-up style with a roll or a bun at the nape of the neck. The word is French, but the hairstyle is linked to ancient Greek styles and was popular in the 1950s.

1 Part the hair from ear to ear and section off the front section of hair.
2 Start by backcombing the ponytail to add volume, then spray with hairspray.
3 Comb over the top lightly to smooth out the hair before making a simple loop out of the ponytail. Use a band to hold the loop in place.
4 Loosely wrap the freely hanging end around the base of the ponytail. The end of the wrap of hair should be fanned out so that it covers the base of the ponytail nicely. Pin the wrap in place.
5 Start working on the front section by dividing into two sections. Tease each section at the roots and lightly brush through to smoothen the hair.
6 Bring one section to the chignon and cover the base with it, then pin at the sides.
7 Wrap the strand loosely around the chignon and pin.
8 One pin should be close to the base while the next one should be a bit lower to create a softer finish.
9 Repeat these steps for the other side and spray.

Step by step: men's quiff

1 Comb clean, dry or damp towel-dried hair to the side.
2 Apply a small amount of styling product, such as wax or gel, to your fingertips and evenly distribute through the hair.
3 With your fingers, sculpt and shape the hair into a quiff using upwards movements.
4 Using either a comb, brush or fingers, blow-dry the quiff up and over, into the desired shape.
5 Secure the quiff using finishing products such as hairspray, pomade, defining paste or additional wax/finishing gel.

▲ **Figure 7.48** Chignon

▲ **Figure 7.49** Men's quiff

Test your knowledge

1 Describe three hair techniques that were popular in the 1980s.

2 Explain the effects of products used to create a 1960s Twiggy-style eye make-up.

3 State two hair techniques and two make-up techniques used in the Victorian era.

4 Explain how art and culture have influenced the catwalk.

5 Describe three social or cultural influences on fashion.

6 Explain the influence of Surrealism on fashion development.

7 Describe two iconic films that have influenced fashion.

8 State four eye techniques and the era in which they were popular.

9 Describe two looks in 1980s fashion.

10 Describe the make-up used by the Ancient Egyptians.

Practical assignment

Scenario

You have been asked to create a show to demonstrate how make-up and hair have changed throughout history.

Task

Document the evidence you would need to supply to the director of the show, detailing the social and cultural influences you would use, the eras you would cover, your inspiration for the looks, the products that will be required and the different techniques that you will use.

CHAPTER 8

FACE AND BODY ART

INTRODUCTION

Make-up artists working in some of the most exciting areas of the industry, such as events, festivals, promotions, film and photoshoots, may be asked to design and apply body art. These make-up artists may be working under the direction of a chief designer, who will have a vision for the overall look, or they may be provided with a brief that they need to work to independently. The designer may ask the make-up artist for help and guidance on the products and techniques to use to complete the finished design.

Body art competitions have become increasingly popular within the industry, and more and more make-up artists are entering them. They are important events for networking and for showcasing your skills. You need dedication and exceptional knowledge and skills to win. The winner of a competition may find that the doors into the make-up industry open a little wider and opportunities become more frequent.

In this chapter, you will learn about:
1   the influences on body art
2   how to apply face and body art designs
3   the requirements for body art competitions.

Body art differs a lot depending on where in the world you are, often due to religious or other beliefs. It has many different meanings and has many different uses. Body art is sometimes used as a sign of bravery, as part of beliefs such as protection from spirits and bringing fertility or as a symbol of power. Body art may also simply be used for creativity or self-expression, including tattoos, piercings and permanent make-up.

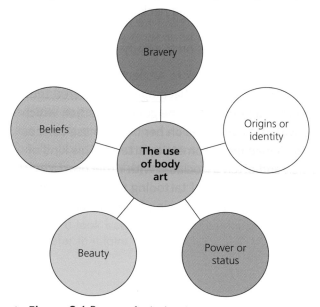

▲ **Figure 8.1** Reasons for body art

▲ **Figure 8.2** Creative body art based on the character Wonder Woman

▲ **Figure 8.7** Scarification

Mehndi: a form of body art, originating in ancient India, where decorative designs are created on the body using a paste made from the leaves of the henna plant.

Other influences

Scarification

Scarification is an ancient tradition that involves purposefully cutting the skin to create a pattern of raised scars. It is practised in Africa, Australia, Papua New Guinea and South, Central and North America. Scarification has been used to emphasise social and political roles, spiritual relationships, sexual attraction and aesthetic values. It is also used as a way of demonstrating the ability to endure pain and as part of medicinal and healing rituals.

Non-Latin characters

Tattoos written in non-Latin scripts, such as Chinese, Japanese and Arabic, have become very popular in body art around the world.

Henna

Henna is a plant that grows in a tropical and subtropical climate, for example, in parts of Africa, southern Asia and northern Australia. It has been used for body art for many centuries, with evidence showing that it was used as a decoration in the Bronze Age (3000–1200BC). It was also used in ancient Egypt to mark special occasions such as weddings.

Mehndi is a form of temporary body art that originated in ancient India. Different colours of henna paste were developed, allowing for more intricate and meaningful designs. It is associated with good luck and positive spirits, with vines and leaves used to signify devotion and vitality. It is traditional to hold a mehndi ceremony the night before a wedding to wish the bride prosperity and good luck prior to making their journey into married life.

▲ **Figure 8.8** Henna designs

Cicatrisation

Cicatrisation is a type of scarification in which the skin is deliberately wounded and irritated to form blisters, to which different pigments may be added to make them stand out. Like scarification, it is used in some cultures to mark milestone changes in both men and women's lives, such as puberty and marriage.

ACTIVITY

Create a look book of your own designs using the cultural influences that you have just read about.

2 APPLYING FACE AND BODY ART DESIGNS

Products, tools and equipment

There is a vast range of different products available for creating body art. There is no right or wrong product or technique to use as long as the finished result is effective.

Your mood board of ideas for the design should include all of the products, tools, equipment and techniques that will be required to achieve the overall finish. Adaptations can be made to the application if an original idea did not go to plan or a different technique could be used to create the look. If changes are being made, they need to be agreed by the whole team, so it meets the original aim.

Table 8.1 describes the products that you may need outside your normal make-up kit to create body art.

HANDY HINT

The purpose of a mood board is to put all theme-based ideas onto a visual aid; it can be a large collage of images/sketches and technical information.

▼ **Table 8.1** Products used to create body art

Product	Application
Airbrush make-up	This can come in a variety of forms. • **Water-based** – this make-up has a matte to semi-matte texture. It has a lightweight appearance so skin needs to be prepared properly prior to application to give a professional finish. • **Silicone** – this is very durable, does not evaporate and stays on the skin longer. Used correctly, it can conceal imperfections, hide discolouration and even out skin tone. It can be moved for a few minutes after application, unlike water-based products, so any errors are easier to correct. Airbrush guns need to be cleaned with a special cleaner if silicone is used. • **Alcohol-based** – this is long-lasting and highly pigmented. It is used for body art, prosthetics, special effects and tattoo stencils. It is not suitable for heavy use on the face as it can act as an irritant and block the pores.
Coloured inks	The Dura brand inks are waterproof and durable and come in a variety of colours. They stay on the skin for up to four days and can be removed with any product containing oil.
Water-based paints/aqua	These body paints are mixed with clean water and applied to the face and body. They dry very quickly and last up to several hours. They are removed with soap and water.

Tools	Use
Stencils and templates	Pre-made stencils and templates can be bought in many different designs, or you can design and make your own. They are great for flower designs, symbols and realistic-looking tattoos. They are especially useful in TV and film work where the tattoo will need to be applied each day of filming. Stencils are normally made out of Perspex so they can be easily held or taped to the skin. Some are reusable while others have a sticky back and are disposable. Templates can be used to draw around to create different shapes.
Metal moulding tool	A metal moulding tool is used to dispense products or to mould and blend the edges of prosthetic pieces and modelling wax.
Brushes	Different-sized brushes can be used to achieve different looks depending on the technique being used, from very small bristles to create fine lines to large brushes for coverage of larger areas. It is very important to have a variety of brushes. It is also a good idea to have a separate set of brushes just for body art as some paints stain the bristles.

Details of airbrushing equipment can be found later in the chapter.

▲ **Figure 8.10** Promotional full body art look

Themes for face and body art

Make-up artists can use just about anything to create eye-opening, jaw-dropping body art designs. Designs can be simple but very effective with intricate detail, or they can be avant-garde and unusual. It is a unique way to captivate and awe audiences on social media sites such as Instagram, Facebook, Twitter and Pinterest.

Body art is used widely throughout the make-up industry, particularly in film, TV, theatre, fashion shoots, music videos and magazines, which makes it a good area to get into. A body art make-up artist has to be very versatile, with a good eye for detail, be artistic, and have the stamina to spend up to eight hours applying a body art design.

It is important to explore different themes in order to create a range of body art looks, and to use a variety of body art techniques to show diversity in your work.

HANDY HINT

The skin should be prepared for body art in the same way as for any make-up application before applying products. See Chapter 4 (pages 107–108) for more details on preparing the skin before the application of make-up.

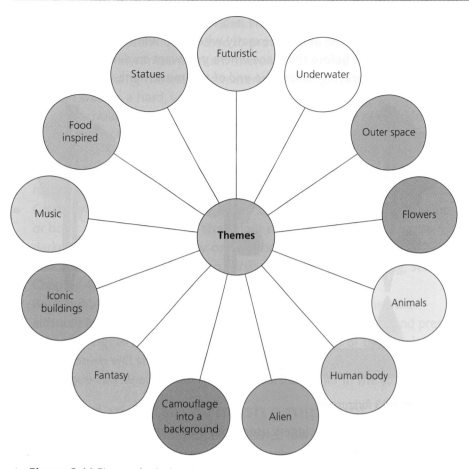

▲ **Figure 8.11** Themes for body art

Airbrushing

Airbrushing is a method of paint application. Compressed air is forced through a gun, where it mixes with paint and is aerosolised into a fine spray that allows for a thin, smooth, even application of make-up.

The compressed air is supplied by a compressor. Compressors can range from light to heavy-duty use. The type of work being carried out will determine the type of compressor needed. The cost of the equipment will also be a factor in the make-up artist's choice of airbrush.

Most compressors used for make-up have an adjustable working pressure, a lead that feeds to the airbrush, a knob for adjusting pressure, a pressure gauge and an airbrush holder. Some may have a moisture filter, which removes water from the air, or an oil filter, which removes oil from the air.

The benefits of using an airbrush compared to sponging on water-based paint include:
- airbrushing gives a very smooth finish to your paint
- alcohol-based body paints are best applied with an airbrush
- you can accomplish certain effects that can only be created with an airbrush
- liquid paints are easier to mix than cream or cake make-up.

▲ **Figure 8.12** Airbrush gun and compressor

"I BELIEVE I HAVE CREATED IN cosmetic colour harmony a life-like naturalness in make-up which every woman will find, as we in Hollywood have proved, to be without equal in accentuating beauty and charm!"

▲ **Figure 9.1** Max Factor

▲ **Figure 9.2** Elizabeth Arden

▲ **Figure 9.3** Sir Archibald McIndoe

Joyce Allsworth

Joyce Allsworth (1923–94) served with the Women's Auxiliary Air Force (WAAF) during the Second World War. She was shocked by the facial burns that she saw and wanted to come up with something that could help wounded airmen with similar injuries.

Records suggest that Allsworth was familiar with the work of some of the other pioneers of skin camouflage, including Sir Harold Gillies and Sir Archibald McIndoe. She studied beauty therapy and theatrical make-up artistry at the London School of Fashion. After the Stockport air disaster of 1967, she transferred her skills to concentrate on camouflage techniques.

Allsworth instigated the camouflage service within the British Red Cross and founded the British Association of Skin Camouflage (BASC). She went on to write and publish *Skin Camouflage: A Guide to Remedial Techniques* in 1985.

Max Factor

In 1904, Max Factor (1877–1938) emigrated from Poland to America, where he soon established himself in the world of make-up. In 1918 he created his 'colour harmony' principle, in which all products were designed to harmonise with the wearer's natural skin, eye and hair colour – a first in cosmetic history. In 1938, the year Factor died, the company's make-up was recognised by the medical profession due to its commercial success for use as skin camouflage to mask injuries. The company was also commissioned to formulate shades of pancake make-up for commandos to use a camouflage during the Second World War.

Elizabeth Arden

Elizabeth Arden (1881–1966) was already a successful entrepreneur with an established make-up business at the time of the Second World War. During the war she developed a 'scar cream' that could be used to help those with injuries to conceal their scars. This established the idea that concealers could be a commercially successful product and led to them becoming a standard part of each manufacturer's range of products.

Sir Archibald McIndoe

Sir Archibald McIndoe (1900–60) was a surgeon working at the Queen Victoria Hospital in West Sussex. He pioneered new ways to treat burn injuries during the Second World War. He worked with the chemist Thomas Blake to develop a topical cream designed to conceal burn scar tissue. This led to the development of Veil Cover Cream, which went on general sale in 1952. Originally, there were only three skin tones available, but Joyce Allsworth persuaded Thomas Blake to extend the range. It was made available on prescription through the NHS in 1975.

Sir Harold Gillies

Sir Harold Gillies (1882–1960) is considered to be the father of modern plastic surgery. Having trained as a doctor, he served in the Army during the First World War, during which he asked the government for a building to deal with the huge number of soldiers injured with facial wounds that could not be treated in conventional hospitals. That building became Queen's Hospital in Sidcup.

Gillies developed new plastic surgery techniques to treat the injured servicemen, focusing on aesthetics and trying to make them look similar to how they looked before they were injured. He went on to write a book called *Plastic Surgery of the Face*, which was published in 1920. He was a major influence on his cousin, Sir Archibald McIndoe.

British Red Cross

In 1959, the British Red Cross was asked to organise a beauty care service throughout the UK to help with the recovery of patients through massage, make-up and other treatments. Joyce Allsworth was one of the instructors working on the scheme and later became the chief trainer.

By the time that camouflage services became available through the NHS in 1975, the Red Cross had trained nearly 3000 beauty care volunteers and offered the most established and experienced skin camouflage service in the UK. In 2012, these services transferred to the charity Changing Faces.

British Association of Skin Camouflage

The British Association of Skin Camouflage (BASC) was founded by Joyce Allsworth in 1985. The main objective of the BASC is 'to alleviate the psychological, physical and social effects that an altered image can have on someone's life by the simple application of specialised skin camouflage products'.

In 2010, the association published *Cover: The principles and art of para-medical skin camouflage*, which is a manual for anyone wanting to extend their knowledge of camouflage make-up and is based on the work of Joyce Allsworth. The BASC is the UK's leading provider for training professionals in the skills needed to apply skin camouflage and the organisation continues to look for ways to improve the current services offered to patients.

> **HANDY HINT**
>
> Changing Faces provides support for anyone with a visible difference on their face or body. They provide guidance and information, advocate to change social attitudes and also provide skin camouflage services. You can find out more about them at www.changingfaces.org.uk.

> **ACTIVITY**
>
> Research different organisations that can help you to learn more about camouflage make-up and working with these clients, for example, the British Association of Skin Camouflage (https://skin-camouflage.net) and Let's Face It (www.lets-face-it.org.uk).

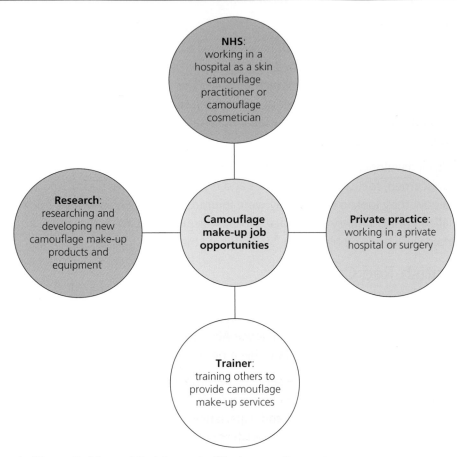

▲ **Figure 9.4** Some of the job opportunities in camouflage make-up

KEY TERMS

Hypopigmentation: patches of skin that are lighter than the overall skin tone.

Vitiligo: a non-contagious skin condition that causes the loss of skin colour (paling of the skin).

Keratinocyte: an epidermal cell that produces keratin, which is responsible for the strength and flexibility of our skin.

Skin conditions that may require camouflage make-up

It is important to know the different skin conditions and their appearance to be able to use the correct techniques and create the best results when applying camouflage make-up.

▼ **Table 9.1** Skin conditions for which people may seek camouflage make-up

Condition	Appearance
Hyperpigmentation	Hyperpigmentation occurs when the skin produces too much melanin. This can make spots or patches of skin appear darker than their surrounding areas. Examples include birthmarks and age spots. Hyperpigmentation is a common skin condition that affects people of all skin types.

→

Condition	Appearance
Hypopigmentation 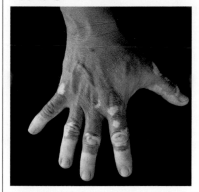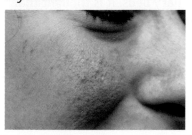	**Hypopigmentation** refers to patches of skin that are lighter than the overall skin tone. This happens when the skin does not produce enough melanin, causing the skin to lighten. These effects can occur in spots or may cover the entire body. **Vitiligo** is a common hypopigmentation condition.
Erythema	Dilation of blood capillaries that come to the surface of the skin, causing redness. Persistent facial erythema can be a symptom of rosacea, a common skin condition.
Scar tissue 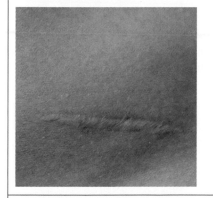	A scar is a mark left on the skin after a wound or injury has healed. Most will fade and become paler over time, although they never completely disappear. Fine-line scars are common following a wound or after surgery. They are not usually painful, but they may be itchy for a few months. On darker skin types, the scar tissue may fade to leave a brown or white mark. A scar may be more obvious on tanned skin because scar tissue does not tan.
Birthmark 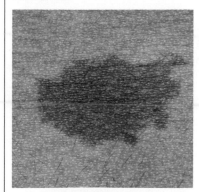	A birthmark is a benign, irregular patch on the skin that is present at birth or appears shortly afterwards. They can come in all shapes and sizes, and appear anywhere on the body. Birthmarks are caused by an overgrowth of blood vessels, smooth muscle, melanocytes, fat cells or **keratinocytes**.

→

Condition	Appearance
Tattoos 	A tattoo is a form of body modification in which ink or dyes are inserted into the dermis layer of the skin to make a permanent design.
Dilated capillaries 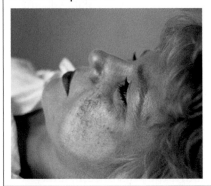	Capillaries are the fine blood vessels responsible for **microcirculation**. They are grouped together in clusters or capillary beds. It is thought that dilated capillaries and spider veins are caused by poor circulation.
Freckles 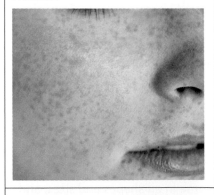	Freckles are small brown marks on the skin that appear due to the overproduction of melanin. They usually appear in areas that are more exposed to the sun, such as the face, arms and chest.
Moles 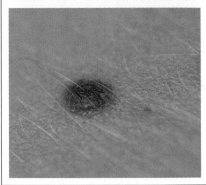	Moles are growths on the skin that appear in early childhood and during the first 25 years of a person's life. They are usually brown or black and can appear anywhere on the skin, either alone or in groups.

→

Condition	Appearance
Dark circles under the eyes 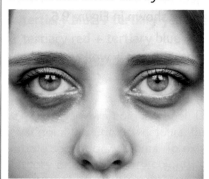	Dark circles under the eyes can be caused by a number of factors, for example, a lack of sleep, poor diet, ageing skin or inherited conditions. The circles may be black, blue, purple or dark brown depending on the person's skin tone.

ACTIVITY

Research the different skin conditions listed in Table 9.1. Collate pictorial evidence and create a booklet of pictures and your own descriptions of the conditions.

KEY TERM

Microcirculation: the blood flow through the smallest vessels in the circulatory system.

Colour theory

The colours that we see depend on the colour of the light source, the colour of any filters used and the colour of objects that reflect the light. Colour theory is both the science and art of using colour. It can explain how the eye perceives colour and the effects of how colours mix and contrast together. Colour theory is one of the most important foundations of make-up artistry and the make-up artist should know about it in order to successfully recognise and match a client's skin tone and underlying tones.

A knowledge of colour theory is essential when applying corrective and camouflage make-up effectively. It relies on the perfect colour match and technique. Colour correction is also discussed in Chapter 4, pages 75–76.

Light waves

Light is a form of electromagnetic energy that travels in waves. Light travels through air nearly a million times faster than sound, which explains why you see lightning before you hear thunder. It takes 8 minutes and 20 seconds for light to travel from the Sun to the Earth.

Light waves travel in straight lines and can be detected by the eye. They are reflected by mirrors and change direction when they travel from air into glass or water.

The eye can perceive different colours because each colour has its own wavelength. When white light passes through a glass prism, its waves split according to their wavelengths and can be seen as different colours – red, orange, yellow, green, blue, indigo, violet – like the colours of a rainbow. These colours are collectively known as the colour spectrum.

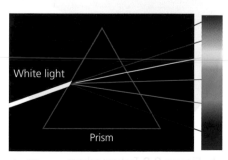

▲ **Figure 9.5** Light waves

It is very important to have a thorough consultation with the client to help them feel at ease and feel able to discuss their needs comfortably. It may take time to build a rapport with the client as they may be reluctant to discuss why they have been referred, so allow them to talk freely and consider their needs. The client may seek help themselves or may have been referred by:

- their GP
- a hospital burns unit
- a dermatologist
- a private clinic
- a counsellor
- a psychiatrist.

The client may show signs of:

- stress and nervousness
- negative body language
- embarrassment
- depression
- anxiety
- tearfulness
- discomfort
- uncertainty about what can be achieved.

Body dysmorphia

People with body dysmorphia are excessively worried about parts of their body that they perceive to have a defect, despite reassurances. Any area of the body may be involved in body dysmorphia.

Applying camouflage make-up

Procedure

Make the client comfortable and complete a thorough consultation in a relaxed, private area.

It is important to get the correct colour match for the client, so study their skin tone and write down what colours you can see in it. Looking at the range of camouflage colours available, pick the closest colour that will match the skin tone – you may need to mix colours to gain the best results. Choose an area near to where the camouflage will be applied and test the colour here to see if it matches the skin tone. If it is flawless and no seams are visible, mix up enough colour to cover the treatment area.

Do not worry if it takes time to colour match and mix colours if needed, as it is essential for performing the treatment correctly. To get the best results, the colour match must be perfect.

The following step by step guide to applying skin camouflage for pigmentation can be used for any area of the face, neck, chest, shoulders, limbs or back.

Step by step: applying skin camouflage

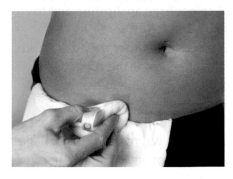

Step 1 – Cleanse the area that you are going to camouflage, to ensure it is free from oils.

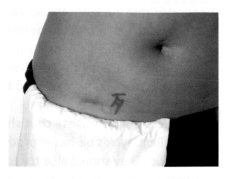

Step 2 – The tattooed area prior to camouflage treatment.

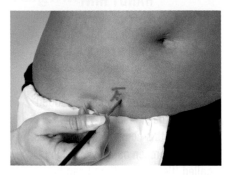

Step 3 – Apply a camouflage cream (D32) to the tattooed area only.

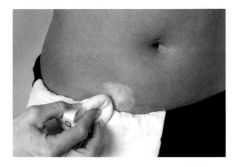

Step 4 – Press a fixing powder onto the area to set the product on the skin. Leave for 10 minutes then sweep away any excess powder.

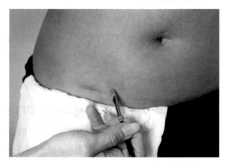

Step 5 – To ensure a perfect colour match, test the colour on the surrounding skin. (It is best to do this in daylight.) Apply the selected colour over the area, being mindful not to press too hard so you do not dislodge the product underneath.

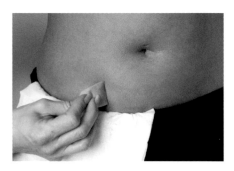

Step 6 – Blend the edges with a sponge to ensure the colour matches perfectly with the natural skin tone.

Step 7 – Press a fixing powder onto the area to set the product on the skin. Leave for 10 minutes then sweep away any excess powder.

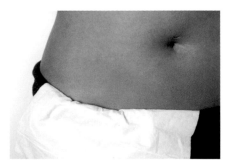

Step 8 – The finished look.

CHAPTER 10

CUTTING AND STYLING TECHNIQUES FOR PERFORMERS

INTRODUCTION

When working in fashion, TV, film or theatre, you may be expected to have some basic hair cutting skills and to be able to maintain a performer's hairstyle for the purpose of continuity, ensuring that the performer's look remains the same for the duration of filming.

This unit covers the basic cutting skills used on both female and male performers, on hair that is long or short, including a one-length haircut, a basic layered cut from a uniformed layer, a short graduation and a long graduation.

You will learn the importance of working safely, communicating effectively during consultations, knowing the right cutting techniques to use – including the correct products tools and equipment for the model or performer's needs – and, most importantly, having a professional approach following a script or a brief and understanding the requirements of the production.

In this chapter, you will learn:

1 how to prepare for cutting and styling hair
2 how to cut and style hair.

1 PREPARE FOR CUTTING AND STYLING HAIR

Influencing factors for cutting and styling

You need to establish the requirements from either the brief or the script, as the haircut will depend on the role that you are working on. This could involve communicating with:

- the production team, so that you understand the requirements of the production set out by the director or producer
- your hair and make-up designer
- the performer.

You must communicate in a professional manner, using positive body language and asking both open and closed questions, so that a clear understanding is established.

While you are communicating with the performer, check for any contra-indications. You can do this verbally or visually, but always do it with empathy and discretion. If you have any doubts, for example, about the performer's suitability for the chosen cut and style, you should consult with a relevant authority for a second opinion, for example, the hair and make-up designer. For more information on different face shapes, see Chapter 5, page 122.

While cutting the performer's hair, ensure that you protect their skin and clothing from products and water at all times. You should also wear appropriate PPE.

Hair texture

You need to consider the texture of the hair. This is how the hair appears and feels when touching it. Hair texture has a major impact on how you can cut and style it.

- **Fine hair** can be easier to cut and style, although it can show every section you cut, so accuracy is paramount. Styles tend to drop out of fine hair more easily, so do not last as long. When using products, choose formulas that are lightweight and will not soften the hair.
- **Thick or coarse hair** can hold and retain water, so it takes a lot longer to dry. However, once the hair is cut and styled it can retain the shape for longer. Thick hair sometimes needs finishing products, such as serums or shine sprays, to make it appear less dry.

Hair movement

Hair movement is an influencing factor. The hair will move differently depending on whether it is straight or curly. It will determine your choice of cutting techniques and how much you take off when cutting the hair. It will also determine your choice of products when styling your model's hair.

Hair density

Hair density is determined by the number of hair follicles on the head. It ranges from sparse to normal, medium or thick. You can feel the density of the hair with your fingers and this can be identified initially when communicating with the performer. The hair density will determine how you are going to style the hair.

Length

Hair length is an important factor in determining whether you can create the required style. If the hair is too short, you may not be able to put it up. If the hair is too long, the weight of the hair could pull, which would be uncomfortable for your model. You should discuss this with your model and the production team, as an alternative style may need to be used. This could include the use of hairpieces or even wigs.

Hair condition

The **elasticity** of the hair determines whether the hair is weak or strong. You can test elasticity by taking a small section of hair – about seven or eight strands – and, from the mid-lengths to the ends, gently pull it. If the hair stretches slightly and retains its shape, it indicates that it is strong. If it stretches but does not have a spring in it, it indicates that the hair is weak and that it has been damaged.

> **HANDY HINT**
>
> When you are cutting curly hair, remember that it will shrink a lot shorter when it dries. Even if the hair is tightly curled, you may wish to cut the hair once you have blow-dried it so that it remains at the length you want it to be.

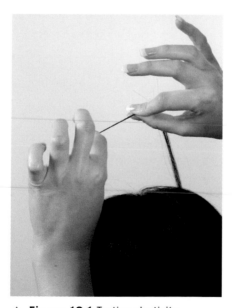

▲ **Figure 10.1** Testing elasticity

You will initially cut a **guideline** as you start to cut the hair. This will determine the amount of hair you are going to cut off for the haircut. The guideline will be an initial starting section that is not very thick. You will then follow this around the entire haircut.

This chapter covers the:

- one-length cut
- short graduation cut
- basic/uniform layer cut
- long graduation cut.

One-length cut

This is one of the most basic haircuts. A classic bob is a one-length cut above the shoulders, but it can also be left below the shoulders. A solid fringe can be incorporated too.

▲ **Figure 10.12** One-length cut

▲ **Figure 10.13** Cutting angle for one-length cut: hair is pulled down at 0°

Step by step: one-length cut

Step 1 – Ensure the model is sitting upright. Let the hair fall down naturally at 0° and comb it so it sits flat against the head. Use the horizontal section at the back for your initial guideline.

Step 2 – Club cut the first section of hair, following the guideline and keeping the hair pulled down. Use a comb to keep the hair in place.

Step 3 – Take the next horizontal section and club cut it, keeping the same tension. Check the balance and remove any graduation or unevenness at the bottom.

→

Step 4 – Continue cutting sections up the head until you reach the desired length, then move round to the side sections. Pull sections down with your fingers to check for balance and evenness throughout.

Step 5 – You can also cut in a fringe if desired.

Step 6 – Check the accuracy and balance of the cut visually, and check the weight distribution of the hair by running your fingers through it. Finally, apply finishing products and style.

Short graduation cut

A short graduation cut has shorter layers at the nape of the neck, becoming longer towards the top and front of the hairstyle. It is also graduated short around the sides.

▲ **Figure 10.14** Short graduation cut

▲ **Figure 10.15** Cutting angles for a short graduation cut: the hair on top may be pulled out at 90°, the back and sides are tapered in and cut at 45°

HANDY HINT

Try to keep hair damp at all times when cutting as this helps to maintain a consistent elasticity and porosity.

Step by step: asymmetric (unbalanced) short graduation cut

Step 1 – The model's hair prior to cutting.

Step 2 – Wash and comb the hair then use clips to section the hair, leaving the back section loose.

Step 3 – Beginning at the nape of the neck, pull the hair down at 0° and cut the baseline. Then bring down the next section of the hair.

Step 4 – Cut the next section, making sure your guideline is still clearly visible to you.

Step 5 – Continue up the back of the head, cutting section by section, until you are happy with the baseline shape.

Step 6 – Continue the cut around the sides of the head, following the shape and pulling the hair down at 0°.

Step 7 – Bring the hair into vertical sections from the occipital bone down to the nape of the neck.

Step 8 – Pull each section out at 45°, cutting to create short graduation and remove bulk.

Step 9 – Continue with the other sections, to just below the crown.

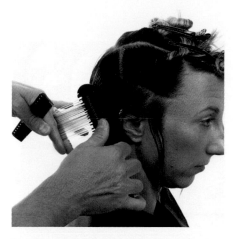

Step 10 – Use a carving comb to cut the back and side sections. This will remove weight while shaping and texturising the hair.

Step 11 – Pull the top sections up at 90° and club cut.

Step 12 – Dry the hair then check the balance of the haircut.

Step 13 – Finish by diagonally cutting in a triangular section at the front.

Step 14 – Apply finishing products to the completed look.

Basic layer cut

The basic layer cut, more commonly known as a uniform layer cut, is a rounded shape following the head around at the same length, with no build-up of weight within the style. A uniformed layer haircut can be at any length as long as the layers are exactly the same length. For a basic layer cut, a cutting angle of 90° is used.

HANDY HINT

If you cannot see your guideline, stop cutting. Go back a few sections to find it. Check that each section is of equal thickness, but not too thick.

▲ **Figure 10.16** Basic layer cut

Step by step: basic layer cut

Step 1 – Establish the first guideline by taking a section of hair along the centre parting, pulling it up at 90°.

Step 2 – Following your guideline, cut the hair in sections, following the shape of the head.

Step 3 – Continue to cut the hair from the top of the head working towards the nape, keeping a constant 90° angle.

Step 4 – Blend the length into the base guideline.

Step 5 – Club cut the internal guideline and work around the back sections, maintaining the 90° angle.

Step 6 – Once you have finished cutting, pull sections out to the sides and cross-check for even weight distribution.

Step 7 – Dry the hair and apply finishing products to complete the look.

Long graduation cut

Long graduation is when the hair has shorter layers around the top and front of the haircut that gradually become longer towards the back of the head, where the hair length is left longer. The shape of the long graduated look is elongated. The interior lengths are shorter than the exterior lengths. Interior layers shorten the hair but keep the bulk at the outer edge of the haircut.

You can comb and cut the hair vertically, horizontally or even diagonally, depending on the shape you are trying to create. If you start combing and cutting the hair vertically, you will have shorter layers around the face. If you start combing and cutting horizontally, the layers would be of equal lengths around the head.

▲ **Figure 10.17** Long graduation cut

▲ **Figure 10.18** Cutting angles for long graduation cut: layers are cut between 90° and 180°

The cutting angle for a long graduation is 90° to 180°. The more the hair is elevated, the longer the hair length that will be left. You can refine the outline around the perimeter of your head shape following your haircut and, by doing so, you will create a more natural fall with a more solid line.

> **HANDY HINT**
>
> Ask the performer where they wear their parting, but always check visually for the natural fall of the hair.

> **HANDY HINT**
>
> Keeping your work area clean and tidy while you are working prevents accidents and injuries and reduces the risk of cross-contamination.

Step by step: long graduation cut

Step 1 – Wash and comb the hair, find the parting and then section the hair. Take the back section and cut the baseline length using club cutting techniques.

Step 2 – Continue cutting the back section, making sure the line remains straight. Use the comb to help with this.

Step 3 – Check that the length of the back section is even by pulling the hair down gently on both sides with your fingertips.

Step 4 – Bring the side sections down and cut to the same length as the back section.

Step 5 – Take the side sections to the front and check for balance.

Step 6 – Section the hair vertically from the lower crown.

Step 7 – Lift the back sections up and cut the layers.

Step 8 – Continue to cut the layers around the back sections and cross-check horizontally.

Step 9 – Elevate the top section and cut to blend into the back layers.

Step 10 – Remove length from the sections using point cutting techniques. This will also add texture.

Step 11 – Lift sections of hair straight up on both sides to check that they are the same length.

Step 12 – Razor cut the sides to create texture and to soften the edges.

Step 13 – Blow-dry the hair and apply finishing products to complete the look.

HANDY HINT

Remember that if the one-length cut, short graduation cut or long graduation cut have been cut with a side parting, the balance of the look may be asymmetrical and the weight distribution could be heavier on one side, giving an uneven balance.

ACTIVITY

Practise the following haircuts on your tuition head:

- one-length cut
- long graduation cut
- basic layer cut
- short graduation cut.

The concept of continuity

Working to a brief or script

When working on TV, film or theatre productions, you will have to follow a script. You should read it and then break it down to help you decide how to achieve and maintain the hair and make-up looks, and also so that you can participate in designing the hair for different characters based on the scenes in the script. You will work closely with the cast and crew as you continue to develop your designs. Some characters may look the same throughout the whole production, while others may change significantly.

Following a shooting schedule

Once you have read and fully understood the script and have agreed the design for each character's hair and make-up, you can consider the shooting schedule or call sheet. The shooting schedule is generally determined by locations and accessibility, so scenes are frequently shot out of sequence. For this reason, continuity of the performers' hair and make-up is paramount. For more on shooting schedules, see Chapter 1, page 26.

Liaising with directors and designers

You need to work closely with the production team to ensure continuity between each scene. On a film set you will usually liaise with the first assistant director, who will take any concerns to the director and producer.

The shooting schedule may require a change of hair and make-up for every scene filmed that day. If this is the case, you must follow your continuity notes or photographic evidence on both hair and make-up and ensure that the cast and crew are fully aware of the timings or time constraints for these changes.

Recording evidence

If it is likely that you will need to recreate the look again the following day or following week, or if a colleague needs to recreate the look from scratch, you need to record evidence in the form of continuity notes. Your notes should include clear photographic evidence of the hair and make-up from every angle; written notes about all products, tools and equipment used; and the time it took to create the look.

Strict rules on confidentiality – about the performer as well as the storyline of the production – need to be followed at all times when working on any kind of production. All information recorded electronically must be managed correctly according to the Data Protection Act (see pages 14–15).

2 CUT AND STYLE HAIR

It is good practice to sit with the performer and ask open questions about anything that might influence your decisions when cutting and styling. Firstly, you should consider any possible contra-indications. Then you need to look at the hair itself: consider the hair type and the current length, as well as any growth patterns that may affect the cutting and styling. You should also analyse the performer's face shape and features, as these will also have a bearing on your chosen cutting techniques.

It is important to establish a good rapport with the performer as you will be working together to create the look that will enhance their role. Be confident and open when discussing the techniques you will be using, and explain your recommendations fully.

HANDY HINT

Use your time effectively to ensure you work to viable times required in industry.

HANDY HINT

Performers will come from a diverse range of ethnic, cultural and religious backgrounds. Make sure you respect other people's culture and religion.

Select products, tools and equipment

Your selection of products, tools and equipment will help you achieve the desired look for the performer. The tools and equipment you may use are outlined in Table 10.1 on pages 242–243, while styling and finishing products are discussed on pages 241–242.

Cut hair following guidelines

As you have already learned, the guideline is the most important part of any haircut as it determines the finished length of the cut and its overall shape and balance. Following your guideline, and using accurate sectioning, ensures that you work methodically through the haircut. It helps with maintaining accuracy, symmetry and the overall neatness of your haircut.

Cross-check the haircut to ensure even balance and weight distribution

Cross-checking is a visual check of your haircut, looking at weight distribution, balance and symmetry. Cross-checking ensures that the haircut is neat and balanced and that it has been cut correctly and accurately. You can cross-check while you are cutting the hair as well as at the end of the haircut.

You can also cross-check your cut by combing the hair in the opposite direction, either horizontally or vertically, as well as by running your fingers through the hair to check the weight of the hair and the evenness of the length.

Style hair to create the finished look

The selection of styling and finishing products will be determined by:

- the performer's hair type – condition of the hair, thickness of the hair, hair growth patterns
- the style you are trying to create – whether you require height or width, volume and extra body, a firm hold or a natural hold and so on
- the environment that the performer is going to be exposed to – it may be outside or inside
- longevity – you will probably need additional finishing sprays to hold the hairstyle in place, especially for outdoor scenes.

Once you have finished hairstyling, you need to log everything that you have done to create the style for continuity purposes. This is especially important if another hair and make-up artist might have to recreate the look, or if there will be long periods of time between filming different scenes that require the same hair design.

> **HANDY HINT**
>
> Protect your client's clothes with a clean towel, gown or cutting collar when cutting hair.

> **HEALTH AND SAFETY**
> Follow health and safety guidelines, ensuring that you sterilise and disinfect tools and equipment after use.

Test your knowledge

1 Identify the one factor that does not need to be considered when cutting hair.

   a density

   b face shape

   c hair colour

   d hair texture

2 At what angle would you hold the hair for a one-length haircut?

   a 45°

   b 90°

   c 0°

   d 180°

3 At what angle would you hold the hair for a uniform layer cut?

   a 90°

   b 45°

   c 0°

   d 135°

4 Give two reasons why you should cross-check the hair once you have completed a haircut.

   a It helps to style the hair.

   b It checks for accuracy.

   c It checks the hair's density.

   d It checks that the length is even.

5 Why is it important to use the correct degree of tension?

6 Describe the 'club cutting' technique.

7 Explain what is meant by 'continuity'.

8 Name two styling techniques that can be used when you have finished cutting.

9 Name a styling product that could be used for fine hair.

10 Name three finishing products that can be used on performers' hair.

Practical assignment

Scenario

You have been asked to design a hairstyle for a performer in a production of *Made in Dagenham*, which is set in the 1960s.

Task

- Create a mood board and a design plan that includes your cutting angles and the performer's hair characteristics. You should also include mention of the period.

- Carry out your haircut, taking photographic evidence, and create a step by step guide to recreating it for the purpose of continuity.

- Recreate the style following your continuity notes. Take photographs to compare the two finished looks.

CHAPTER 11

AVANT-GARDE HAIR AND MAKE-UP

INTRODUCTION

Avant-garde hair and make-up is an exciting area to work in because anything goes and there is no rule book. Rather than having to conform to traditional styles, avant-garde designs allow you to think outside the box and interpret things your own way.

This chapter will stretch you and challenge you to work in experimental ways, using unconventional tools, products and equipment. The unique styles that you create could set future trends.

In this chapter, you will learn about:

1 the current fashion industry
2 how to create an avant-garde hair and make-up look.

1 THE CURRENT FASHION INDUSTRY

Contemporary fashion designers have a great influence on the hair and make-up industry. Notable European designers include:

▲ **Figure 11.1** Contemporary fashion influences the hair and make-up industry

- Stella McCartney – a British fashion designer known primarily for her fur- and leather-free apparel, as well as her celebrity clientele
- Nicolas Ghesquière – a French designer who has been the creative director of Louis Vuitton since 2013
- Phoebe Philo – a British fashion designer known for her beautiful and understated designs
- Iris van Herpen – a Dutch fashion designer renowned for her futuristic looks based on multi-layered kinetic sculptures
- Simone Rocha – an Irish fashion designer who is the daughter of designer John Rocha
- Vivienne Westwood – a British fashion designer known for her controversial designs and for popularising punk fashion.

Leading fashion houses include:

- Calvin Klein
- Versace
- Valentino
- Giorgio Armani
- Chanel
- Ralph Lauren
- Alexander McQueen
- Louis Vuitton.

Art movements also influence contemporary designers. You can read more about these in Chapter 7, pages 182–183.

Iconic influences in the make-up, hair and fashion industry

The make-up, hair and fashion industry is influenced both by the designers and artists working within it and celebrities who set trends with their unique style.

These are some of the notable figures within the make-up industry.

- Pat McGrath is one of the most influential make-up artists in the world. She is recognised for her unique, adventurous and innovative techniques, for example, using her hands rather than brushes when working on fashion shows and for magazines such as *Vogue*. She worked as cosmetic director for companies such as Giorgio Armani and Procter & Gamble, creating collections for CoverGirl and Max Factor, and has since launched her own brand of make-up.
- Val Garland has worked on projects ranging from highly conceptual catwalk shows for Alexander McQueen to commercial shoots with Kate Moss. She was a judge on the BBC series *Glow Up*.
- Alex Box is known for her surreal and experimental looks. She has worked as a make-up director for international fashion shows and with numerous celebrity clients.

Hairdressing icons include Vidal Sassoon, who created the five-point bob of the 1960s, and Patrick Cameron, who is known for his ability to dress long hair, as well as John Frieda and Lee Stafford.

Celebrities also have an influence on fashion.

- Madonna rose to fame as a pop singer in the 1980s. She has constantly reinvented herself as a performer and remains current today.
- Lady Gaga is notorious for her experimental hair, make-up and clothing, for example, the dress made from meat.
- David Beckham is a former professional footballer who is equally famous for his hair and style, which has a massive following.

Hair, make-up and fashion trends

Although there is no rule book for creating avant-garde looks, and the artist has free licence, we can still look to the past for inspiration. This could include historical fashions, hair and make-up, which could be combined with more contemporary influences, such as **fashion week**, to create an avant-garde look. You could also take inspiration from fashion designers, photographers, leading global brands and iconic celebrities.

Carry out broad, in-depth research using a wide range of sources, including the internet, social media, books and magazines. Find out what people in the industry are doing.

▲ **Figure 11.2** Recent trends influence avant-garde looks

KEY TERM

Fashion week: when leading fashion designers, brands or fashion houses present their latest collections for the upcoming season, usually spring/summer or autumn/winter.

HANDY HINT

If you cannot attend London Fashion Week in person, follow the live streams on social media.

You can also take inspiration from music videos, museums and art galleries. See Chapter 3, pages 57–60, for more possible areas of research.

Once you have your initial idea, you are free to take your own innovative approach.

What is avant-garde?

Avant-garde means something that is new, experimental or out of the ordinary. Avant-garde designs are creative and original, and can be extreme and dramatic.

▲ **Figure 11.3** Avant-garde is…

Except for needing to work safely, there are no rules when creating avant-garde looks. You can be completely experimental in your approach to hair, make-up and costumes, using unconventional methods, techniques, products, tools and equipment. Being inventive and pushing the boundaries enables you to demonstrate your flair, individuality and creativity.

ACTIVITY

1 Come up with some creative ways to use paper and material in your designs.
2 Consider how you could use alternative items, such as pencils, when setting hair.

2 CREATE AN AVANT-GARDE LOOK

Hair, make-up and costume techniques

The following techniques can be used to build a unique and original avant-garde look.

- **Contouring** can be used as a corrective or to define the model's face shape. For more on contouring see Chapter 4, pages 85–86.
- **Shading** is generally used to make features recede. It can be used in the opposite way for an avant-garde make-up application.
- **Highlighting** is used to emphasise the face shape. Again, it can be used in an unconventional way to create high points on the face.

HANDY HINT

Being original will get you noticed.

HEALTH AND SAFETY

Unconventional or alternative products must be hygienic and safe to use. Always work safely and never create a design that could obstruct the model's airway.

Product	Uses and types
Mixing medium	Mixing media have multiple uses in make-up applications. They can be used to thin down cream bases or added to loose powders, such as eye pigment pots, to give them intensity and make them water resistant. They can also be used to change the use of a product, for example, added to an eyeshadow to create a liner.
Body paint products	Aqua or cake paints can be applied with a range of brushes and sponges using body art techniques (see Chapter 8, pages 206–207, for details). Greasepaints or oil-based paints can also be used in body art to create a vivid range of colours. Coloured inks can be used to create henna-inspired designs.
Wax	This can be used for blocking out brows and other special effects.
Brush cleaner	This is an essential product to keep your make-up kit clean and hygienic. Always clean your brushes between each model, first using an alcohol-based brush cleaner and then using soap and water.
Make-up remover	This is another essential product. It is used to remove all the make-up at the end of the day. They come as creams, lotions and oils.

HANDY HINT

You can be experimental with food products as long as you ensure you are working safely.

ACTIVITY

Choose a food product to incorporate into your avant-garde make-up.

Apply the avant-garde total look

Developing the look based on the design brief

When you are given your design brief, you can start to consider the look or theme and begin your research. Many factors will influence your design plans for the hair, make-up and costume.

Your primary research will include your own knowledge, experiences and memories. You could also refer to other resources, such as books, images, films or even stories. Broaden your ideas with secondary research, such as:

- researching iconic fashion and textile designers and viewing past and present fashion shows
- researching award-winning hairdressers
- researching iconic make-up artists
- researching fashion houses and brands
- visiting libraries for reference books, magazines and even comics
- visiting museums, art galleries and any relevant exhibitions
- reviewing editorial images, for example, in *Vogue*, *Harper's Bazaar*, *Tatler* or *Elle*.

For more information about researching a look, see Chapter 3, pages 57–60.

HANDY HINT

Take inspiration from your different areas of research.

You also need to consider your model's characteristics when planning your hair, make-up and costume. What gender are they? How tall are they? How long is their hair? What size of costume will you need? Finally, consider the budget for your products, tools and equipment, including any unconventional products that you will be working with. Your research will help you produce mood boards and then progress to designing the hair and make-up.

▲ **Figure 11.8** Creating an avant-garde look

Health and safety considerations

You must follow health and safety protocols at all times. If skin sensitivity testing needs to be carried out, ensure that you can do this before creating your avant-garde look. Always ensure that your model is comfortable, making sure that they know what you intend to do with the hair and make-up and that they feel completely comfortable with it. For more on health and safety considerations, see Chapter 1, pages 20–23.

Preparing for work

Initially, you will have in-depth discussion about the requirements of the job with your designer or production team. This is your opportunity to ask questions about the looks that the designer wants you to create. Your first steps will be researching and working on mood boards or look books for inspiration, then developing face, hair and costume designs.

Once you have prepared your research, look books and planning, you will meet with your designer or production team again to present your looks and explain your designs. You should receive constructive feedback and make changes as necessary to fit the brief. You should also discuss the dates and times of the job, as well as the location and logistics of getting there, including travel expenses.

> **HEALTH AND SAFETY**
> Make sure that your electrical tools and equipment have been PAT tested.

The effect of the environment has to be considered. Is it an indoor or outdoor location? Will the lighting be natural or key lighting? Is it going to be a night shoot or day shoot? You will also be given information about how many models you will be working on, as well as their gender. You can then start to liaise with the models, asking important questions about skin and hair types, colour and length of hair, and whether they have any preferences for certain products or any allergies. This gives you the information to carry out skin testing, take measurements and to prepare additional hairpieces or ornamentation.

You can discuss with your designer and production team the requirements for your budget, including all make-up, hairdressing products and any additional products or materials. Ensure that you have all the relevant PPE for you and your models.

Your working environment also needs to be considered. The table, mirror and chair needs to be comfortable for the model, as well as allowing you to work in the correct posture. Always ensure the model's modesty is preserved and make sure that anything you plan to do is completely safe. You will need to organise your work area so that you can work productively and achieve your look in the time you've been allocated. Your work area should have everything in place that you'll need to create the hair and make-up while following your design. Your equipment should be clean, sterile and hygienic, and you must follow best working practices for health and safety at all times. For more on current legislation affecting health and safety, see Chapter 1, pages 10–17.

HANDY HINTS

- Make sure you work equally with both hair and make-up, rather than focusing on one or the other.
- Trial the hair and make-up beforehand so that you gain better results.

Test your knowledge

1 Name three iconic hairdressers.

2 Describe what is meant by 'avant-garde'.

3 What alternative tools could be used for an unconventional set?

4 Name an unconventional product that could be used for contouring.

5 What is ombré and how is it used?

6 What is a catwalk in the fashion industry?

7 Name three iconic make-up artists.

8 Which one of these products should not be used when blocking out eyebrows?

   a soap

   b spirit gum

   c wax

   d gel

9 What is colour blocking?

10 Which one of these products is **not** a finishing product?

   a serum

   b wax

   c mousse

   d hairspray

Practical assignment

Scenario

A magazine has contracted you to write a feature in their special avant-garde edition. They also want you to create an avant-garde look for the front cover.

Task

Write a 300-word article on Vivienne Westwood detailing current trends in avant-garde hair and make-up.

Design an avant-garde hair and make-up look influenced by Vivienne Westwood for the front cover of the magazine. Annotate your face and hair charts with the processes and techniques that will be required to create this look.

CHAPTER 12

APPLY PROSTHETIC PIECES AND BALD CAPS

INTRODUCTION

This chapter is about applying small, ready-made prosthetic pieces and bald caps to create a range of different characters. Prosthetic pieces can be made from latex, foam and silicone. You will be able to experiment with a range of different products, tools and equipment in order to find out what works best for you. Prosthetic pieces and bald caps can be used to create realistic looks or fantasy looks, such as witch, clown or sci-fi make-up looks. Bald caps can create realistic baldness or can have hair laid over them so that the look is not completely bald.

To make your look accurate and authentic, your application of prosthetic pieces needs to be seamless and blend them perfectly with the skin. You will be able to apply different make-up products to enhance 3D prosthetic pieces and make them look more realistic. You will learn to apply noses, ears, chins, brows, fingers, teeth, horns, half-face and full-face pieces, as well as wounds. This chapter also considers the importance of following health and safety protocols at all times, as well as communicating effectively with the performer.

In this chapter, you will learn about:

1 the use of prosthetic pieces and bald caps
2 how to apply prosthetic pieces and bald caps.

1 THE USE OF PROSTHETIC PIECES AND BALD CAPS

Areas where prosthetic pieces may be used

Prosthetic pieces are widely used to create a diverse range of characters by changing a person's facial or body features. Prosthetics are usually applied for theatre and TV productions and feature films in order to create a look that is aesthetically accurate for the storyline. Prosthetic pieces are also occasionally incorporated for photographic and creative fashion shoots, for example, when creating an avant-garde look.

If it is written into the script that prosthetic pieces are to be included, they will usually be made during **pre-production**. The performer will have their face cast by a prosthetic specialist who will sculpt and make the prosthetic pieces, ensuring a perfect fit for the performer's face.

The make-up artist working on the production would then apply the prosthetic pieces or bald cap. The prosthetic piece is positioned correctly, then adhered securely to the skin and the edges are blended seamlessly using the correct products, tools and equipment.

KEY TERM

Pre-production: the time spent planning and organising before the production (of a film or TV show, for example) begins.

The make-up artist then colours the prosthetic piece so that it blends into the skin and looks realistic. Longevity is an extremely important consideration because the prosthetic piece may need to withstand very long periods of performance or filming, either indoors or outdoors.

Prosthetic pieces

Prosthetics can be vast and complex – they can completely change the way a person looks by altering their entire body shape, although this would probably require a small team of specialist prosthetic make-up artists. You are more likely to work on the following small prosthetic pieces.

- **Ears** – these are applied on the performer's natural ear with the correct adhesive to change their looks and come in a range of designs. They could be used for a fictional character, such as a pixie. The ears have to be placed correctly and look equal and symmetrical. All the edges need to be secured down and the ears must stay in place for a long period of time. The make-up artist needs to colour the ears using greasepaints, alcohol-based paints or an airbrush.
- **Nose** – these come in a range of different shapes and sizes to suit the character. They need to be placed and fitted symmetrically using the correct adhesive to secure them in place. The edges need to be blended out seamlessly for longevity and you would colour for realism, either while making the piece or after application, depending on the technique that is used.
- **Chin** – these come in a range of shapes and sizes depending on the look that is being created. They are applied to the performer's chin using the correct adhesive, with all edges smoothed out so that it looks seamless. It should be coloured for realism.
- **Brows** – these come as separate brows or two brows in one piece. They can be built up, making them higher or deeper in width, depending on the look you want to create.
- **Fingers** – these come as separate fingers to be used as props as well as extensions to the width or length of the performer's fingers.
- **Teeth** – variations of teeth can be used. They need to be measured and fitted correctly to avoid any discomfort to the performer.
- **Horns** – these can be separate horns applied individually or a set of horns applied as one piece. They come in a range of sizes and shapes, depending on the design.
- **Wounds** – these can be made from silicone moulds and applied directly to the performer's skin as small prosthetic wounds. You can also apply larger wounds that have been cast beforehand.
- **Half-face** – ready-made half-face prosthetic pieces can be purchased, but they may not fit the performer's face shape as well as one created from a cast of their face. If it is not a perfect fit, you may have adjust the edges to fit and work with colour to blend them.

> **HANDY HINT**
>
> Colour match the make-up to the performer's skin type and skin tone before you apply a prosthetic piece or bald cap.

▲ **Figure 12.1** Liquid latex

- **Full-face** – as with half-face pieces, ready-made full-face prosthetic pieces can be purchased, but they may not fit your performer's face shape as perfectly as one cast from their own face. They may require more problem solving, such as working with adhesives and blending the edges more to fit the performer's face.

The cost of prosthetic pieces varies depending on what they are made from, so the products that you work with will depend on the budget of the production.

Products used in prosthetics

Latex

Latex was commonly used for prosthetic pieces before the development of more advanced materials that more closely resemble skin and flesh. Latex is made of rubber, which can be a disadvantage as some people are allergic to it. Because of this, skin sensitivity testing prior to using latex is essential. Latex products are considerably cheaper to purchase compared to the more advanced silicone-based products that are also available.

Latex can be light, which is an advantage in terms of it staying in place, but it can also be stiff and rigid, making it unrealistic and meaning that it restricts the performer's movements. Latex can be blended out with more latex or Pros-Aide, using stippling techniques to build the edges to create a seamless edge. The edges can be disguised using texturising techniques and materials such as tissue and latex.

You can make your own prosthetic pieces by layering liquid latex. You could even use tissues or cotton wool to add to the density of the latex, making it more durable.

Foam latex

This is far more advanced than latex but it can also be more expensive. It is also more complex to work with in terms of health and safety, and you need to have the correct equipment. There are two types of foam latex:

- **hot foam** – this is cured in an oven, which can be expensive and take up a lot of room
- **cold foam** – this does not need an oven, but the environment needs to be at the correct temperature for it to set into a solid form (this process is called **going off**).

When using either hot or cold foam, it is essential to follow the manufacturer's instructions on mixing ratios. If these are not followed, the foam will not develop properly.

Foam is extremely lightweight so it sits on the skin very well. It is also very malleable. Foam also needs an outer layer of cap plastic, which is used for making bald caps. Using cap plastic as a top layer over cold foam enables you to blend out the edges on the performer's skin, making your application seamless.

Silicone

Silicone is a superior, specialised product that moves realistically and closely resembles flesh and skin. It is expensive and mainly used for high-budget theatre, film and TV productions. It does not need an oven, unlike hot foam, but it must be mixed accurately for the silicone to go off. Health and safety protocols must be followed closely, but there are fewer safety issues with silicone than with hot and cold foam.

Gelatin

This is a pork-based food product, so it is a lot cheaper than foams or silicone. It is easy to work with, but some people may not want to use it for religious or ethical reasons, for example, because they are vegan. It cannot be stored either as it is a food product and can become mouldy.

It is straightforward and easy to prepare, although you still have to measure out the key ingredients accurately. It is also heavy, so it is better for small prosthetic pieces. Colouring it can be challenging because it is a high-sheen product, so you need to add a primer and key product before you start to colour your prosthetic piece to create long-lasting colour. Gelatin pieces are generally used on low-budget productions.

Bald caps

Bald caps are used in theatre, film and TV productions when bald characters are written into the storyline, perhaps to show illness or ageing. To make them look authentic and realistic, the application process has to be carried out correctly, beginning with concealing the performer's natural hair.

Bald caps can be made from latex, cap plastic and even silicone. All three products vary considerably in texture and thickness, as well as realism and accuracy. They also differ in price, with the latex being the cheapest and silicone the most expensive. The hair is prepared in exactly the same way for all three types of bald caps, but the application can vary.

- **Latex** can be applied with adhesive. The edges can be blended out by applying more latex, using stippling techniques to build the edge so that you create a seamless edge. The edge can also be disguised using texturising techniques and materials such as tissue and latex.
- **Cap plastic** is applied using contact adhesive. Once it is secured, you can **bleed** the edges to the performer's skin using acetone, making sure they are seamlessly dissolved. Care must be taken when using acetone.
- **Silicone** bald caps use the same methods as cap plastic.

Full details on how to apply a bald cap are given on pages 274–276.

Bald caps are generally transparent when they are made or purchased, so you will be able to see the performer's hair under it when it is first applied. It therefore needs to be coloured by the make-up artist, either to colour match it to the performer's skin tone or whatever colour is required for a fantasy character.

> **HANDY HINT**
>
> Use disposable latex foam wedge when stippling the edges of latex pieces.

> **KEY TERM**
>
> **Bleeding**: blending the edges of a prosthetic piece or a bald cap onto the performer's skin for a seamless finish.

▲ **Figure 12.8** Wooden spatulas

HANDY HINT

You can purchase recyclable single-use applicators.

Tools

- **Brushes** – a range of small, medium and large professional make-up brushes are used when working with prosthetics and bald caps. Body art brushes and even just a selection of art brushes can also be used.
- **Sponges** – foam sponges and orange and black stipple sponges can be used. Black sponges are coarser and are used to create texture. Orange sponges are softer and more dense, creating a softer texture that is not so harsh.
- **Moulding tools** – these sculpting tools come in a range of different shapes and sizes, and can be made from plastic, metal or wood.

Equipment

- **Palette** – this can be used for mixing make-up products, greasepaints, alcohol-based paints and powders.
- **Spatula** – wooden or metal spatulas are used for decanting and mixing products, as well as smoothing edges on prosthetic pieces.
- **Make-up cape** – this is an essential part of your PPE. It protects you and your performer from spills on clothing or costumes.
- **Disposable applicators** – these are used to prevent cross-infection as well as to prevent ruining your better brushes when working with latex.

Application of prosthetic pieces and bald caps

Preparation

Before you apply any prosthetic pieces or bald caps, the skin has to be completely clean, without any oils or make-up. You need to cleanse the skin of make-up first and then use a toner to ensure the adhesives will stick properly.

Wrapping hair before applying a bald cap

Preparation of the hair before applying a bald cap is one major part of creating an accurate, authentic bald cap. The hair should not be plaited and hair grips should not be used. It has to be wrapped around the head completely and must be totally flat against the head to avoid lumps or bumps showing through the bald cap.

Hair wrapping is a technique that needs to be practised until you get it right. It can be done with soap and water or with hair gel or hair slick. However, hair gel can remain wet and run down inside the bald cap, affecting the bald cap's security at the nape of the neck.

Once wrapped, the gel or soap can be set with a hairdryer to make it more secure and not so wet. This technique is used for TV and film productions.

Step by step: wrapping hair before applying a bald cap

1 The night before, put a bar of soap in a bowl of water and let it dissolve. When you come back to it the next day, the soap will have dissolved and the water will have a slightly slimy texture.

2 Brush the hair thoroughly so that it is free from knots. Start by taking small sections and use your hands to rub the water and soap solution through the hair, starting at the roots and working to the ends of the hair. Work your way up the head until you have covered all of the hair with the soap and water solution.

3 Taking a cutting comb, start with small sections and comb the hair flat to the head, working clockwise around the entire head.

4 Continue to do this until all of the performer's hair has been wrapped around their head. Use your hands to press the hair down onto the head to secure it in place.

5 Use a hairdryer to blow hot air onto the soap and water. It will dry solid, making it more secure and keeping the hair in place under the bald cap.

6 Pick up the bald cap and blow hot air into it with the hair dryer. This makes it more malleable so that it can stretch and move over the head. Place the front of the bald cap on the forehead and stretch it over the wrapped hair, gently pulling it down to the nape of the neck. Once the bald cap is in place, use your fingers or a tail comb to sweep any stray hair back up under the bald cap.

ACTIVITY

Using your tuition head, practise wrapping the hair around the head correctly and fitting the bald cap over it. Time yourself and see if you can increase your speed.

Applying bald caps using adhesives

Using contact adhesive will ensure that the bald cap is secure and will stay in place for long periods of times.

Step by step: applying a cap plastic bald cap with adhesive

1 Roll the bottom of the bald cap back on itself and apply the contact adhesive to the skin all the way around, where the bald cap is going to be applied and also on the bald cap.

2 Contact adhesive is white when you apply it but becomes transparent as it starts to dry. Make sure that all the adhesive dries and is transparent before folding the cap back. It will not stick properly if it is not fully dry.

3 When the adhesive is dry, fold the bald cap down. Using your hands and fingers, brushes, sponges or even a powder puff, add pressure to the bald cap to secure it. The bald cap should be slightly stretched so that it is smooth and there are no creases or folds in it. When you secure the nape, ask your model to tilt their head very slightly forward.

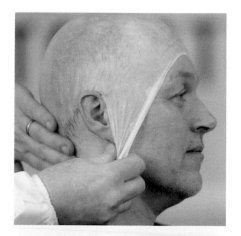

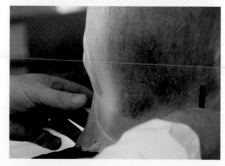

▲ **Figure 12.9** Applying a plastic bald cap with adhesive

HANDY HINT

Acetone cannot be used on latex bald caps.

HANDY HINT

Use large latex sponges to build up a base colour on your bald cap. Camouflage make-up gives a good coverage and base colour for creating flesh tones on bald caps.

HANDY HINT

To create a splatting effect with alcohol-based paints, use a paint brush and cut the bristles shorter.

ACTIVITY

Try colouring your prosthetic piece prior to application to practise covering the piece fully. Use blending and stippling techniques, and create freckles and veins on it.

4 Using a small brush dipped in acetone, start to gently dissolve the cap plastic just below the part where you have secured the bald cap to the skin. Hold a tissue in your other hand to prevent any drips running into the performer's eyes.

5 Take your time bleeding all around the bald cap, ensuring that the cap plastic is blended out smoothly so that you cannot see any edge and it is impossible to tell that the performer is wearing a bald cap.

Step by step: applying make-up to a bald cap

1 First, block out the natural hair colour that is showing through, using camouflage make-up or greasepaint. Use a pink tone to block out the dark tones of varying hair colours under the bald cap, stippling the colour and building it up. Try not to pull or rub the bald cap too much – you do not want to disturb it.

2 When you are happy with the coverage of the corrective colour, you can set it with transparent powder. Use a powder puff with a rolling motion to do this, making sure that you fully press the powder into the make-up, then leave it for a few minutes.

3 You should have already colour matched the make-up to your performer's skin type and skin tone. Using either a sponge or brush, apply the make-up using stippling effects so that you do not disturb the camouflage colour.

4 Take your time building up the coverage and colour, taking it down onto the performer's forehead and the tops of the cheekbones to distract from the bald cap. If you only colour the bald cap, it may still be noticeable and could give the appearance of wearing a hat.

5 When you are happy that the colour is a good match and has good coverage with no hair showing through, you can set with powder again. Leave it for a few minutes, then lightly brush off the excess powder with a large soft brush.

6 Use alcohol-based paints to imitate freckles, age spots or even veins. Try flicking or splatting with a toothbrush to create freckles or age spots. Use a very fine make-up brush to create fine blue/purple veins.

Applying prosthetic pieces using the appropriate adhesive

When applying a small prosthetic piece, the performer should sit at a height that is comfortable for the performer and allows you to work in an upright position. Ensure that all health and safety protocols are followed at all times, including the wearing of PPE. All skin tests should have been carried out before applying the prosthetic piece.

Step by step: applying a prosthetic nose

1 Place the prosthetic piece on the performer's face to see the correct position and how well it fits. Make a mental note or pinpoint where to position the piece and where the edges of the piece sit on the face, checking the balance and symmetry by standing directly in front of the performer as well as checking in the mirror.

2 Once you have mapped it out, put the piece on your work station and start applying the contact adhesive to the skin where the prosthetic will be placed. Use a brush or sponge to apply the contact adhesive. A small brush may give you more control than a sponge.

3 Apply contact adhesive to the edges of the prosthetic piece. You need to let the contact adhesive on the skin and prosthetic piece dry before you apply it. Contact adhesive does not work properly if it is wet.

4 When the contact adhesive is dry, gently position the piece so that it is just hovering above where you want to place it. Think about the edges and make sure the piece is symmetrical and balanced. Once you have done this, you can press it down onto the skin.

5 Using a very fine brush, powder puff or spatula, gently apply pressure to the edges, ensuring that they are stretched with no folds or creases so that the prosthetic piece has a seamless finish.

6 If it is not sticking down to the skin, you will have to apply a little more contact adhesive to the skin and also the prosthetic piece. Remember that the contact adhesive must be fully dry or it will not stick the prosthetic piece down.

7 If you have a slight edge on your prosthetic piece, add a little adhesive with a sponge and stipple this across the edge of the piece.

8 If the edge is quite prominent, you may have to use a product more like latex or silicone. These will fill the edge of the prosthetic piece more easily. Make sure that you follow the manufacturer's instructions for mixing and curing silicone.

▲ **Figure 12.10** Applying a prosthetic nose

Create a character using prosthetic pieces and bald caps

The biggest challenge with prosthetic pieces is making them look realistic. They tend to lack colour and can have a grey appearance as they do not have blood pumping through them like our skin does. They need to look as though they are really are part of the face or body, rather than a prosthetic piece that has just been stuck on.

To create warmth, start with stippling effects using a brush or sponge to creating the flesh tone, using yellows, pinks, oranges and reds for all skin tones as you build up colour over the prosthetic piece. Start to stipple onto the performer's skin as well – it can look very obvious if you only colour the prosthetic piece, especially if the colour is not an exact match. Flesh skin tones do vary, but with all skin types it is paramount to get the underlying warm tones, so do not be afraid to be heavy-handed with these initially.

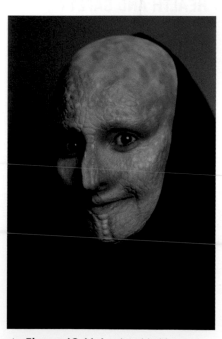

▲ **Figure 12.11** A painted bald cap

▲ **Figure 12.12** Greasepaint

You can stipple greasepaints or even alcohol-based paints. Either way you will have to build up the colour. If you have used greasepaints, you have to set the make-up with setting powder and a powder puff for longevity. Once you have done this, you could add more detail, such as freckles and veins, using alcohol-based paints.

If you want to create a more mottled effect with colour, use alcohol-based paints because of their pigmentation and consistency. You do not have to set alcohol-based paints – once they dry, they are waterproof and will stay in place until they are removed with isopropyl alcohol. This is why alcohol-based paints are also a good choice when you need longevity in a range of different environments, so they are commonly used in theatre, film and TV productions.

Contouring the face or body around prosthetic pieces is done with the products mentioned on pages 272–273. By shading and highlighting, the artist can enhance the look of a bald cap or the 3D appearance of prosthetic pieces. Shading makes features recede, adding more depth, while highlighting adds further emphasis.

Colour wash is another technique that can be used on prosthetic pieces and bald cap applications, particularly if you are incorporating a prosthetic piece in a body art design.

You can also work creatively by making additional props to incorporate in your character design. Props could also be included in your prosthetic pieces, for example, papier mâché, moss, bark, shells or even gold leaf.

Removing prosthetic pieces

Take care when removing prosthetic pieces – you do not want to damage them and you also need to take care of the performer and their skin.

1   Ensure that the performer is sitting comfortably at a height that you can work from easily. Both you and the performer should be wearing the correct PPE.
2   Dip a small brush into adhesive remover and gently start to dissolve the adhesive. Holding a tissue underneath with your other hand to catch any drips, rub your brush gently over and under the prosthetic piece. Do not pull the prosthetic piece at any time – you need to keep it intact and avoid causing any discomfort to the performer. Work slowly and gently around the prosthetic piece until the adhesive has been fully removed and the prosthetic piece can be gently removed.
3   Using a cotton pad and adhesive remover, wipe the area of the performer's face where the prosthetic piece was to remove any last remaining sticky residue. Follow this with cleanser, toner and moisturiser, as the adhesive and other chemicals can be very drying.
4   Using your tissue to catch any drips, wipe the prosthetic piece with adhesive remover to remove any sticky residue. Place it in a container to prevent it from getting damaged, then store it in a cool, dark, dry place until you need it again.

Removing bald caps

Follow these instructions to remove a bald cap.

1 Ensure that the performer is sitting comfortably at a height that you can work from easily. Both you and the performer should be wearing the correct PPE.

2 Use small brush and an adhesive remover to work at the edges of the bald cap, working slowly and gently to start to dissolve the contact adhesive. With your other hand, hold a tissue underneath to catch any drips and stop anything running into the performer's mouth or eyes.

3 Work in small sections around the circumference of the head, continuing to protect the performer from any spills.

4 When you know that all the edges have been dissolved and that the bald cap is totally free from your performer's skin, you can lift it off.

5 Using a cotton pad and remover, wipe over the performer's skin to remove any remaining sticky residue. Follow this with cleanser, toner (if required) and moisturiser, as the adhesive and other chemicals can be very drying. If using a toner, it must be a mild one that is not too astringent as that would irritate the skin.

6 Finally, shampoo the performer's hair to restore it to its original state. Just add warm water to the soap and it will just break down naturally and rinse out. Once it has rinsed out with a little massage, you can shampoo, towel dry and blow-dry the hair.

Test your knowledge

1 Describe what 'wrapping hair' means.

2 What is an adhesive?

3 What is an adhesive remover?

4 Which one of these products resembles flesh more realistically?

 a latex

 b latex foam

 c gelatin

 d silicone

5 Which of these products is totally waterproof?

 a aqua colour

 b greasepaints

 c alcohol-based paints

6 What technique could you use a toothbrush for when applying make-up to a bald cap?

7 What is the bleeding technique used for?

8 Can you dissolve latex edges?

9 Name six prosthetic pieces that can be used on the face.

10 What colour would you use to neutralise a blue tone?

Practical assignment

Scenario

You have been asked to design a fantasy or fairy character for a corporate event.

Task

Incorporate a small prosthetic piece (or pieces) into your design to enhance your fantasy character.

CHAPTER 13

SPECIAL EFFECTS MAKE-UP

INTRODUCTION

Whether you want to create a unique look for a theatre, TV or film production, or for a Halloween party, special effects make-up allows you to transform any face into something amazing. Using techniques to imitate burns, bullet wounds, cuts, severed fingers, animal bites and broken bones, you can create effects for crime scenes, war scenes, accident scenes and hostage scenes.

The world of special effects make-up is a fantastic and rewarding industry that is continually changing, thanks to advances in technology and techniques. Special effects make-up will allow you to explore many other avenues, for example, working within a training organisation for the police, fire, hospital and ambulance services to recreate scenarios that these first responders could deal with on a daily basis.

In this chapter, you will learn about:

1 the range of special effects products and their uses
2 how to create casualty make-up using special effects techniques and products.

1 SPECIAL EFFECTS PRODUCTS AND THEIR USES

Advancement of special effects make-up

Special effects products and technology have evolved considerably throughout the years and they continue to do so. As new technology develops, the line between computer-generated imagery (CGI) and special effects make-up has become increasingly blurred. The combination of both ensures that the performer can be given a physical look to work with and use to get into character, that can be enhanced with CGI.

Past and present technology
Shakespeare's plays

The Elizabethan era (1558–1603) was famous for its theatre, particularly the works of William Shakespeare. Only men were allowed to be actors in this era, so they would be made up to look like a woman if playing a female character. As there was no artificial lighting, plays were often performed in the afternoon to make best use of the available natural light, or by oil lamps or candlelight.

Some of the most famous plays by Shakespeare include:

- *Hamlet*
- *Macbeth*
- *Romeo and Juliet*
- *Julius Caesar*
- *The Winter's Tale*
- *Twelfth Night*
- *A Midsummer Night's Dream.*

Actors in the Elizabethan era would have worn white face make-up that contained lead. Soot or chalk powder were used to accentuate the actors' features, to make them more visible to the audience, while burnt cork would be used to apply dark lines to actors' faces.

The ingredients used to create special effects smelled bad and could sometimes be dangerous. Sulphur, which smells like rotten eggs, and saltpetre made from dung were used to make gunpowder. Chemicals were mixed to create smoke effects, for example, alcohol burned with salts to create flames.

Hammer

Hammer Film Productions was originally founded in 1935 in the UK. It is famous for the gothic horror films it made from the mid-1950s to the mid-1970s and for the 1980s TV series *Hammer House of Horror*. Famous Hammer horror films include:

- *The Curse of Frankenstein* (1957)
- *Dracula* (1958)
- *The Revenge of Frankenstein* (1958)
- *The Mummy* (1959)
- *The Curse of the Werewolf* (1961)
- *The Phantom of the Opera* (1962)
- *The Kiss of the Vampire* (1963)
- *The Plague of the Zombies* (1966).

Roy Ashton was the man behind many of Hammer's make-up effects. He began working at Hammer in 1957, assisting on *The Curse of Frankenstein* and *Dracula*. In 1959, Ashton became head of the make-up department in 1959 and created the visual look of many of Hammer's films, including *The Phantom of the Opera* and *The Mummy*, creating special effects on a small budget.

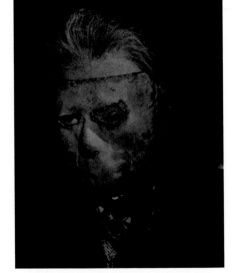

▲ **Figure 13.1** The Phantom in the 1962 film, *The Phantom of the Opera*

ACTIVITY

Watch video clips from Hammer horror films and Shakespeare stage performances. Make notes on the special effects that were used before the development of more recent technology, such as CGI.

Computer-generated imagery

Computer-generated imagery (CGI) is the use of computer graphics to produce images for films, TV shows and video games. CGI can create 2D effects, but it is more commonly associated with the creation of 3D images for characters, scenes and special effects. CGI can be used to animate whole locations but can also be used on a smaller scale, such as on props.

CGI is now used extensively to create visual effects because the results are higher quality and the effects are more controllable than those achieved using physical processes. It allows film-makers to produce content without the use of actors, expensive sets or props. The first use of CGI was in the 1973 science-fiction film *Westworld*, which used 2D computer graphics. *Superman* (1978), *Star Wars* (1979) and *Alien* (1979) were some of the first films to use 3D computer graphics.

CGI can be used to create background special effects as well as characters. The film *Terminator 2: Judgment Day* (1991) features a CGI character – a robot made of liquid metal that is capable of transforming into human form. In the film *Forrest Gump* (1994), CGI was used to create the effect of Lieutenant Dan missing his legs. Other notable films made using CGI include:

- *Avatar* (2009)
- *High Life* (2018)
- *Star Wars: The Rise of Skywalker* (2019)
- *Terminator: Dark Fate* (2019)
- *Gemini Man* (2019).

▲ **Figure 13.2** A scene from the 2009 film *Avatar*

Digital technology

Digital technology has progressed to a very advanced point. 3D rendering can create entire scenes and characters digitally, while digital buffing can make an actor look older or younger, give the illusion that they have gained or lost weight and create effects such as artificial tears.

ACTIVITY

Research the impact that CGI and digital technology have had on make-up artists within the film industry.

▲ **Figure 13.3** The Sorting Hat was a prop used in the *Harry Potter* films

Prop-making

The props used in film, TV or theatre productions can become iconic. People working in props might have to make masks and costumes, prepare props using methods such as casting and moulding, and paint materials to create special effects. The introduction of CGI has had an impact on prop-making within the film industry, but props are still regularly used to help the actors visualise the effects. For example, the *Harry Potter* films used many props, including clothing, wands and doors. Props are also used widely in TV and theatre.

Animation

Animated films are those in which the images have been drawn or created using models rather than by filming actors. Computer animation has developed rapidly and images of models or drawings can now be computer-generated and manipulated in many different ways.

Prosthetics

Prosthetics were used in films as early as the 1920s, long before CGI was developed. An early example was the use of fish skin, which was stuck onto the nose to achieve the effect of the nose being tilted up. Foam latex was developed in the 1930s, allowing artists to create false facial features. It was used in *The Wizard of Oz* (1939) to create the Scarecrow and Cowardly Lion characters. More realistic effects have been developed as newer products have become available. The development of silicone has allowed make-up artists to create more convincing character make-up and prosthetics continue to be an important aspect of film-making.

▲ **Figure 13.4** Prosthetics helped to transform actor Jim Carrey into the Grinch in the film *How the Grinch Stole Christmas*

Animatronics

Animatronics refers to high-tech mechanical puppetry. They were first introduced into films by Disney in the 1964 film *Mary Poppins*, which featured animatronic birds. Modern animatronics tends to use robotics and this was used to create the character of Buckbeak in the *Harry Potter* films, but CGI is replacing it for many realistic uses.

▲ **Figure 13.5** Animatronics were used to create the E.T. character in the film *E.T. the Extra-Terrestrial*

ACTIVITY

Take a look at the making of some of the iconic characters in the *Harry Potter* films, for example, the Basilisk, Buckbeak and the Gringotts goblins: www.wbstudiotour.co.uk/explore-the-tour/creature-effects.

Products, tools and equipment
Products

▼ **Table 13.1** Products used to create special effects

Product	Uses
Liquid latex	This can be used to create realistic special effects make-up, including cuts, burns, lacerations and ageing effects. Make sure you do a skin sensitivity test prior to application, and use an old brush as it is difficult to remove liquid latex from bristles.
	Liquid latex can be used with tissue to give a look texture. Apply a thin layer of latex, allow to dry, then apply 1 ply tissue. If required, you can carry on layering latex then tissue to build up the thickness.
	To create a wrinkle effect, apply thin layers of latex against the direction you want the wrinkle to go in, keeping the skin taut with your fingers. Allow the latex to dry until it is transparent, and be mindful not to apply too much otherwise it will bobble.

→

Product	Uses
Bruise wheel	This is a compact wheel that contains four cream colours ideal for creating bruise effects on skin. Green, blue, purple and maroon tones are used to replicate the various stages of a bruise. See pages 305–306 for a step by step guide to creating a bruise.
Bruise gel	These are used to simulate ultra-realistic skin injuries. Its unique formula and properties make the colour appear to be in the skin, which is ideal for use directly on skin or on prosthetic pieces.
Greasepaint	This is a thick oil-based make-up that comes in a huge variety of colours. It can come in a palette or as a single product. It can be used on both skin and prosthetic pieces, and it stays greasy on the skin after application.
Water-based paint	This comes in a huge variety of colours and can be used on skin and prosthetic pieces. It needs to be mixed with water. It can come in a palette with a mix of colours or as a bigger one-colour product. It is mainly used for facepaints as it does not smudge and dries on the skin quite quickly.

→

Product	Uses
Alcohol-activated paint	This is incredibly durable because it is applied with alcohol. It is waterproof, smudge-proof and non-transferring. It comes in a variety of colours and must be activated with isopropyl alcohol. It can be used on skin, hair and prosthetic pieces.
Isopropyl alcohol (IPA)	A solvent used in many different ways in make-up artistry. It works as a cleaning product for brushes and tools. Be careful to apply IPA only to the bristles of a brush as it can corrode wooden handles. When the bristles are clean, wipe away any excess IPA. Do not leave brushes soaking in IPA as this will ruin them. IPA can also be used to activate alcohol-activated paints. Using a spray bottle, spray IPA directly onto the paint to activate it, then use a brush to apply it.
Petroleum jelly	This is used for a variety of different effects, such as for brow taming, for highlighting, as an adhesive for glitter, for protecting lips and for creating a wet look on eyelids.
Barrier cream	This is used to protect skin from harsh cosmetics, special effects products and paints. Apply a thin layer of barrier cream over the area you will be applying the product to and let it dry before applying the product. Barrier cream is particularly useful for someone with sensitive skin.

Product	Uses
Tuplast	This is a gel-like substance that is applied directly from the tube to create realistic scars and other skin anomalies. When tacky, it can be reshaped easily using a spatula. After it has dried, the scar is waterproof and can be peeled off. Tuplast can dry out very quickly so make sure you put the lid on straight away after use.
Collodion	This is a special effects make-up product used to create scarred-looking skin. It comes in liquid form with a brush. Apply it to a small area of skin, then pinch the skin to create an indentation. Allow this to dry and repeat to enhance the scarring effect. To remove, peel gently from the skin or use spirit gum remover. Make sure you do a skin sensitivity test prior to application.
Cereals and seeds	These are used to thicken up special effects products to give them texture, and for effects such as vomit.
Coffee	This can be added to artificial blood to create a thick, coagulated old blood or to create a gravel effect in cuts. You only need a small amount so be sure to add a little bit at a time.

→

Product	Uses
Airbrush	This can be used to spray make-up onto the skin using an airbrush instead of being applied with sponges, brushes, fingers or other methods. There are three types of airbrush make-up. • **Water-based** products need to be mixed with water before application. They dry quickly on the face and have a matte to semi-matte finish. • **Silicone-based** products are resistant to water and sweat and will not smudge. They give a soft-focus effect that gives the skin a radiant glow. • **Alcohol-based** products are mainly used for body art, tattoo colouring and prosthetic pieces. They are resistant to water and sweat so are good for using underwater or in a very hot climate.
Gelatin	This is good for making quick effects such as burns, open wounds and scars. It has a clear gel-like consistency and can be sprayed through a bottle or pipetted onto the skin. It is gentle on the skin and easy to apply and remove. Gelatin contains pork so some people may not want to use it for religious or ethical reasons.
Glycerine	This is a clear, gel-like formula that is used in special effects make-up to create realistic, quick and easy tears and sweat, as well as oozing or wet wounds.
Artificial blood	There are many different types of artificial blood. These are detailed in Table 13.2 on pages 294–295.

Product	Uses
Wound filler	This is a gel-like blood effect product used to create realistic injuries. It comes in a variety of colours and can be used directly on the skin or on prosthetic pieces. It is waterproof which makes it very durable. Wound filler should be placed into the lower part of the created scar or injury with a spatula to produce a natural-looking blood effect.
Modelling wax	This is used for the alteration of natural facial shapes and for simulating realistic-looking injuries such as cuts and lacerations on the skin. It can also be used to smooth the edges of prosthetic pieces. It comes in a variety of shades to suit different skin tones, is easy to use and soft enough to be moulded by hand. It works best when heated up in the palm of the hand. If it gets a little sticky, add some petroleum jelly to stop the wax from sticking to the hand or fingers when applying to the skin.
Eyebrow wax	This is a wax product used to block out the eyebrows so you can create different eyebrow shapes or effects or move the brows. It can also be used to make small 3D effects to go onto the skin. This is an easy product to use which can be applied thinly to give the illusion of an invisible brow, ensuring a smooth surface to work over the top of.
Tooth enamel	This is a special product that can be used on teeth. It comes in a variety of colours from white to yellow to black, allowing you to create many different effects. It is incredibly effective and easy to apply, providing realistic colours as well as giving the effect of broken, missing or decayed teeth.

→

Product	Uses
Flocking	This is a colour additive made from very fine polyamide fibres. A little can be added to into Artex, gel foam or other transparent or semi-transparent carriers to create the effect fine veining of the skin. It can also be used to disguise the edges of prosthetic pieces and add texture to prosthetic pieces where needed.
Sculpt gel	This enables make-up artists to apply prosthetics easily. Once mixed, it can be applied directly onto prepared skin without creating moulds or life casts. It also creates realistic scars, cuts and swellings, either in moulds or directly on the skin. Paint can be added to give the desired colour.
Adhesives	A variety of adhesives are available. These are used to adhere hair, beards, wigs, prosthetic pieces and bald caps. Make sure you use the correct adhesive and adhesive remover. You can get adhesives specifically designed for sensitive skin.
Translucent powders	Some translucent powders set foundation and others set special effects make-up.

Product	Uses
Sealer	This is a clear synthetic liquid used over latex, foam and wax models, putty noses, chins and other prosthetic pieces to provide longevity and protection.
Foam capsules	These are filled gelatin capsules. When they are chewed, they create a white foam in the mouth.
Food colouring	This is used to create blood. It can also be added to special effects products to change their colour.
Texturising materials	These are used to create texture within special effects make-up to give the realistic effect desired. For example, you could use tissue paper, seeds and food such as strawberries. Anything can be used as long as it is safe.

→

Product	Uses
Crepe hair	This is used to create single-use beards, stubbly beards, moustaches, eyebrows and sideburns. It can also be used to conceal the edges of fake beards.
Soap	An unperfumed solid bar of soap can be used to block out eyebrows.
Glue sticks	These can be used to block out eyebrows.
Removers	These are used to remove prosthetic pieces and special effects make-up. Make sure you use the correct remover for the adhesive that has been used for best results.
Ready-made prosthetics	There are many ready-made prosthetic pieces that can be applied to the skin with adhesive and blended in. The most popular are noses, ears, chins and bullets wounds. They are made from a variety of different materials, including foam latex, silicone and gelatin.

ACTIVITY

There are many effective ways of blocking out an eyebrow. Research the following methods and try them out yourself. Write down the benefits and drawbacks of each method and take photographic evidence.

- Soap
- Hydro Mastix or water-based spirit gum
- Brow wax
- Concealer or airbrush
- Bleach
- Glue stick

When creating blood special effects, remember that different types of blood may be needed.

- Arterial blood – this is bright red in colour.
- Venous blood – this is dark red in colour but looks purple through a person's skin.
- Dried or old blood – this is brownish red in colour and creates a crust or scab to help heal the wound. This is because blood thickens as it leaves the body due to oxidation.

▼ **Table 13.2** Artificial blood products used for special effects

Product	Description and use
Crusty blood	This is a latex containing dark red/brown blood paste that looks scabby when it dries.
Special film blood	This is a realistic artificial blood that flows slowly. It is used to simulate fresh wounds.
Fix blood	This is a blood paste that dries on the skin. Its dark colour is good for creating dried-blood effects and scabs.
Fresh scratch	This comes in two colours: dark and light. Dark is used to simulate an older scab on a wound. The light version can be used to simulate fresh wounds, giving a shine that makes it look real.
Blood capsules	These are gelatin capsules filled with a specific blood powder. Once bitten, the blood powder colours the saliva, giving a realistic bleeding-from-the-mouth effect.
Blood sachets	These are fine plastic bags filled with runny blood that break easily under pressure.

→

Product	Description and use
Eye blood	This comes with a dropper so that blood can be dropped into the eyes to create a bloodshot eye effect.
Blood powder	This is used to simulate the sudden appearance of blood, for example, from a bleeding wound. Blood powder is placed onto the skin then, when water is applied, a blood effect appears immediately and starts trickling according to the amount of water applied. This product can stain skin and clothing.

HANDY HINT

Regular special effects blood has a tendency to separate on silicone, so artificial blood has been developed specifically for use on silicone.

▲ **Figure 13.6** A selection of special effects blood products

Tools and equipment

▼ **Table 13.3** Tools and equipment used to create special effects

Equipment	Uses
Pipettes	These are used to dispense small amounts of liquid product, such as eye blood, onto an area.

→

Equipment	Uses
Scissors	These are used to cut prosthetic pieces or materials.
Hairdryer	This is used to dry products, such as latex, for an ageing effect or collodion when creating a scar effect.
Tissues	These are used for hygiene, for example, to place brushes on. They can also be used to create texture when applied with latex to the skin.
Metal moulding tools	These are used when moulding prosthetics or wax to create effects such as cuts. You can also use them to dispense products onto a palette.

→

Equipment	Uses
Stipple sponge	This is a highly textured sponge used to create stubble effects for theatrical make-up as well as cuts, grazes and texturising skin effects. It can also be used to blend thicker make-up. When doing so, apply the sponge with care as you do not want to ruin the effect. You may need to cut the sponge to a more usable size.
Sponges	These are used to apply make-up, particularly bases, and to blend the edges of special effects make-up. They come in different shapes and sizes and also different density, for example, some are stiff whereas others are soft and pliable.
Brushes	Better quality brushes give a more professional result. There are many different brushes on the market, but brushes made from sable hair are the most popular. Your kit should include a variety of different-shaped brushes, including round, pointed, fine, thick, flat, firm and soft. No specific type of brushes are required for any particular technique in special effects, but having a variety of brushes is very useful. Be mindful of using products such as latex because they will stick the bristles together when they dry.
Mixing palettes	These are used to mix all types of make-up and special effects products, for example, sculpt gel. They come in different shapes and sizes. Metal palettes are easier to wash so they are more hygienic.

Special effects make-up artists need specialised skills to transform actors into realistic characters. The techniques outlined in Figure 13.7 will need to be practised and perfected to become a qualified make-up artist within special effects.

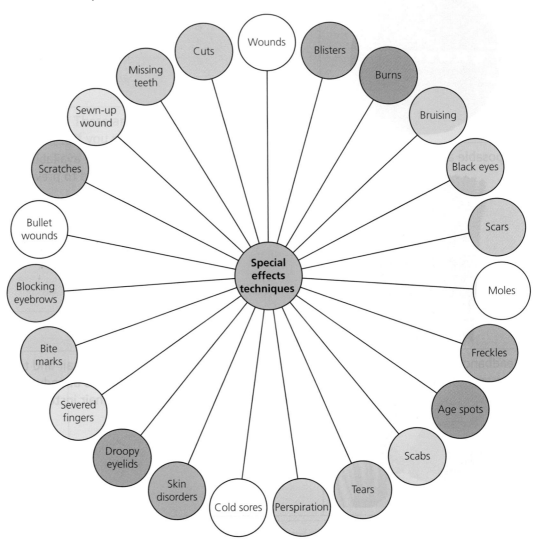

▲ **Figure 13.7** Some of the special effects that a make-up artist can create

ACTIVITY

Suggest which products could be used to create:

- blisters
- droopy eyelids
- a skin disorder such as psoriasis or eczema
- scabs.

Every make-up artist will use different products and create their special effects in different ways. There is no right or wrong with special effects make-up, as long as it is created with health and safety in mind and the end result looks realistic and meets the brief or the script.

For all of the following step by step techniques, remember that they each provide only one way to approach the creation of each effect. Other methods may also be used in the industry to create the effect.

Cuts

Step by step: cut wrist

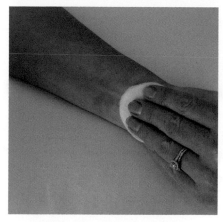

Step 1 – Clean the area of skin to be used. For more on cleansing the skin, see Chapter 4, pages 107–108.

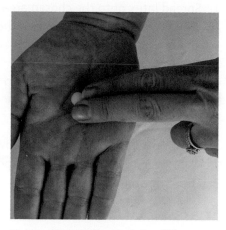

Step 2 – Take a small amount of modelling wax and warm it up in your hand. If it gets sticky, apply a small amount of petroleum jelly to your fingers.

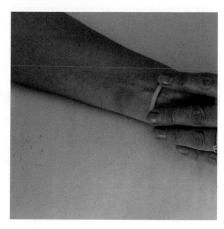

Step 3 – Roll the wax into a sausage shape and place it on the desired area.

Step 4 – Blend the edges as close to the skin as possible, making it seamless, and leave a raised lump in the middle.

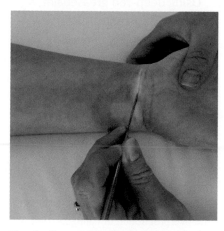

Step 5 – Carve a deep line down the centre of the wax shape, creating a small lip on both sides.

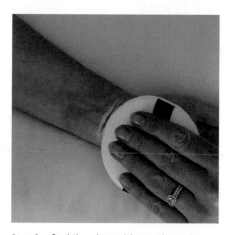

Step 6 – Seal the edges with a sealer and powder generously.

Step 7 – Apply a red blood down the centre of the cut, in between the lips. The amount needed depends on how deep the cut is.

Step 8 – Apply a small amount of red greasepaint to the edges of the cut if required (this will depend on the severity of the cut and not if used in high-definition TV work).

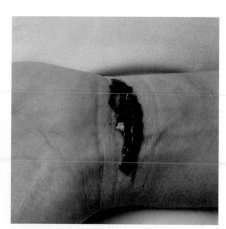

Step 9 – The final look.

KEY TERMS

Hypertrophic: thickened and often raised skin that develops where it has been injured.

Hypotrophic: sunken scar tissue over an old wound, which is often hypopigmented in appearance.

Grazes and scratches

One method is as follows.

1 Spread latex onto the chosen area.
2 Use an orange stick to roughen the surface by rubbing it backwards and forwards.
3 Leave it to dry.
4 Use a brush to apply red make-up in the grooves.
5 Apply spots of running blood over the rough area. This gives a fresher finish.

Alternatively, you could use the following technique.

1 Apply red make-up to a stipple sponge.
2 Drag the stipple sponge over the required area to create a graze effect.

Scars

New scar (hypertrophic)

1 Clean the area of skin being used.
2 Using deep-red greasepaint, lightly draw a line where the scar will be, blending the edges slightly.
3 Apply moulding wax along the line. While it is still wet, mould it into the desired shape with a modelling tool.
4 Apply more red greasepaint around the edges, making sure it is not too neat so that it looks realistic, and blend the edges out slightly.
5 Leave it looking shiny.

HANDY HINT

Different types of scars have different characteristics. Keloid scars are caused by the overproduction of collagen. They are hard and thick.

Step by step: old scar (hypotrophic) application

1 Clean the area of skin being used.
2 Draw a line where the scar will be, using greasepaint in a shade lighter than the skin tone.
3 Apply collodion to the skin. Place the edge of the metal tool into the centre of the collodion and pinch the skin around it. You may need an extra pair of hands for this.
4 Dry with a hairdryer on a cool setting.
5 Remove the metal tool, which will have left an indent in the 'skin'.
6 Apply a line down the centre of the scar using greasepaint in a shade slightly darker than the skin tone.
7 Powder the area all over.

Blood and foam capsules

These products can be used to create lots of different characters. For example, a blood capsule could be used to create a character who has been in a fight, and a foam capsule could be used to create a character who has had a drug overdose. They are completely safe to have in your mouth but be mindful not to swallow the product.

Step by step: using blood and foam capsules

Step 1 – Sip a small amount of water and leave it in the mouth.

Step 2 – Place the blood or foam capsule in the mouth and chew it to generate the blood or foam effect.

Step 3 – Open the mouth slightly to allow the blood or foam to come out of the mouth.

Blocking out eyebrows
Step by step: blocking out eyebrows using eyebrow wax

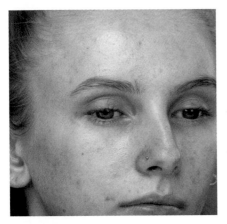

Step 1 – Clean the eyebrow area.

Step 2 – Comb the natural eyebrows upwards.

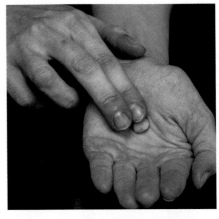

Step 3 – Warm and soften a small amount of eyebrow wax in the palm of your hand.

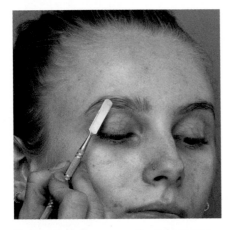

Step 4 – Apply the wax over the eyebrow area with the flat end of a metal tool, keeping the wax as thin as possible.

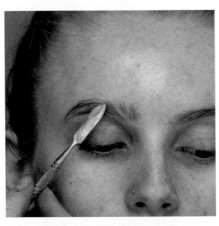

Step 5 – Use a small amount of petroleum jelly to smooth the area and prevent cracking.

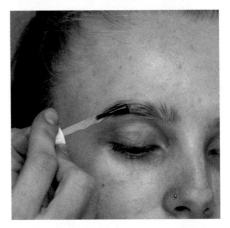

Step 6 – Apply a sealer over the area and wait until it is completely dry.

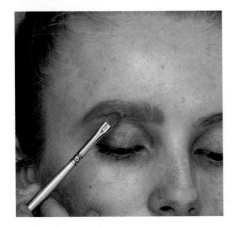

Step 7 – Apply a small amount of a pink base to just the darkened eyebrow area. This will neutralise any darkness of the natural hairs. This may not be necessary on light-coloured eyebrows.

Step 8 – Apply a light dusting of powder.

→

Step 9 – Apply cream make-up to match the skin tone and powder to finish.

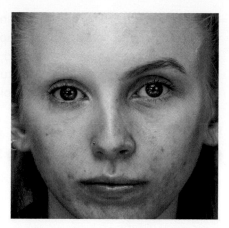

Step 10 – The final look.

Using soap

1 Clean the eyebrow area.
2 Dampen a bar of soap and scrape a small amount off with a metal tool.
3 Brush this soap paste onto the eyebrow area in an upward motion, flattening all the hairs. Allow it to dry.
4 Apply a small amount of a pink base to just the darkened eyebrow area. This will conceal any darkness of the natural hairs. This may not be necessary on light-coloured eyebrow hair.
5 Apply a light dusting of powder.
6 Apply cream make-up to match the skin tone and powder to finish.

Bruising

Realistic bruising effects can be created with make-up alone. The key is to make sure that the colours are correct. A new bruise will be a very different colour to a week-old bruise due to the healing process.

● At first, the bruised area will look red because a bruise is a patch of blood that has seeped into the flesh under the skin.
● One to two days later, the blood begins to lose oxygen and change colour. The bruise will appear blue, purple or even black.
● After five to ten days, the bruise turns yellow or green. These colours come from compounds called bilirubin and biliverdin. The body produces these when it breaks down haemoglobin, which is found in blood.
● After 10 to 14 days, the bruise will turn a shade of yellowish-brown or light brown.

It is important that you understand the stages of these colour changes, which are outlined in Figure 13.8. This is particularly important for continuity in TV and film.

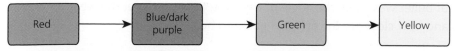

▲ **Figure 13.8** Colour changes in a bruise as it heals

KEY TERMS

Severity: how bad a condition is.
Eye pouches: the bags that appear under the eye as part of the natural ageing process.

When creating a bruise, it is important to consider what has caused the bruise as this could affect its shape and **severity**. You will often be required to create bruising around the site of more severe injuries, for example, a deep wound. If you study a bruise, you will notice that it is irregularly formed with a depth of colour that fades at the outside edges.

Black eye

Step by step: applying a new black eye

Step 1 – Using greasepaint, apply a strong red colour in the deep corners of the eye socket.

Step 2 – Use the same colour under the **eye pouch**.

Step 3 – Apply a deep purple greasepaint under the lower eye socket and on the inner corners of the eyebrow.

Step 4 – Fade out with deep red into a subtle colour.

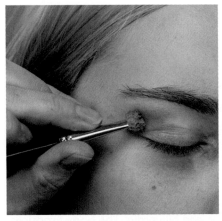

Step 5 – If the eye looks too colourful, or the colours look disjointed, blend with a sponge. If you want the bruise to look swollen, apply some petroleum jelly for a shiny effect.

Step 6 – The final look.

HANDY HINT

When creating special effects make-up research pictures of real-life incidents to ensure that your make-up gives a realistic impression.

Bullet wounds

A bullet wound can be either an entrance or an exit bullet hole. Other factors to be considered when creating this effect are what size and type of bullet was used, the angle of the shot, how powerful the weapon was and how close-up the effect is going to be seen.

Step by step: entrance bullet wound

Step 1 – Model before make-up application.

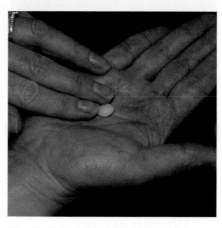

Step 2 – Warm up some wax with your fingers and roll it into a ball.

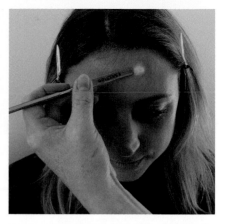

Step 3 – Apply the wax to the skin, blending the edges with your fingers so that the wax sticks. Use spirit gum to keep the wax stuck to the skin.

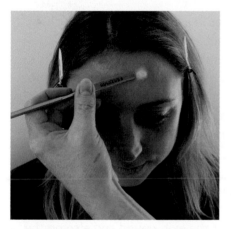

Step 4 – Blend the edges with a metal tool.

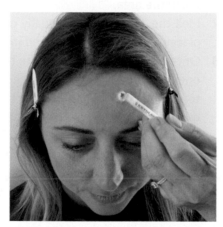

Step 5 – Cut out a hole in the middle of the wax using a metal tool.

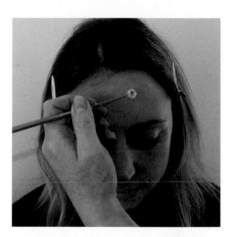

Step 6 – Fray the edges of the wax so that they look jagged.

Step 7 – Apply black greasepaint to the centre of the wax.

Step 8 – Apply red greasepaint to the centre and edges of the wax, blending the colour outwards.

Step 9 – Apply congealed blood to the centre of the wax.

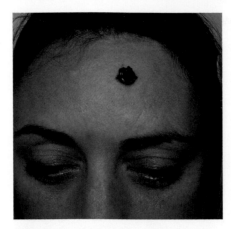

Step 10 – The final look.

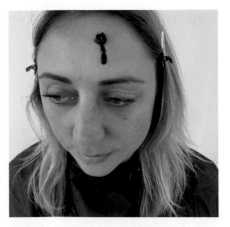

Step 11 – The final look with runny blood coming from the bullet wound.

Exit bullet hole

1 Clean the area.
2 Melt the gelatin (which usually comes in a plastic bottle or pouch) by placing the product unopened into hot water.
3 Once melted, remove from the hot water and use a pair of scissors to open the product by cutting the top off the pouch, or the nib off the top of the bottle. With a metal tool or spatula, apply the gelatin to the desired area in a figure-of-eight motion to give texture and dimension by creating divots in the gelatin. This will give a realistic appearance.
4 Apply red greasepaint to the divots, blending the colour around the edges and blending onto the skin.
5 Apply dark blood to areas to give the effect of the bullet taking flesh away as it exited the body.
6 Drip some blood down the body near the exit wound and also on the wall behind the performer if there is one.

Burns

There are different types of burn that you might need to create.
- **First-degree burn** – a slight burn that only affects the top layer of the epidermis. It causes redness and sometimes a small blister.
- **Second-degree burn** – a burn that causes severe blisters, affecting the epidermis and dermis layers of the skin. When creating this effect, remember to start with a first-degree burn and build the redness and blisters around it.
- **Third-degree burn** – a severe burn that damages all layers of the skin, including muscle, and causes nerve damage. The flesh may look charred and black. It can sometimes look white and leathery when it starts to heal.
- **Acid burn** – damage to tissue caused by exposure to an acid. The severity of the burn is determined by the strength of the acid and the duration and extent of exposure.

First-degree burn

1 Clean the area.
2 Redden the desired area with greasepaint.
3 Apply three thin layers of latex, making sure that the latex dries fully between layers.
4 Pinch the latex to create a couple of circular holes to look like blisters.
5 Apply red greasepaint to the skin where the latex has been removed, and to the edges of the latex where the holes have been made.
6 Make sure the redness is blended into the skin.
7 Tiny veins can be applied with a slightly darker red greasepaint.

Second-degree burn

To transform a first-degree burn into a second-degree burn, add some blistering using Tuplast or latex and redden the area further.

Step by step: acid burn to side of face

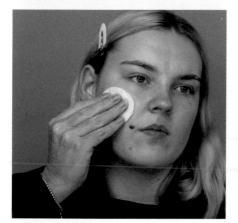

Step 1 – Clean the area.

Step 2 – Melt the gelatin in a container of hot water.

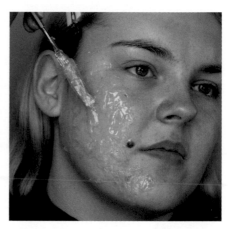

Step 3 – Check that the gelatin is not too hot, then apply it to the desired area with a metal spatula.

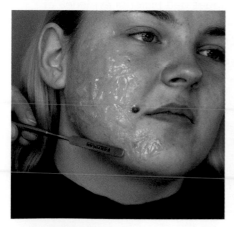

Step 4 – Smooth out the edges of the gelatin to ensure they are not too thick.

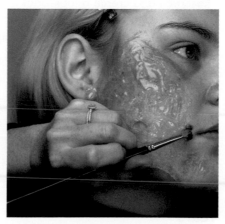

Step 5 – Apply a red greasepaint to the area.

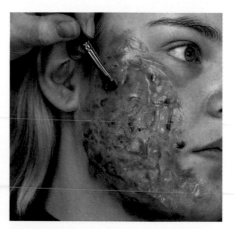

Step 6 – Apply a darker red greasepaint to the divots of the gelatin.

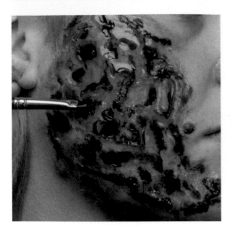

Step 7 – Apply some dark artificial blood to the divots.

Step 8 – Apply some glycerine to the area to give a little shine.

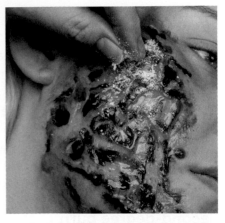

Step 9 – For an instant acid burn effect, sprinkle a crushed water-dissolving tablet on the area.

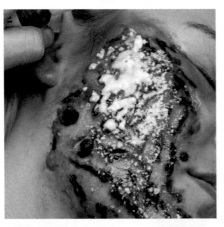

Step 10 – Spray water on the area to activate the tablet, which will fizz and foam up to give a realistic effect.

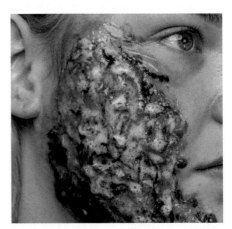

Step 11 – The final look.

ACTIVITY

Research and create a look book of images and pictorial evidence of your recreation of the following scenarios:

- someone who spilled boiling water over their hands
- someone who has had acid thrown over their face and neck
- someone who has been burned in a house fire with 45 per cent third-degree burns to their body.

HANDY HINT

To create a real teardrop, apply a tear stick close to the eye. This will irritate it enough for it to water. To make it more realistic, apply a small amount of red greasepaint around the eye.

Tears and perspiration

This can be used to give the effect of someone crying or sweating, for example, someone who is very upset or drug-addicted.

Tears

To simulate tears, fill a dropper with pure glycerine and place drops of glycerine into the corners of the eye to create a teardrop.

Perspiration

1 Fill a spray bottle with three-quarters glycerine and one-quarter water.
2 Spray on to the skin where required.

Sewn-up wound

This can be applied anywhere on the body.
1 Clean the area.
2 Redden the area with greasepaint, lightly and realistically.
3 Cut a length of black thread and tie knots at intervals along the thread, cutting the thread in between the knots.
4 Apply a small amount of latex with a metal tool along the wound. Working quickly, apply the thread ends into the latex at regular intervals.
5 Apply a small amount of red greasepaint around the latex with a fine brush, blending outwards.
6 Apply a small amount of congealed blood around the latex edges.
7 Using a dropper, apply thick blood to a few of the threads.

Skin pigmentation

Creating different types of pigmentation on the skin is very effective and is used in all areas of make-up, including TV, film, theatre and the catwalk.

- **Moles** – moles can be created easily using modelling wax and skin-coloured cream make-up, depending on the size of the mole required.
- **Freckles** – creating freckles has become very popular, especially for character make-up. Freckles are created by using a brown-based make-up, either water- or cream-based or a greasepaint. Clusters of small dots can be flicked onto the skin or added with a small fine brush. They do not have to be the same size. Freckles are not as large as age spots.
- **Age spots** – it is easy to create age spots using water-based make-up or greasepaint. Make sure that they are not completely symmetrical and use a darker colour than the performer's skin tone. Age spots are not normally as dark as a freckle so be careful not to get them mixed up.

Cold sores

Cold sores are very easy to create. They could be needed for a few different scenarios, for example, a character who is run-down, drug-addicted or homeless.
1 Clean the area.
2 Apply a small amount of Tuplast to the area.
3 Apply a sealer.
4 Using a fine brush, apply red greasepaint around the Tuplast and blend.

Severed finger

This could be required for a number of reasons. For example, it could have been caused by an animal bite or cut off in a hostage situation.

KEY TERM

Cold sores: blister-like lesions that can appear on the lips or around the mouth and occasionally on the nose and cheeks.

HANDY HINT

Special effects for TV and film have to be as realistic as possible. You should research real-life images to get a true picture of what needs to be re-created with special effects make-up.

ACTIVITY

Skin disorders such as psoriasis and eczema can be created realistically with special effects make-up. Research the appearance of both eczema and psoriasis. Then, using latex and greasepaint, recreate them on yourself and take pictorial evidence.

Step by step: severed finger effect

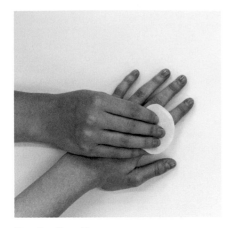

Step 1 – Clean the area.

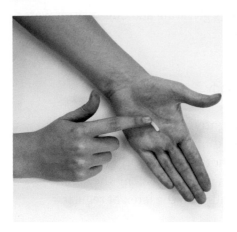

Step 2 – Take a small amount of wax and roll it into a cylinder shape.

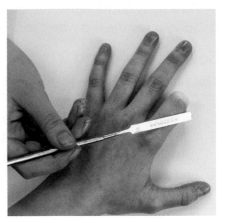

Step 3 – With the performer's finger bent under, apply the wax to the knuckle and blend it into the skin, softening the edges with petroleum jelly to prevent it from going sticky.

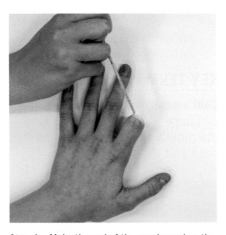

Step 4 – Make the end of the wax jagged so the skin looks torn and open.

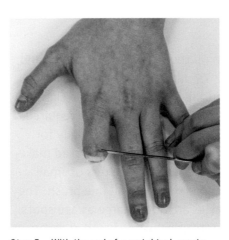

Step 5 – With the end of a metal tool, create lines on the knuckle to make it look realistic.

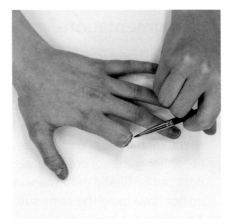

Step 6 – Apply a red greasepaint at the end of the finger and within the creases that have been created on the knuckle.

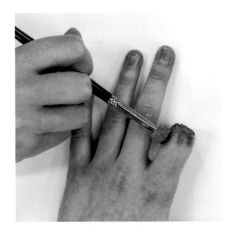

Step 7 – Apply red greasepaint down the finger using a stipple sponge. To make it look realistic, add a little blue in places to give the illusion of a lack of blood circulation.

Step 8 – Add congealed blood to the end of the finger.

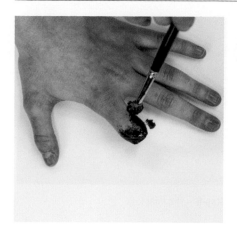

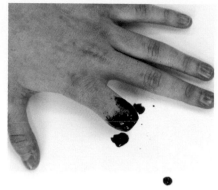

Step 9 – Apply dark blood for a realistic effect.   **Step 10** – The final look.

Bite marks

There are a lot of different types of bite marks that can be created using special effects make-up. Zombie, human or animal bites are all created in a different way. Looking at pictorial evidence when creating a human or an animal bite is very important to get the best realistic results.

HANDY HINT

Try to remember that less is more with special effects make-up. Do not go over the top as it will become unrealistic.

Step by step: bite mark application

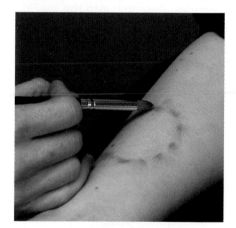

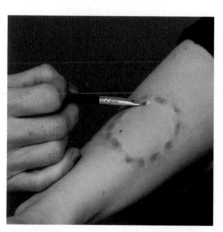

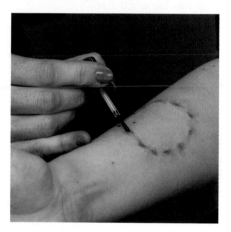

Step 1 – Apply a red greasepaint with a fine brush, creating the shape of the tooth marks.

Step 2 – Apply a white highlighter in between the tooth marks to add definition and to help when applying the collodion, as it is a clear substance.

Step 3 – Apply three or four layers of collodion to create the build-up of the bite.

→

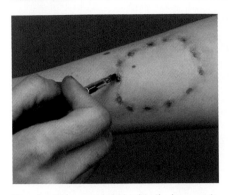

Step 4 – Add congealed blood to the inner parts of the bite mark.

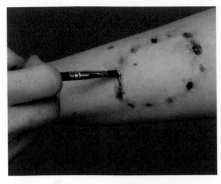

Step 5 – For an irritation effect around the edges, add a small amount of red and blend around the bite mark.

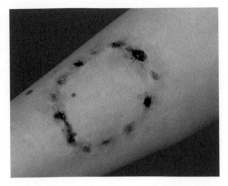

Step 6 – The final look.

ACTIVITY

Research the appearance of a infected hand and the techniques that are required to create the look with special effects. Recreate the look on your own hand. Write a step by step guide to how you achieved it, including pictures for each step.

2 CASUALTY MAKE-UP USING SPECIAL EFFECTS TECHNIQUES AND PRODUCTS

Casualty scenarios

As a make-up artist, you need to understand how to create a variety of casualty characters based on different scenarios. Research into the specific casualty scenario is paramount in order to create a realistic interpretation of the look required. Figure 13.9 lists a number of different scenarios that you may have to recreate using the techniques given in this chapter.

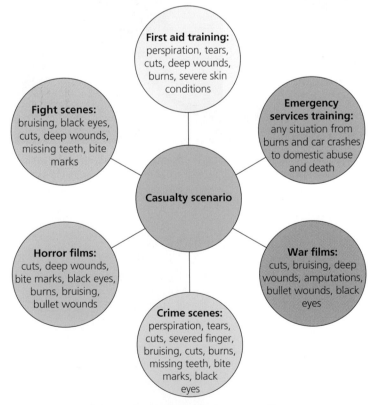

First aid training: perspiration, tears, cuts, deep wounds, burns, severe skin conditions

Emergency services training: any situation from burns and car crashes to domestic abuse and death

Fight scenes: bruising, black eyes, cuts, deep wounds, missing teeth, bite marks

Casualty scenario

War films: cuts, bruising, deep wounds, amputations, bullet wounds, black eyes

Horror films: cuts, deep wounds, bite marks, black eyes, burns, bruising, bullet wounds

Crime scenes: perspiration, tears, cuts, severed finger, bruising, cuts, burns, missing teeth, bite marks, black eyes

▲ **Figure 13.9** Scenarios that may involve a casualty

Step by step: make-up application for a drug-addicted character

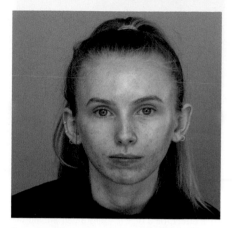

Step 1 – Remove all make-up from the skin.

Step 2 – Apply a foundation to the face that is paler than the model's skin tone.

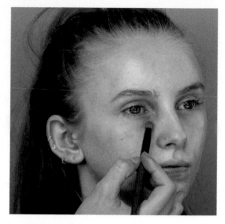

Step 3 – Apply either greasepaint or a matte dark brown powder under the eyes, around the eye sockets and under the cheekbones to give a deepened sunken effect.

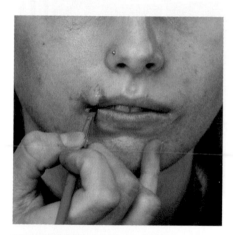

Step 4 – Create a cold sore using Tuplast or Artex and use a red greasepaint around the edges.

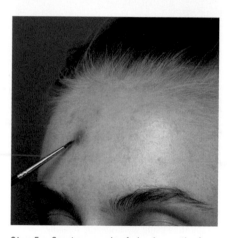

Step 5 – Create a couple of pimples on the face using either Tuplast or Artex.

Step 6 – Powder the whole face with a translucent powder.

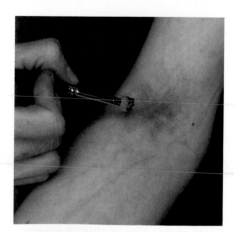

Step 7 – On the inner wrist or arm, use purple greasepaint on either side of the natural vein.

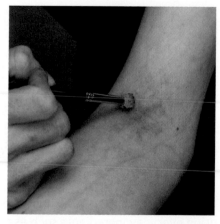

Step 8 – Fade or use a lighter colour purple and blend the colour so the purple is lighter away from the vein.

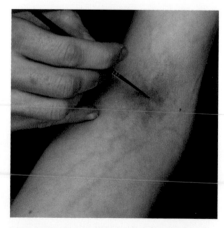

Step 9 – Draw along the vein using a dark purple/black greasepaint, blending the edges.

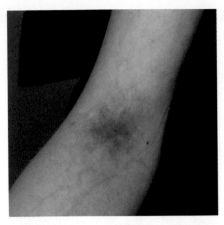

Step 10 – Dot red pinprick needle puncture marks. Use a black pen or greasepaint to put tiny dots on top, making some stronger than others.

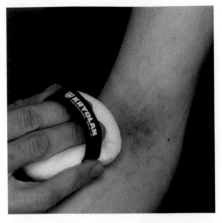

Step 11 – Powder and apply fixing spray. For extra effect, tie a rope or apply a belt around the upper arm.

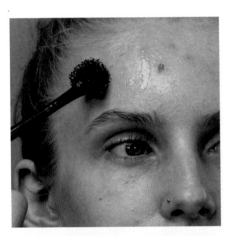

Step 12 – To simulate an overdose, apply perspiration using glycerine and foaming capsules for the mouth.

Step 13 – The final look.

ACTIVITY

Create a look book of the different side effects for a substance abuser.

HANDY HINT

To create a realistic look for someone who is drug-addicted, research the effects of addiction online, bearing in mind that there are many different drugs and side effects.

HANDY HINT

To create a realistic bone effect, visit your local butcher to see what bones they have. Any bones that you use must be fully disinfected by boiling prior to use.

Creating special effect products (low budget)

Make-up artists often experiment to create their own special effects using everyday ingredients such as breakfast cereal, tinned soup, bananas, coffee, flour, honey and food colouring.

Figure 13.10 shows some special effects and how they can be made using items from the kitchen cupboard or in a make-up artist's kit.

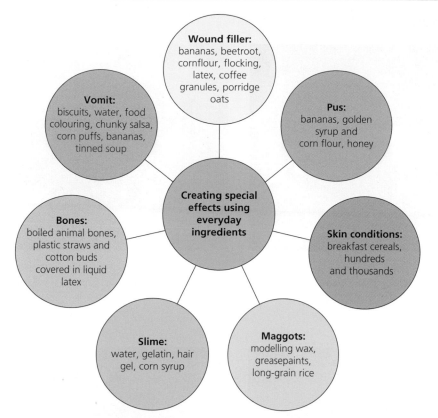

The following bubbles surround the central concept:

Creating special effects using everyday ingredients

- **Wound filler:** bananas, beetroot, cornflour, flocking, latex, coffee granules, porridge oats
- **Vomit:** biscuits, water, food colouring, chunky salsa, corn puffs, bananas, tinned soup
- **Pus:** bananas, golden syrup and corn flour, honey
- **Bones:** boiled animal bones, plastic straws and cotton buds covered in liquid latex
- **Skin conditions:** breakfast cereals, hundreds and thousands
- **Slime:** water, gelatin, hair gel, corn syrup
- **Maggots:** modelling wax, greasepaints, long-grain rice

▲ **Figure 13.10** Creating special effects products

Wound filler for a meaty skin effect

1 Pour a small amount of latex into a plastic container.
2 Add some red flocking to the latex and mix it in.
3 Add some isopropyl alcohol to the latex and flocking mixture.
4 Use a metal tool to add some texture to the mixture and create the required shape.
5 Place the mixture on a piece of paper towel to absorb the excess liquid.
6 Leave to dry for 48 hours, then use when creating a fleshy wound.

Step by step: vomit

Step 1 – Mix milk, biscuits and water together in a large bowl.

Step 2 – Add in food colouring as needed to get the effect required for the scene. Mix to create a thick, lumpy texture.

Step 3 – The mixture can be placed on the floor next to the performer and a small amount can be placed in or around their mouth.

Step by step: maggot-infested wound

Step 1 – Roll modelling wax between two fingers to create small maggot-size rolls. Bend them over a brush handle to create a curved shape. Paint them with whitewash to give them the correct colour.

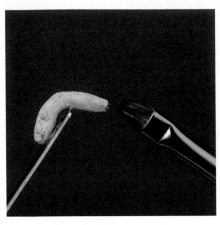

Step 2 – Using a small, thin brush, apply a black dot at one end to look like the head.

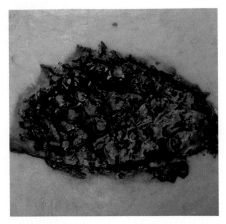

Step 3 – Create a wound with wax to the desired area and seal the edges.

Step 4 – Use a small brush and yellow/orange and brown greasepaint, or alcohol-activated paints, to give the wound an infected look. Add dark red to areas of the wound and around the edges to create depth and to make it look realistic.

Step 5 – Apply the maggots to the wound, some burrowed in and some half out.

Step 6 – Apply glycerine to give a wet pus-like effect.

Step 7 – The final look.

HANDY HINT

As well as creating realistic special effects that match the script, it is important to consider continuity when working in film and TV, as scenes are often shot out of sequence. Make-up artists need to take photos of every step to refer back to, so that they can make sure the make-up looks exactly the same each time it is created.

Test your knowledge

1 Describe how special effects make-up has changed over the years and how it has affected the work of make-up artists.

2 Explain what computer-generated imagery (CGI) is and the impact it has had on the work of make-up artists.

3 What effect does collodion have on the skin?

4 Describe four special effects characteristics that could be used to create the appearance of a drug-addicted character.

5 State five special effects products that might be used to age the face of a young performer and that require a skin sensitivity test.

6 Why is it important to understand continuity when working with special effects?

7 Name three effects that can be created using modelling wax.

8 Describe the different types of burns that can be recreated by special effects make-up artists.

9 Describe what digital technology is and why it may impact a make-up artist.

10 What could you use to create vomit when making your own special effects products?

Practical assignment

Scenario

You have been contracted to design and create two characters for a remake of *Hammer House of Horror*.

Task

Discuss the factors that you should consider when designing and creating the characters.

CHAPTER 14

CREATE, DRESS AND FIT FACIAL POSTICHE

INTRODUCTION

Facial postiche are false hairpieces used on the face, such as beards, moustaches and sideburns. It is widely used in film, TV and theatre.

This chapter describes a range of facial postiche pieces and explains how to use the correct products, tools and equipment to make them. You will understand the process of making facial postiche, cutting and styling it, applying and removing it, and how to maintain it.

In this chapter, you will learn:

1 how to create and dress facial postiche
2 how to fit and maintain facial postiche.

KEY TERM

Facial postiche: false hairpieces used on the face.

1 CREATE AND DRESS FACIAL POSTICHE

Types of facial postiche

Facial postiche are generally made for a specific look for characters in a production. Using facial postiche that has a particular shape and style can help to depict a certain era. You can also use facial postiche to create fictional and fantasy looks.

- **Beards** – these can be made specifically for a performer's face. The colours can be knotted to the requirements of the brief or the production.
- **Moustaches** – these can be made to measure for the performer in the specific style, shape and colour required for the character or era being depicted. They should sit securely above the top lip.
- **Sideburns** – these sit on either side of the face, above the ear and below. The style and shape can be made to the specifications of the brief or the production.
- **Eyebrows** – these can be measured and made in the exact shape, style and colour required.
- **Ears, nose and chin** – facial postiche for these areas would probably be minimal but, as above, all could be made to the specifications of the production in any shape, length, style and colour.

When you start to make facial postiche, you need to identify the type of hair that is most suitable for the method you are using to make the facial postiche, which will depend on the type of production that the facial postiche is needed for. The quality and authenticity required will also affect your selection of hair type. The hair types you might use include:

- human hair – European or Asian
- animal hair – yak or horse
- crepe hair – wool
- synthetic hair – acrylic or nylon.

Human hair

Human hair is mostly used for knotting and making wigs and eyebrows as it creates an authentic look. It is rarely used for facial pieces, however, as it does not have the same texture as facial hair. Asian hair is more commonly used for wig-making and if the colour does not fit the production's requirements, the wig may be coloured.

Animal hair

Yak and horse hair are used to make facial postiche pieces for theatre, film and TV where authenticity is essential, for example, for the character of Gandalf in *The Hobbit* films. It is thick in texture and has a coarse feel that resembles real facial hair.

Wool

Wool, more commonly called crepe hair, can be knotted however it can tear and break when too much pressure is put on it. It can also be cut and applied directly to the skin to create a small facial postiche. This is not as authentic as a knotted facial postiche but it can be built up in layers and could be enough for an extra in a crowd scene, for example. You would never use a crepe hair facial postiche on an actor unless for a low-budget production.

Synthetic hair

Synthetic hair is made from acrylic or nylon and is mass manufactured. It is very glossy and shiny, so it does not look like authentic facial hair, although it could be used in a production if a fancy dress facial postiche is written into the script or for a comic scene. You cannot apply heat to it as it will melt.

Ready-made facial postiche pieces

There are two important points to remember when considering the use of ready-made pieces.

- They are mass produced using synthetic materials and could only be used as fancy dress or for a comedic scene.
- A wig-maker can prepare a higher quality, realistic, ready-made postiche that is individually knotted onto **hair-lace** for a specific look that fits the performer perfectly.

KEY TERM

Hair-lace: the netting base that hair is knotted to when creating wigs and facial postiche.

HANDY HINT

Hand-knotted facial postiche are almost always made to order following specific measurements.

Construction and application techniques

Measuring and creating a template

Once you have all the information regarding the requirements for a facial postiche, you need to create a template.

- Use an eyebrow pencil to mark on the performer's skin, following the natural shadow if creating a template for a beard.
- Apply a layer of cling film around the face, taking care not to obstruct the performer's breathing.
- Use a permanent marker pen to map out the desired shape of the postiche on the cling film over the performer's face.
- Place tape over the cling film to create a stronger, more rigid template and to prevent the marker rubbing off onto the hair-lace.
- Use scissors to cut out your drawn-out shape and transfer it onto paper to make a template. You can then transfer this to your **wooden block** so you can start knotting.

KEY TERM

Wooden block: a solid wooden head used for knotting wigs and facial postiche.

▲ **Figure 14.1** Creating a template and transferring it to a wooden block

Padding

You need to secure the template to your wooden block accurately. If the template is not flush to the wooden block or has gaps or creases in it, the postiche will not be the correct size. Padding, such as cotton wool, tissue or crepe hair, may need to be added to secure the template in place so that the shape is completely accurate when you start knotting.

Every stage of the construction process needs to be as accurate as possible. The better the facial postiche fits the performer's face shape, the more authentic and realistic it will look.

Selecting hair-lace

Hair-lace comes in a variety of thickness and density. If the facial postiche is for a stage production, the hair-lace can be slightly thicker and slightly more visible. If the facial postiche is for a film production shot in high definition, the hair-lace needs to be ultra-fine and virtually invisible.

The choice of hair-lace will depend on how fine and how invisible you require it to be. You could choose one of the following types.

- Veg net, caul net and power net are commonly used for wig-making. They are strong, durable and the amount of give in them depends on the size of the holes:
  - veg net has very small holes and does not stretch
  - caul netting is stretchy and has holes that are larger as it is used in the centre of the wig to bulk up hair
  - power net is a more refined net with very small holes.
- Fronting lace and foundation lace are the best ones to use for facial postiche. Fronting lace has very small holes but it stretches and is very lightweight. It is almost invisible against the skin, which adds to the authenticity of facial pieces. The downside is that it is so fine that it can tear easily, so great care needs to be taken while knotting. Fronting lace runs from ear to ear at the very front of wigs and is nearly invisible when worn. It is frequently damaged and is the most common piece of the wig to be replaced in a process called wig refronting. Different densities tend to be used in theatre productions than that for film or TV.

Blocking lace

When you secure hair-lace to the wooden block over the top of your template, it needs to be at least 2.5 cm longer or bigger than the template. This enables you to have plenty of edge when it comes to cutting around the facial postiche. The excess can be trimmed back after you have finished knotting.

Position the hair-lace over the template so that the holes are running vertically, which will help with knotting. Keeping the tension taut to the block, start pinning in the centre, slightly higher than the template – the pins cannot be where you are knotting. Then pin the bottom, the top left corner, the top right corner, the bottom left corner and the bottom right corner.

Darts are folds or tucks sewn into a fabric to help fit it to the body's shape. If any darting is required on your facial postiche, for example, when knotting a beard, a simple crease can be incorporated with a technique called whipping, described on the next page, although not all facial postiche will require this.

Hair teasing

The hair that you will be using needs to be gently teased to separate the chosen colours of hair from their bunches. Loosening and shaking it will remove any dust and separate it so that it is not clumped together. Once you have a pile of loose hair, you can start mixing the hair.

Hair mixing

You may need to mix two or even three shades of hair to achieve a natural colour. To add grey to the shade, add white hair to the mix. To add more warmth to a colour, mix in orange and red tones. A hackle is used to mix hair: the hair is split with one hand and flicked through the hackle with the other. Keep doing this until you eventually see the hair mix together.

KEY TERM

Blocking: securing the foundation base or net to a wooden block when creating postiche or securing postiche to a malleable block for cutting, styling or dressing.

▲ **Figure 14.2** Securing hair-lace over the template

Whipping

Whipping is the term for creating folds in hair-lace using a knotting hook and nylon thread. This technique is used to join different sections of hair-lace together when making wigs but it can also be used when constructing some facial postiche. If you have any folds in the hair-lace, whipping can be used to secure them in place.

Knotting

Knotting describes the way in which the hair is attached to the hair-lace. It is done with a tool called a knotting hook, which comes in a range of different sizes.

- **Single knotting** is one of the most common forms of knotting. The knotting hook is used to knot the hair once.
- **Double knotting** is the same process as single knotting but you repeat another single knot over the original knot to create a double knot.
- **Point knotting** is a technique of knotting with the points of the hair that can be used to finish off fine detail on facial postiche, giving it an extremely realistic finish. On wigs it is used for the fine detail around the facial perimeter, where the hair needs to look most natural.
- **Under knotting** is when hair is added to the underside of a wig, either to hide or soften the edge of the cap. It is often used at the nape of the neck.
- **Cross knotting** is when knotting is carried out in opposite directions. This replicates the random patterns of human hair growth and allows separation to occur, giving the hair more lift.

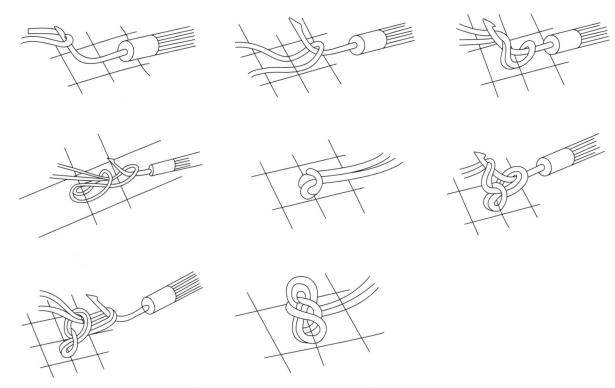

▲ **Figure 14.3** Single and double knotting

Pre-curling hair

Three methods that can be used to curl the hair are:

- frisure force, for hair that is 15 cm or longer
- crop curl, for hair under 15 cm in length
- creoling, for long hair that needs to be crimped.

This can be carried out before or after the facial postiche has been constructed. The hair is wound round a roller, then it is boiled and baked for permanent curls. This can create a range of curls, depending on the size and shape of the rollers.

You can also perm facial postiche once it has been knotted, following the same process as if you were perming the hair on somebody's head.

Dyeing hair

Temporary hair dye can be used on any facial postiche, for example, water-based cake make-up applied with a mascara wand. The postiche can also be dyed with alcohol-based colours, changing it from light to dark or vice versa.

Products, tools and equipment

As well as the types of hair and hair-lace already mentioned, the following products may be used when producing facial postiche and affixing it to a performer's face.

Products

- **Cleanser** – this is used to cleanse the skin prior to the application of the facial postiche. An astringent cleanser is recommended to ensure that there is no residue of natural oils on the skin as this can affect the adhesive.
- **Astringent wipes** – these can be used on the skin to remove any residue or oils that would prevent the adhesive from working properly.
- **Barrier mousse** – this can protect the skin from the harshness of some adhesives. It has a mousse-like consistency. It should not be mixed with greasy barrier cream, however, as this will prevent the adhesive from sticking to the skin.
- **Adhesive** – a range of adhesives specifically for facial postiche are available. Hydro Mastix is a water-soluble adhesive, while Mastix has to be removed with adhesive remover.
- **Adhesive remover** – isopropyl alcohol is generally used as an adhesive remover, although specific adhesive removers are available. They work by dissolving the adhesive.
- **Facial hair wax** – this is used as a finishing product to smooth and control the hairs of the facial postiche, as well as to form shapes and keep the hairs in place.
- **Toupee tape** – this is a double-sided sticky tape that is applied to hair-lace to hold it in place on the performer's skin. It is a quick fix and is more commonly used on stage than for TV and film.

Tools and equipment

- **Pin tail comb** – this is used to comb the facial postiche. The pin tail can be used to section the facial postiche when setting, dressing and styling the hair.
- **Paper** – this is used to make your patterns for facial postiche.
- **Permanent markers** – these are used to draw out your initial shape on cling film.
- **Scissors** – all-purpose scissors are used when cutting cling film and paper. You will also need professional hairdressing scissors to cut the facial hair to the length that you want.
- **Hackle** – this is a sharp object set on a wooden base with upright nails that are used to separate and mix human, animal and crepe hair.
- **Drawing mats** – you will put the hair on drawing mats when knotting. They prevent the hair clumping together and knotting up.
- **Wooden block** – this is a solid wooden head used for knotting the hair on to.
- **Malleable block** – this is used for blocking wigs and facial postiche onto for cutting, styling and dressing.
- **Nails** – these are used to keep hair-lace in place when you are knotting hair on to your wooden block.
- **Hammer** – this is used to secure the nails into the wooden head before you start knotting.
- **Pins** – this is used to secure facial postiche to the malleable block when you start to cut, dress and style it.
- **Template** – this is the cling film template that you created.
- **Tape measure** – this is a standard plastic or material tape measure used to measure the face when creating facial postiche.
- **Knotting hook** – this is a small tool with a hook on the end that is used to knot hair on to hair-lace. It comes in a range of sizes.
- **Oven** – this is a heater specifically for the tongs used for working on facial postiche and wigs. Some ovens have a built-in thermostat. If yours does not, test the heat of the tongs on paper first to avoid singeing the hair. If the tongs scorch the paper, let them cool down before using on the hair.
- **Tongs/irons** – these are specifically designed to be used with an oven. They come in a range of different sizes and are used on wigs as well as facial postiche.

Create a facial hair postiche

Start by deciding which facial postiche you are going to create, for example, a moustache or a beard. If you are creating something for a production with historical influences, such as a period drama, research the era thoroughly to create an authentic piece.

Wrap cling film around the area that you are going to take a template from, for example, the top lip or the chin. Make sure that the cling film sticks closely to the skin but does not obstruct the performer's airway.

KEY TERM

Malleable block: a head-shaped block filled with sand and sawdust and covered in material, which is used for blocking wigs and facial postiche onto.

HEALTH AND SAFETY

Be careful when using the oven and tongs. Tongs can become exceptionally hot and can burn the hair. Remember, all electrical equipment should be PAT tested.

Once you have secured the cling film in place (you may need a second person to help with this part) mark out the facial postiche with a permanent marker. You can design the shape and style directly onto the cling film on the performer's face. This way, you see how the facial postiche will look on the performer.

Add tape on top of the marked-out facial postiche to create a more solid template. The template can then be removed from the performer's face. Cut around it, leaving at least 2.5 cm around the perimeter. The template can now be secured to your wooden block so that you can begin constructing your facial postiche. Attach the template to the wooden block with sticky tape, then secure your chosen hair-lace over the template using nails.

Have your tools and equipment in place ready to start the construction, including your knotting hook and hair ready in your drawing mats.

The hair-lace you have chosen needs to be secured over your template, keeping it close and taut, with no folds or creases. The holes in the hair-lace should run across the template if you are making a moustache.

Start knotting from the top of the facial postiche, working your way down. You need to rotate periodically from opposite side to side when knotting a moustache – this means that you are not knotting in one direction, ensuring that the hair resembles the natural direction of growth. Continue to follow the same format until you have completed all knotting.

This method is used to create moustaches, beards, eyebrows and sideburns, using different templates to reflect the different sizes of the facial postiche being created.

▲ **Figure 14.4** Mark out the postiche on the cling film with a permanent marker to create your template

▲ **Figure 14.5** Apply tape to the marked-out facial postiche

---

HANDY HINTS

- Place the drawing mats with the teeth facing away from you. This will detangle any loose hairs inside the drawing mats.
- Placing coloured paper underneath hair-lace can help you to see it more easily when knotting.

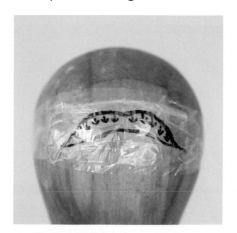

▲ **Figure 14.6** Secure the template to the wooden block

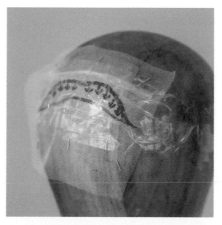

▲ **Figure 14.7** Secure the hair-lace over the template

▲ **Figure 14.8** Knot the postiche

Dress a facial postiche

Once the facial postiche has been constructed, you can start to dress it, cutting and styling it into the shape you want it to be.

You will need to take the facial postiche off the wooden block and trim around the hair-lace edge. How closely you trim will depend on the purpose for which the postiche will be used: you can usually leave more hair-lace in theatre productions, but it is cut quite close for TV and film.

Secure your facial postiche to your malleable block. Cutting facial postiche requires a very different approach than when you are cutting hair into a hairstyle. Firstly, the hair should be dry – there is no need to wet it. You will mainly cut freehand, trimming into shape visually, looking closely at the hair as you cut it to check that it is symmetrical and well balanced.

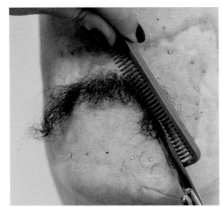
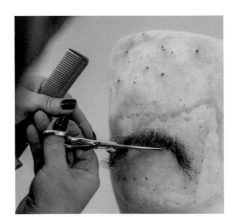

▲ **Figure 14.9** Cut and style the postiche

Once you have cut the facial postiche into shape, you can move on to tonging. The tongs need to be heated in your tong oven. They must be hot, but not so hot that they damage the hair, so test them first on a piece of tissue or paper.

Use your tail comb to take small sections, starting from the top. Place the tongs at the roots and start by adding lift at the roots to resemble the natural root lift of facial hair. Then work your tongs to the ends to curl them over slightly or style them into the direction that you require.

Use a little facial wax rubbed into your fingers to smooth and finish the style of the facial postiche. This will help it keep its shape. A little hairspray can also be used to hold it in place.

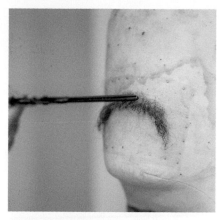

▲ **Figure 14.10** Tong the postiche

ACTIVITY

Practise knotting on a 10 cm square of hair-lace. Secure the lace to your wooden block and use the single knotting technique across five rows.

2 FIT AND MAINTAIN FACIAL POSTICHE

You will need various products, tools and equipment to apply facial postiche. Most of these were described earlier in this chapter.

- Start by ensuring that the skin is completely free of make-up and oil by using an astringent cleanser or toner before applying the facial postiche.
- Consider using a mousse to protect the performer's skin prior to applying the adhesive.
- Select the adhesive that will give you the longevity required and secure the facial postiche in place. You could use either a water-soluble adhesive or an adhesive that has to be removed with adhesive remover. Carry out a skin sensitivity test before applying adhesives and record the results in line with the provisions of the Data Protection Act (see pages 14–15).
- Once you have applied the facial postiche and you are happy that it is very secure and positioned correctly, you could carefully add a little facial hair wax to complete the styling and create the perfect shape.
- If you have not used water-soluble adhesive, you will need an adhesive remover to remove the facial postiche. It will dissolve the adhesive so that you can remove it from the performer's skin without pulling.

Prepare hair and skin for fitting facial postiche

The skin has to be prepped before applying facial postiche to ensure that it is completely clean and make-up free. Any oils left on the skin will cause problems with the adhesive and the facial postiche will not stick.

HEALTH AND SAFETY

Skin sensitivity testing to the adhesive and adhesive remover is essential and must be carried out 24–48 hours beforehand. See page 39 for how to carry out a skin sensitivity test. Remember to record the results in line with the Data Protection Act.

HEALTH AND SAFETY

Always use PPE for you and the performer.

The skin also has to be completely free of hair – no beards, moustaches or sideburns – so ensure that the performer knows they need to be clean-shaven before you apply facial postiche.

Apply facial postiche

Sit your performer in a make-up chair at a height you can work at comfortably and check that they are comfortable. You should both be wearing adequate PPE.

Begin by holding the facial postiche in place on your performer's face to visualise where it is going to be, checking for symmetry and balance. Once you know where the facial postiche will be positioned, you can apply a little adhesive with a make-up brush and allow it to become tacky. If you are using Mastix, you can tap it gently with your finger to speed up the drying process and make it become stickier.

Once the adhesive is tacky, position your facial postiche over it and press down firmly, taking care not to disturb or flatten your styling.

Use the end of your pin tail comb or the end of a make-up brush to press the edges of the hair-lace down onto the adhesive, going around the facial postiche to make sure that all edges are securely stuck to the skin and that the hair-lace is not visible.

If some of the edges of the hair-lace are not quite stuck down, you can add a little more adhesive underneath the hair-lace with a fine brush, leaving it to go off. When it has done so, use your finger or end of your pin tail comb to gently push down and put pressure on the hair-lace so that it sticks to the skin this time.

If the facial postiche looks slightly flat or squashed, run your pin tail comb through it lightly, combing it back into shape, or even just use the end of the comb to lift the hair back up.

▲ **Figure 14.11** Apply adhesive where the postiche will be positioned

▲ **Figure 14.12** Applying the postiche

Remove facial postiche

To remove facial postiche, sit the performer in a make-up chair at a height you can work at comfortably and check that they are comfortable. You should both be wearing adequate PPE. You will be working close to the performer's face, so make sure that you communicate well with them and explain what you are doing.

Pour a little adhesive remover into a bowl and use a small brush to work the remover into the edge of the hair-lace. Place plenty of tissue underneath where you are working to catch any excess remover that drips before it runs into the performer's eyes, nose or mouth. If this does happen, rinse immediately with cold water. Be confident in asking the performer to move their head into the best position for you to work and to avoid remover running into their face.

As the remover dissolves the adhesive, the facial postiche will start to lift away from the skin. Keep working around the edges and under the postiche so that it comes away. Do not pull the facial postiche off – it would damage the performer's skin and could also damage the facial postiche.

When all the adhesive has dissolved, the postiche should come away from the performer's face easily. Place it gently onto a tissue on your work station. Clean any remaining adhesive from the skin by placing some adhesive remover on a cotton wool pad and gently holding this onto the performer's skin. Tap your finger gently on the skin to feel whether it is free from adhesive. It will not feel tacky if the remaining adhesive has been dissolved.

Once there is no adhesive left on the performer's face, gently work cleanser into the skin and wipe off with a warm damp cloth. Follow this with a toner and moisturiser, as adhesives can leave the skin feeling dry. Pat dry with a tissue, then the performer can go.

Maintain facial postiche

After removing the facial postiche, place it into a handful of tissues and start to clean away the adhesive. Work the adhesive remover onto the hair-lace with your small brush. Be careful not to rub too hard as you may dislodge the knotted hair – facial postiche are fragile and can be damaged if you are too heavy-handed.

Feel for any sticky residue that might have been left over from the adhesive. If the facial postiche still feels tacky, go over that area with more adhesive remover. Once it is completely clean, it is ready to put away.

If you are working on a production that requires continuity, the facial postiche needs to be maintained each time you remove it from the performer's face. If this is the case, once it is clean, place it onto your

HANDY HINT

Trim stubborn stray hairs with scissors after placing the postiche on the face to neaten it without having to remove it. Take care with scissors near the performer's face.

HEALTH AND SAFETY

Ensure you have ventilated the room to reduce the effect of adhesives and adhesive removers in a confined space.

CHAPTER 15

MEDIA MAKE-UP BLOGGING

INTRODUCTION

Blogging and using social media platforms are important ways in which make-up artists can promote their work and engage with potential models and clients. A blog is a written piece consisting of facts, thoughts and expert opinions related to your business. It is normally published on a website and can be viewed by all visitors to your website. However, it can be hard for a make-up artist to stand out from the crowd in the digital marketplace.

Effective blogging is a way to boost your business's brand and online visibility and build relationships with your target audience. People enjoy reading blogs, whether they want to learn how to do something, solve a problem or keep up to date with particular topics.

Blogging can be an inexpensive way to advertise your work and drive traffic to your website. It is an effective way to attract new clients by informing them of the services you offer and it also encourages you to keep up-to-date and stay one step ahead of the rest of the industry.

This chapter will cover different online blogging platforms, explore the use of language in blogs and the key features that blogs should include.

In this chapter, you will learn about:

1 the different blogging platforms used in the make-up industry
2 features of blogging used in the make-up industry.

1 DIFFERENT BLOGGING PLATFORMS USED IN THE MAKE-UP INDUSTRY

Purposes of online blogging

It is important to understand the purposes and benefits of online blogging and how it is used within the make-up industry. Blogging has increased in popularity since the early 2000s, when blogs with 'how-to' instructions first began to appear.

Blogging has several purposes.

- Blogging is a great search engine optimisation (SEO) tool. Consistently adding new content to your website and social media channels, as well as using key words and tagging content, is a good way to keep it high in the rankings for Google® and other search engines.
- Blogging is an easy way to keep your customers and clients up to date with new make-up trends and to provide them with tips.

- Blogs allow make-up artists to build rapport with and gain the trust of their audience. As well as showing off their skills, make-up artists can use blogging to build expertise and credibility. Because people can post comments and interact, they can get to know the make-up artist and hopefully come to trust them, which may lead them to book a make-up service or a job.

Benefits of blogging and social media platforms

- **Engage with your target audience** – it is important to engage with your audience. The more you engage with them, the more followers you'll gain and more potential job opportunities you will create. You can do this by writing about current trends, popular make-up products and by demonstrating seasonal make-up, for example, at Halloween or Christmas.
- **Manage your online identity and build trust** – blogging allows you to build and control your online identity. People searching for a make-up artist can read your blogs to get to know your work, product advice and tutorials and to see pictures of looks you have created.
- **Learn new skills and techniques** – you can learn new techniques through blogging as you need to research the subject matter thoroughly to be able to write your blogposts.
- **Build confidence** – the more blogging you do, the more confident you will become doing it. The thought of putting yourself in front of an online audience can be nerve-wracking when you start out, but the more blogging you do, the easier it becomes.
- **Improve writing skills** – even if writing is not one of your strong points, the more you do it, the better you will become. Checking tools can be used to help you with the basics, such as punctuation, spelling, sentence structure and style.
- **Connect with new people** – one of the greatest benefits of blogging is networking with others. Some people can even develop a fan base. Once a make-up artist has a name in the blogging world, it opens up many doors into the industry. For example, in 2008, Sam Chapman and Nicola Haste set up Pixiwoo, a vlog that now has over 2 million followers. It has led to them getting to work with large companies and celebrities as well as the development of their own line of brushes.
- **Demonstrate expertise** – real experts never need to call themselves experts because others will do that for them. As a make-up artist becomes more recognised in their subject area, they will be invited to take part in interviews and events and will be asked by top brands to blog about their products.
- **Become an author** – a make-up artist's blog is their portfolio. Bloggers who have interesting insights, exceptional writing skills, and large audiences have an advantage if they want to become a published author. Many top bloggers have been recognised by publishing companies and offered book deals.

Facebook

Facebook is a large social networking website where people can share text, photographs, videos and links to other websites and also post comments on other people's content. It can also be used to chat online and stream live video.

Like any other social networking platform, Facebook enables make-up artists to get their work seen by lots of people. It is a good way to target an audience and deliver posts directly to the people most likely to want your products or services. Liking and sharing are excellent tools for marketing purposes. Once someone likes your page, followers will receive your updates and their friends will also see them and be directed towards your page.

2 FEATURES OF BLOGGING USED IN THE MAKE-UP INDUSTRY

Features of an online blog

It is very important that you understand the different features that can be included in the content that you share online and how to use them to best effect.

Subject knowledge

It is essential for your reputation that the information you share in your blog is correct, whether it is information about a technique, a product or a brand. Of course, make-up artists can and do create looks and techniques in different ways – that is not a problem, so long as it is easily understood by others and easy to follow. When you are talking about a brand or a product, it is important to have done your research and tried the product before writing a blog about it.

Text

The written elements of your blog are very important. Tips on the use of language, spelling, grammar and punctuation are given later in this chapter. In addition to this, you need to consider the layout and use headings to break the text up. Your blogposts need to be eye-catching and not too lengthy, but have enough content to keep the reader interested. An ideal length for a blogpost is between 1000 and 2000 words.

Photographic images

Images are very important, especially when talking about techniques and skills. Images need to be clear and focused with a clear background – there is nothing worse than trying to showcase work with a plug socket or a curtain in the background. The person reading the blog needs to focus purely on the technique and the skilfulness of the artist.

Video

Video content is a powerful and engaging way to communicate with your target audience and increase your brand visibility. Make-up artistry is inherently visual and all about showing off make-up skills and techniques.

Branding

When blogging about a specific make-up brand, it is very important to make sure that all your facts about the brand are correct. Understanding the product and the brand is imperative as the readers or listeners will be homing in on every detail.

The brands themselves may send products to make-up artists to encourage them to blog about the products. The more followers a make-up artist has and the more blogposts they write, the more interested brands will be in working with them to get their products in the public eye.

Linking social media profiles

As you have seen, there are many platforms that a blogger can use. Most of the blogger's profiles can be linked together so that a new blogpost will be published on all of them at the click of a button. Working across multiple platforms will widen your audience and increase interest in the topic being blogged about.

Language to use

It is very important to understand the language and tone that are suitable for use in a blog. The language you use might be professional and formal or relaxed and informal, depending on the target audience that you have in mind. Whichever type of language you use, it should be authentic and used consistently.

Whether your blogposts are short or nearer the thousand-word count, make sure that the information you have included is communicated to the reader clearly.

When filming a vlog, articulate the words correctly and talk slowly enough that the audience can take in all the information. Use the correct language and show each product or technique as they are discussed.

Formal language

A formal writing style has a professional tone and is usually used for business purposes. You may use formal language when you do not know who will be reading the blog.

- The tone of the blogpost should be polite.
- The content should be age-appropriate.
- Spelling, grammar and punctuation must be correct.
- Avoid repeating subject-matter and words.
- Sentences are fully explained and make sense.
- **Jargon** should not be used.
- If you use statistics to make a point, you need to explain where they come from.

HANDY HINT

Your followers may be likely to purchase a product that you talk about positively in your blogposts, so it is important that you are upfront and transparent if you are blogging about products that brands have sent you for free. Your followers will expect an honest review.

HANDY HINT

One of the most basic yet most important parts of writing an effective blogpost is knowing your audience.

KEY TERM

Jargon: specialised or technical language that may not be understood by those outside the relevant field of expertise.

HANDY HINT

Readers have a natural pace at which they read comfortably. Constant interruptions due to bad spelling slows down this pace. This unnecessary stopping and starting prevents the reader from getting to the end of the sentence in one go.

Informal language

An informal style of writing uses more casual and friendly language. It has a more emotional tone. You might use informal language in a blogpost aimed at a younger audience or when you want to write something more personal.

- Shorter sentences, abbreviated words and slang can be used.
- The writing can have a looser structure.
- The tone can be subjective and personal.

Professional language

When writing about make-up or hair brands and techniques, it is important to use professional language. However, the audience will not always understand make-up jargon, so explain things in simple terms to make them more user-friendly.

Correct spelling, grammar and punctuation

Spelling mistakes in a blogpost interrupt the reader's flow, causing them to stop and mentally correct them before moving on. Slowing down someone's reading pattern can prevent them understanding what you mean and can affect the reader's overall focus and attention on the blogpost.

Correct spelling and grammar are a big deal for some readers. Mistakes can come across as unprofessional and sloppy, which can give a bad impression of the blogger, damaging their credibility and causing them to lose opportunities.

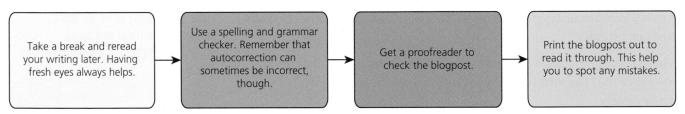

▲ **Figure 15.3** Ways to improve spelling and grammar

Be clear and coherent

When creating a vlog, it is important to speak slowly and clearly while facing and looking at the camera. This helps viewers to understand what you are saying and to engage with the content. Do not to shout or speak too loudly, and make sure there are no distractions or noises in the background that will prevent the viewers from listening to you.

If you are new to vlogging and not used to appearing onscreen, it can be a little daunting at first. Make sure that you rehearse what you are going to say and do – this will help you to deal with any nerves and to be more confident. You may find it useful to create a script or to have an outline to work from to keep you focused as you deliver your vlog.

Present information in a logical sequence

Written blogs should be laid out in a way that makes them easy to read and both blogs and vlogs should follow a logical sequence.

- Establish a flow for the blogpost so that the information unfolds for the reader in an order that is easy to follow. Make sure you have a beginning, middle and end.
- Keep your choice of font clean and simple.
- Use headings, bullet points and diagrams in your blog so it is easy for the reader to follow.
- The information that you include should be relevant and interesting to your audience.
- Avoid duplicating too much information.

HANDY HINTS

- Think before you start writing. Use a pen and paper or a notepad app to plan what you want to write about. This structure will form the skeleton of your blogpost.
- Every blogpost needs to have a catchy title that reveals the theme of your content. Those first few words are key to engaging the reader.

ACTIVITY

Read the following guidelines on how to structure the perfect blog, then create your own plan for a blogpost: https://socialtriggers.com/perfect-blog-post.

Online safety

Users of social networks need to be aware of the risks involved in being online, from the possibility of becoming a target for cyberbullying or cyber predators to the importance of safeguarding their identity, privacy and data from cyber criminals.

Dangers and risks associated with online profiles

Identity safety

Identity safety means taking care of how you share your personal information. This information can be shared in a variety of ways, both voluntarily and involuntarily, so it is important to know who will have access to the information that you share on the internet. This information includes your:

- name
- age
- sex
- appearance
- phone number
- email address
- home address
- usernames and passwords
- bank and debit or credit card details.

Sharing personal information places a blogger at risk of identity theft. You should use strong passwords for your accounts and change them often.

Cyberbullying

Cyberbullying is a form of bullying that takes place online. It can take place on all social networking sites, such as Facebook, Instagram, YouTube and Twitter, as well as through messaging apps, gaming sites and chat rooms.

There are many ways of being bullied online.

- **Harassment** – this means repeatedly sending messages that are rude, insulting or offensive, either as replies to social media posts or as comments on videos, photos and blogs.
- **Denigration** – this could involve posting false information about someone online or using a photo or video of someone to ridicule them.
- **Impersonation** – this could involve either:
  - creating a false profile impersonating someone else and making fake social media posts and comments pretending to be that person
  - hacking into someone's account and using their identity to send embarrassing or hurtful comments to others.
- **Cyber stalking** – this means repeatedly sending messages that are harmful, threatening or intimidating or behaving online in a way that makes someone else afraid for their safety.

Being bullied can impact on a person's self-esteem, confidence and social skills. Everyone online should consider the impact that words can have and think twice before posting.

HANDY HINT

If someone posts an abusive or threatening message online, they can be traced by the police. Every time someone visits a website or makes a post, the internet service provider has an electronic note of the activity. Even if someone creates an anonymous email address, they can still be traced.

Privacy and plagiarism

Using text, videos, music or images without permission from the person who created them is against copyright law and passing off other people's content as your own is called **plagiarism**. Bloggers are not allowed to copy and paste anyone else's work and pass it off as their own. If you want to use a quote from someone else's material, you need to include a reference to the original material.

Most online platforms allow people to set their profile as 'private'. This allows the person to vet who they want to accept as a follower or friend online.

KEY TERM

Plagiarism: copying another person's ideas, text or other creative work and presenting it as your own without permission.

Cyber predators

Many cyber predators pretend to be someone else or lie about themselves to gain the trust of their victims. Never respond to messages that make you feel uncomfortable, and report any improper activity to a person of authority.

To stay safe:
- never post content that reveals personal information about yourself (such as your home address or phone number)
- never meet up with people who you only know through the internet.

Data protection

The Data Protection Act (see Chapter 1, pages 14–15, for more information) protects models' confidentiality. Information about the models who appear in your blogposts, photos or videos must not be divulged to anyone. Information that must be kept confidential includes their personal details, the services that you have provided for them and products that they have purchased.

Elastin: protein that holds bundles of collagen fibres together and makes up less than five per cent of the weight of the skin.

Emphasise: make something stand out.

Enhance: improve or make an area stand out, for example, enhancing cheekbones using a highlighter.

Excretion: expelling waste from the body.

Eye pouches: the bags that appear under the eye as part of the natural ageing process.

Facial postiche: false hairpieces used on the face.

Fashion week: when leading fashion designers, brands or fashion houses present their latest collections for the upcoming season, usually spring/summer or autumn/winter.

Fauhawk: a hairstyle similar to a mohawk but done without shaving the rest of the head. The hair is combed toward the centre and made to stand up with gel or wax.

Finger dry: using your fingers to style the hair into shape as you blow-dry it.

Fungi: simple life-forms including moulds, yeasts and mushrooms.

Geisha pins: long, thick pins that are generally used to secure heavy wigs and hairpieces. They are strong so can cope with weight and thickness.

Going off: when a product cures and sets.

Greasepaint: an oil-based professional make-up product that can be used for special effects, theatrical and media applications. It comes in an array of colours, from foundation tones to bright colours.

Greyscale: a range of shades of grey without apparent colour. The darkest shade is black and the lightest shade is white.

Hair-lace: the netting base that hair is knotted to when creating wigs and facial postiche.

Harmonious colours: colours that sit next to each other on the colour wheel.

Hashtag: a word or phrase preceded by the hash symbol (#) that helps people to identify topics of interest to them.

Hazard: anything that could potentially cause harm.

Henna: a flowering plant, the leaves of which contain a natural and very effective colouring pigment called lawsone.

Hue: the name of the colour, for example, red or blue. The variety of hues is increased by varying the amount of primary colour added.

Humid: having a lot of moisture in the air.

Hygienic: clean and sterilised.

Hyperpigmentation: patches of skin that are darker than the overall skin tone.

Hypertrophic: thickened and often raised skin that develops where it has been injured.

Hypopigmentation: patches of skin that are lighter than the overall skin tone.

Hypotrophic: sunken scar tissue over an old wound, which is often hypopigmented in appearance.

Iconic: well-known or characteristic of a particular idea or time.

Industry portfolio: a collection of pictorial evidence of a make-up artist's best work that showcases their creativity and versatility to others.

Infestation: an invasion of small parasites that live in the folds of the skin or the hair.

Intensity: the strength of a colour. Vivid colours have a strong intensity and dull colours are weak in intensity.

Jargon: specialised or technical language that may not be understood by those outside the relevant field of expertise.

Keratin: a protein that makes up the hair, skin and nails.

Keratinisation: the process that turns the skin into a hard, protective cover. It can also happen to skin that is overused, for example, marathon runners' feet.

Keratinocyte: an epidermal cell that produces keratin; it is responsible for the strength and flexibility of our skin.

Light shaper: a piece of equipment used in photography to create different lighting effects.

Longevity: how long something will last.

Look book: a collection of visual resources that communicates and demonstrates a make-up artist's progression from the initial design stage through to the finished look.

Malleable block: a head-shaped block filled with sand and sawdust, and covered in material which is used for blocking wigs and facial postiche on.

Mehndi: a form of body art, originating in ancient India, where decorative patterns are created on the body using a paste made from the leaves of the henna plant.

Melanin: the pigment that gives human hair, eyes and skin its natural colour. It protects the skin from the harmful effects of ultraviolet light and is responsible for the changes in skin tone and texture when exposed to sunlight.

Melanocyte: a cell that produces melanin, the pigment responsible for skin tone.

Micellar water: a cleansing liquid that contains tiny balls of oil molecules (micelles) which attract dirt and oil to remove impurities without drying out the skin. It can be used as an all-in-one make-up remover, facial wash and moisturiser.

Microcirculation: the blood flow through the smallest vessels in the circulatory system.

Model: a person employed to wear clothes or make-up for fashion- and editorial-based work.

Monochromatic colours: all the colours of a single hue, including the tones, tints and shades of the hue.

Mood board: a collage of images, text, sketches and material that communicates your ideas for a given theme.

Non-pathogenic: incapable of causing disease.

Non-striated: involuntary muscle that is smooth in appearance.

Normal contra-action: a reaction to a product that creates sensitivity, such as a reddening of the skin or watery eyes. These can be dealt with by the make-up artist, but if the contra-action worsens, the model or client should seek medical advice.

Ombré: the gradual blending of one colour to another, from dark to light.

Organic oxides: natural minerals used in make-up. The most common is iron oxide, but talc, silica and mica might also be used in make-up products.

Original state: the hairstyle that your model or client had before you styled their hair.

Ornamentation: any form of hair, body or face decoration.

Padding: a hairstyling accessory designed to achieve volume or create structure. It is extremely useful when styling hair up.

Pathogenic: capable of causing disease.

Performer: a person employed to act in production-based work, for example, film, TV and theatre.

Pigmentation: the natural colour of someone's skin.

Plagiarism: copying another person's ideas, text or other creative work and presenting it as your own without permission.

Postiche: a small hairpiece that clips into the hair to give it more fullness, volume and coverage.

Pre-production: the time spent planning and organising before the production (of a film or TV show, for example) begins.

Prevented contra-indication: a contra-indication that means you cannot carry out the make-up service.

Referral traffic: people who land on a website after clicking a hyperlink on another website, bypassing search engines.

Restricted contra-indication: a contra-indication that means you can carry out the make-up service, but you may have to limit it or work around the area.

Risk: the chance or probability that harm may occur.

Runway: a narrow platform between seating areas that is used by models to demonstrate clothing and during a fashion show.

Sanitise: kill some, but not all, micro-organisms.

Scenario: a written outline of a film, novel or stage work, giving details of the plot and individual scenes.

Scrunch dry: scrunching the hair with your hands and using the heat of the hairdryer to create a slightly wavy or curly look.

Sebaceous glands: small sac-like pouches found all over the body, except on the soles of the feet and the palms of the hands, that produce an oily substance called sebum.

Sebum: a slightly acidic (pH 4.5–5.5) fatty substance secreted by sebaceous glands. It lubricates the skin and hair, making them soft and supple.

Secretion: the production of substances that the body uses, for example, sebum.

Severity: how bad a condition is.

Shade: a colour created by adding black to a pure colour.

Spoolie brush: similar to a mascara wand with a tapered head and soft bristles.

Sterilise: kill all micro-organisms.

Strategy: a method or a plan chosen to bring about a desired outcome.

Striated: voluntary muscle that is marked by a band pattern.

Sun protection factor (SPF): protects the skin from ultraviolet rays.

Sweat glands: simple coiled tubular glands that open directly onto the surface of the skin. They regulate body temperature and help eliminate waste products.

Texture: the thickness of each individual strand of hair.

Texturise: create a surface that is not smooth but has a raised pattern on it.

Time-based media: the Guggenheim Museum describes this as contemporary artwork, including video, film, slides, audio or computer technologies, that have duration as a dimension and unfold to the viewer over time.

Tint: a colour created by adding white to a pure colour.

Titanium dioxide: a fine white powder that occurs naturally. It is used in a variety of make-up products, including sunscreens, pressed powders and loose powders.

Tone: a colour created by adding grey to a pure colour.

Trade test: a test that assesses the skill level of an individual. A make-up artist may be required to perform a trade test for an interview so the employer can check the make-up artist's ability to carry out a certain look or techniques. This helps the employer decide whether the make-up artist is suitable for the job.

Viruses: micro-organisms that are smaller than bacteria and can only reproduce within living cells.

Vitiligo: a non-contagious skin condition that causes the loss of skin colour (paling of the skin).

Vlog: a video blog shared on a platform such as YouTube®.

Volume: body and lift in the hair.

Wooden block: a solid wooden head used for knotting wigs and facial postiche.

Picture credits

Every effort has been made to trace and acknowledge ownership of copyright. The Publishers will be glad to make suitable arrangements with any copyright holders whom it has not been possible to contact.

Fig.1.1 © Gnepphoto/stock.adobe.com; Fig.1.3 © Mino21/stock.adobe.com; Fig.1.4 © Alan Stockdale/stock.adobe.com; Fig.1.6 © Yakobchuk Olena/stock.adobe.com; Fig.1.10 © FotoHelin/stock.adobe.com; Fig.1.11 © Alessandro Grandini/stock.adobe.com; Fig.1.12 © Tampatra/stock.adobe.com; Fig.1.13 © Lyudmila/stock.adobe.com; Fig.1.14 © DR P. Marazzi/Science Photo Library; Table 1.7 (top to bottom): © ThamKC/stock.adobe.com, © Uwimages/stock.adobe.com, © Tony Mcconnell/Science Photo Library, © Praisaeng/stock.adobe.com, © Olavs/stock.adobe.com, © Joloei/stock.adobe.com, © Milan Lipowski/stock.adobe.com, © DR P. Marazzi/Science Photo Library, © Alessandro Grandini/stock.adobe.com, © DR P. Marazzi/Science Photo Library; Fig.1.15 © Phil Jones Photography; Fig.2.1 © Sofia Zhuravetc/stock.adobe.com; Fig.3.1 © Jane Hobson/Shutterstock.com; Fig.3.6 Hannah Brown; Fig.4.5 © Chloe Johnson/Alamy Stock Photo; Fig.4.6 © Daxiao Productions/stock.adobe.com; Fig.4.7 Melianiaka Kanstantsin/Shutterstock.com; Table 4.2 (top to bottom): © Fotosmile777/stock.adobe.com, © Roman Samborskyi/Shutterstock.com, © Iconogenic/stock.adobe.com, © ArtFamily/stock.adobe.com, © Irina Bg/Shutterstock.com; Figs.4.8–4.10 © Kryolan Professional Make-up; Fig.4.11 © Phil Jones Photography; Figs.4.12–4.16 © Kryolan Professional Make-up; Figs.4.18–4.22 © Kryolan Professional Make-up; p.92 bottom left and right City & Guilds, bottom middle © Phil Jones Photography; p.93 top © Phil Jones Photography; pp.95–9 © Phil Jones Photography; Table 4.6 © Kryolan Professional Make-up; Figs.4.23–4.24 © Kryolan Professional Make-up; Fig.4.25 © Tiler84/stock.adobe.com; Fig.4.26 Lucy Jayne Blanchard; Fig.4.27 © Phil Jones Photography; Fig.4.28 © Andy Gaden, Fareham Studio; Fig.4.29 © Phil Jones Photography; Table 5.1 (top to bottom): © Wella Professionals EIMI Perfect Setting Hair Spray Available in salons and at wellastore.com, © Shockwaves Instant Root Lift Gel Spray £2.69 Available nationwide, © Wella Professionals EIMI Shape Me Shape Memory Hair Gel Available in salons and at wellastore.com, Image provided courtesy of L'Oréal Professionnel, © Wella Professionals EIMI Extra Volume Hair Mousse Available in salons and at wellastore.com, © Wella Professionals EIMI Super Set Hairspray Available in salons and at wellastore.com, © Wella Professionals INVIGO Nutri-Enrich Finishing Serum Available in salons or at wellastore.com, Image provided courtesy of L'Oréal Professionnel, © Wella Professionals EIMI Grip Cream Hair Styling Available in salons or wellastore.com, © Shockwaves Messy Matt Clay Available in Sainsburys, © Wella Professionals EIMI Shine Glam Mist Available in salons or wellastore.com, © Wella Professionals EIMI Ocean Spritz Available in salons and at wellastore.com; Table 5.2 (top to bottom): City & Guilds, © Syda Productions/stock.adobe.com, City & Guilds, © Sunwaylight13/stock.adobe.com, City & Guilds, © Blackday/stock.adobe.com; Table 5.3 (top to bottom): © Jon Le-Bon/stock.adobe.com, © Siraphol/stock.adobe.com, City & Guilds, City & Guilds, © Voyagerix/stock.adobe.com, © Sixsmith/stock.adobe.com, © Alter_photo/stock.adobe.com, © Natavilman/stock.adobe.com, © Sergey Baibak/stock.adobe.com, © Yakobchuk Olena/stock.adobe.com, © Juanje Garrido/stock.adobe.com; Fig.5.1 © Barbicide.com; Fig.5.3 City & Guilds; Fig.5.4 © Luckyphoto/stock.adobe.com; pp.126–9 City & Guilds; Fig.5.5 City & Guilds; p.131 © Phil Jones Photography; Fig.5.6 © Sergej/stock.adobe.com; Fig.5.7 © Dimid/stock.adobe.com; pp.132 bottom–134 © Phil Jones Photography; Fig.5.8 City & Guilds; pp.135 bottom–136 top City & Guilds; Fig.5.9 © Nat bowornphatnon/stock.adobe.com; p.137 City & Guilds; p.138 © Phil Jones Photography; Fig.6.1 © Kryolan Professional Make-up; Fig.6.2 Hannah Brown; Figs.6.3–6.4 © Andy Gaden, Fareham Studio; Fig.6.5 © Pixel-Shot/stock.adobe.com; Fig.6.6 Hannah Brown; Figs.6.7–6.8 © Phil Jones Photography; p.149 © Phil Jones Photography; Fig.6.9 © Marinafrost/stock.adobe.com; Fig.6.10 Hannah Brown; Fig.6.11 © Andy Gaden, Fareham Studio; pp.152–3 Lucy Jayne Blanchard; Fig.6.12 Hannah Brown; Fig.6.13 © Eugenepartyzan/stock.adobe.com; Fig.6.14 Ellie Bishop; Fig.6.15 Lauren Jones; Table 6.1 image 10 © Midonovatamara/stock.adobe.com, image 13 © Dzimin/stock.adobe.com, others © Kryolan Professional Make-up; Fig.6.16 © New Africa/stock.adobe.com; Fig.6.17 © Andy Gaden, Fareham Studio; Fig.6.18 © Creatopic/stock.adobe.com; Fig.6.19 © Veles Studio/Shutterstock.com; Fig.6.20 © Masson/stock.adobe.com; Fig.6.21 © Jim

Index